KICK-ASS 2 PRELUDE:
HIT-GIRL

KICK-ASS 2 PRELUDE: HIT-GIRL. Contains material originally published in magazine form as HIT-GIRL #1-5. First printing 2013. ISBN# 978-0-7851-6597-2. Published by MARVEL WORLDWIDE, INC., a subsidiary of MARVEL ENTERTAINMENT, LLC. OFFICE OF PUBLICATION: 135 West 50th Street, New York, NY 10020. Copyright © 2012 and 2013 Mark Millar and John S. Romita. All rights reserved. $24.99 per copy in the U.S. and $27.99 in Canada (GST #R127032852); Canadian Agreement #40668537. "Hit-Girl," "Kick-Ass," and the Hit-Girl and Kick-Ass logos, and all characters and content herein and the likenesses thereof are trademarks of Mark Millar and John S. Romita, unless otherwise expressly noted. The events and characters presented are intended as fiction. Any similarity to real events or to persons living or dead is purely coincidental. This work may not be reproduced, except in small amounts for journalistic or review purposes, without permission of the authors. "Icon" and the Icon logo are trademarks of Marvel Characters, Inc. "Millarworld" and the Millarworld logo are trademarks of Millarworld Limited. **Printed in the U.S.A.** ALAN FINE, EVP - Office of the President, Marvel Worldwide, Inc. and EVP & CMO Marvel Characters B.V.; DAN BUCKLEY, Publisher & President - Print, Animation & Digital Divisions; JOE QUESADA, Chief Creative Officer; TOM BREVOORT, SVP of Publishing; DAVID BOGART, SVP of Operations & Procurement, Publishing; RUWAN JAYATILLEKE, SVP & Associate Publisher, Publishing; C.B. CEBULSKI, SVP of Creator & Content Development; DAVID GABRIEL, SVP of Print & Digital Publishing Sales; JIM O'KEEFE, VP of Operations & Logistics; DAN CARR, Executive Director of Publishing Technology; SUSAN CRESPI, Editorial Operations Manager; ALEX MORALES, Publishing Operations Manager; STAN LEE, Chairman Emeritus. For information regarding advertising in Marvel Comics or on Marvel.com, please contact Niza Disla, Director of Marvel Partnerships, at ndisla@marvel.com. For Marvel subscription inquiries, please call 800-217-9158. **Manufactured between 1/7/2013 and 2/18/2013 by R.R. DONNELLEY, INC., SALEM, VA, USA.**

10 9 8 7 6 5 4 3 2 1

KICK-ASS 2 PRELUDE:

HIT-GIRL

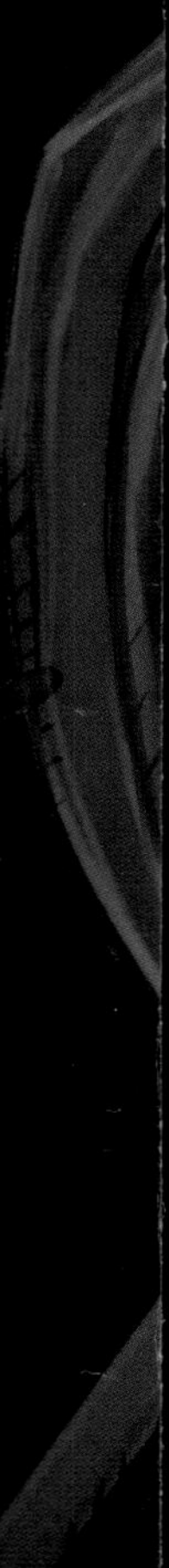

Writer & Co-Creator
MARK MILLAR

Breakdowns & Co-Creator
JOHN ROMITA JR.

Finishes & Ink Washes
TOM PALMER

Colorist
DEAN WHITE
with MICHAEL KELLEHER

Letterer
CHRIS ELIOPOULOS

Editor
JENNIFER LEE

Collection Editor: **JENNIFER LEE**

Book Designer: **SPRING HOTELING**

SVP of Print & Digital Publishing Sales: **DAVID GABRIEL**

SVP of Operations & Procurement, Publishing: **DAVID BOGART**

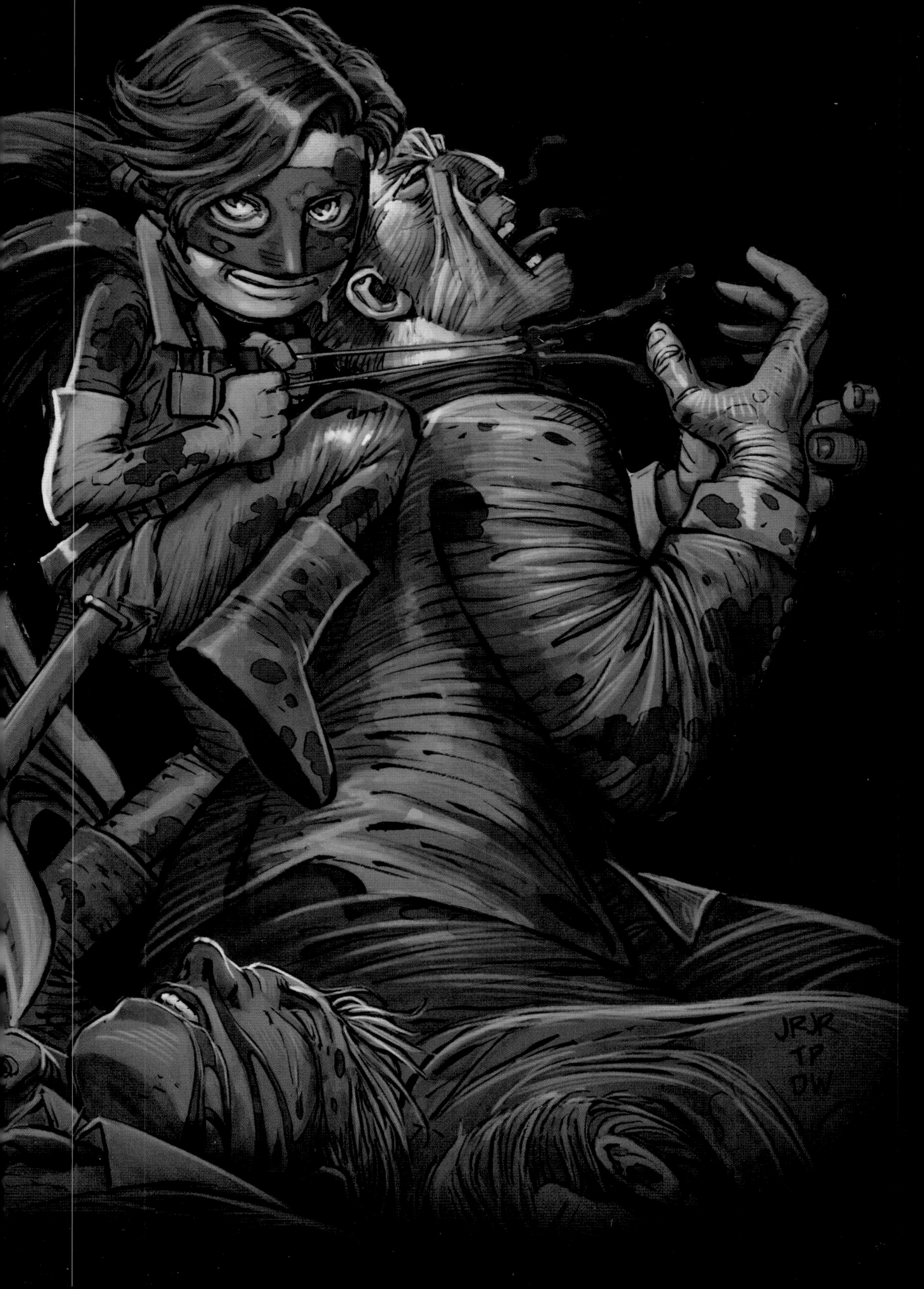

INTRODUCTION

am writing this to you from Mark Millar's dank, Scottish cellar. He says if I don't keep typing, he's going to turn on those jumper cables he's got hooked up to my balls! He went for a pint though, so please, I have seconds, seconds only! Someone send help! Please, I hear him coming bac—

ZZZttt!!!

Aagh!!

So, maybe that's not exactly true. Maybe I'm actually writing this from the comfort of my desk in Long Island. But you'd believe it, right? It's exactly the sort of thing you expect from a man who's written more gut-wrenching ultraviolence, more earth-shaking action than anyone I know. Hell, it's the kind of thing I expected, too, when I first met him.

Which brings me to London, spring 2012. I was there for my first Kapow!Con, and I had barely dropped off my bags when I got a text from Mark, asking me to come meet him for a drink. We had chatted through emails a bit in the weeks leading up to the convention, but I'd never met the man face-to-face. I was nervous. I half expected to walk up to the convention center and see some douchebag come flying through the glass, Mark stepping out after him, swords strapped on, pint in hand, delivering some awesome quip in a growling brogue before chopping the guy's feet off.

But that's not the man I found sitting there at the café by the convention offices. The man I found, Mark Millar, was cradling and feeding his newborn daughter, sipping at a coffee. As soon as he saw me he smiled and waved me over. "Young man!" he said, offering me a seat.

You can probably guess this initial meeting didn't end with the death of untold hundreds. It was really just a great conversation. I have young children myself, and so we got lost for a while, trading stories about these beautiful kids who keep us up all night like fucking maniacs, but whom we love more than the world. Honestly, it surprised me a little, how open and down-to-earth Mark was from go, and above all, how heartfelt his conversation was. Thinking back now, though, I know it shouldn't have surprised me. Because the ugly truth is that at its core, for me, Mark's work has always been about heart.

Now I can hear you out there: "Heart? Fuck off Snyder!" But hear me out…

Because for me, what makes Mark's work beloved by fans around the world isn't really the ball-zapping thrills or the incredible action. It's his love for his characters. It's the way he makes you relate to and care deeply about each of his creations from the first turn of the page. The craftsmanship in each voice, the quirks in each character's thinking—Mark makes his characters' hearts beat for you, makes them live for you in the most immediate, gripping ways. Better than just about anyone. So at the risk of offending you guys (and maybe even you, Mark), I'd say that at the very heart of Mark's work is, well… heart. Yes, this book has the

by SCOTT SNYDER

hyper-violent awesomeness you want and expect from Mark (wait 'til you get to the teddy-bear execution!)... but the magic of the book is how Mark brings to life Mindy's everyday problems side-by-side with the badassery. Here, in HIT-GIRL, we see her vulnerable for the first time, really vulnerable. Don't get me wrong, this is the Mindy you know and love—the vigilante, raised to be the toughest, deadliest hero in the world. But it's also Mindy the kid, trying to figure out how to be child, a daughter, a friend... a Mindy I'm sure you'll come to know and love even more.

Now if Mark's writing is the heart of this book, then John Romita Jr.'s storytelling is its soul. After all, what awesome thing is there to say about his work that hasn't been said before? His signature style is here in all its glory, so expressive and dynamic. His storytelling has never been better than it is in HIT-GIRL. And of course, here there's an extra thrill of getting to see him cut loose, shake off the restraints of all things kid-friendly, and get totally down and dirty. You can just tell from the art how much fun he's having, and it makes for an incredible read. And there's no overestimating the contribution of the crew John has with him here. Between Tom Palmer's rich line-work and finishes, Dean White's evocative colors and Chris Eliopoulos' artful lettering, you've got one of the best teams in visual storytelling.

So friends, to finish up, what follows here is a great book, by a great team, featuring the most bad-ass character currently in comics... There's no way you can read this book and not get swept away by the characters, the mindblowing action, and the adoration of comics inherent on every page. Because, like all the KICK-ASS books, this one is also about the transformative power of comics, about their ability to inspire wonder and desires—good and bad. Like I said, it's a book made with much love, and I couldn't be more honored that Mark decided to reach out to me to write this. Savor this book; it's a wonder.

Still, the next time Mark invites me for a drink, he better bring his fucking swords. Swords, Mark!

Scott Snyder is a novelist and the award-winning writer for BATMAN, SWAMP THING, SEVERED, and AMERICAN VAMPIRE.

ONE

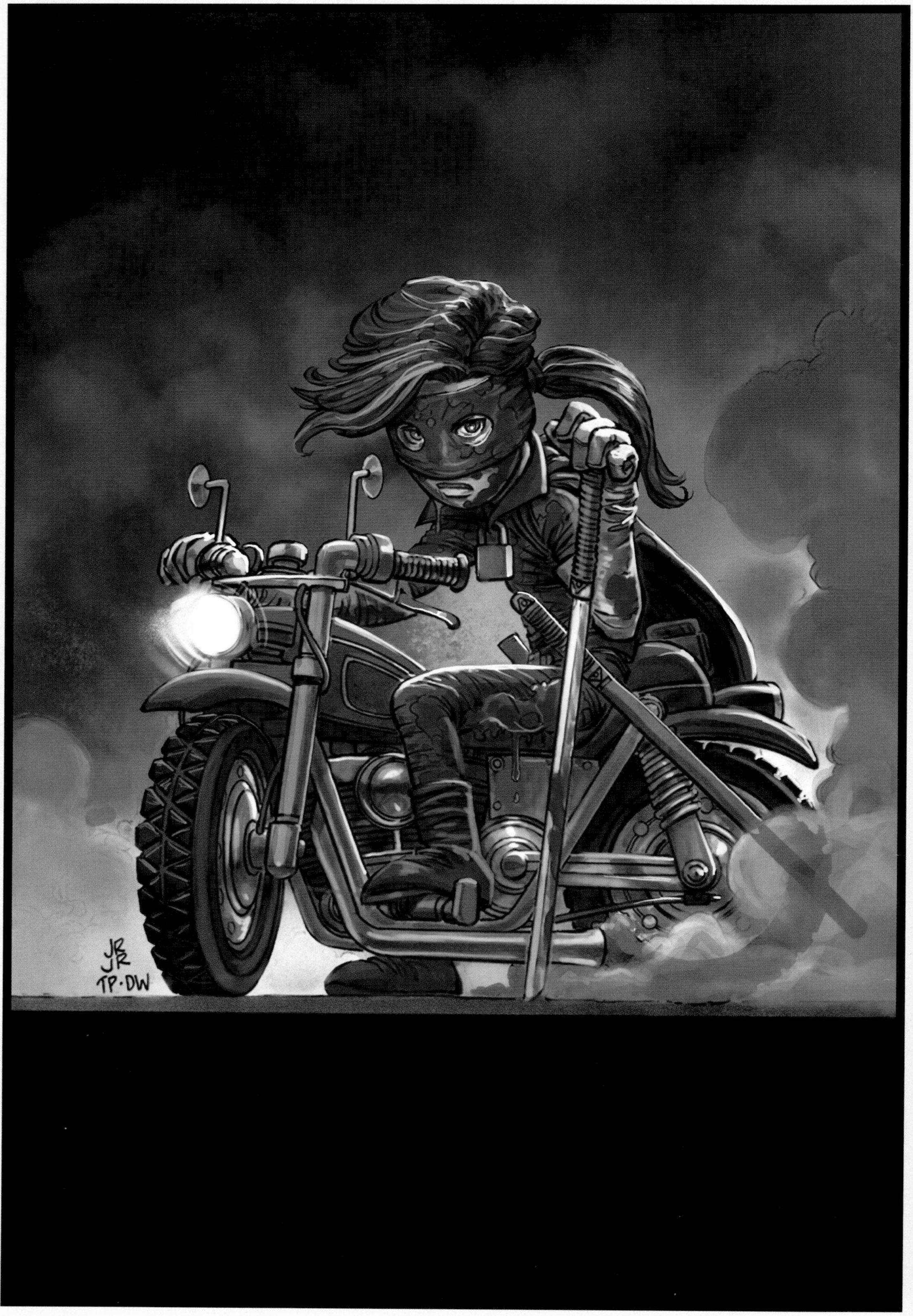

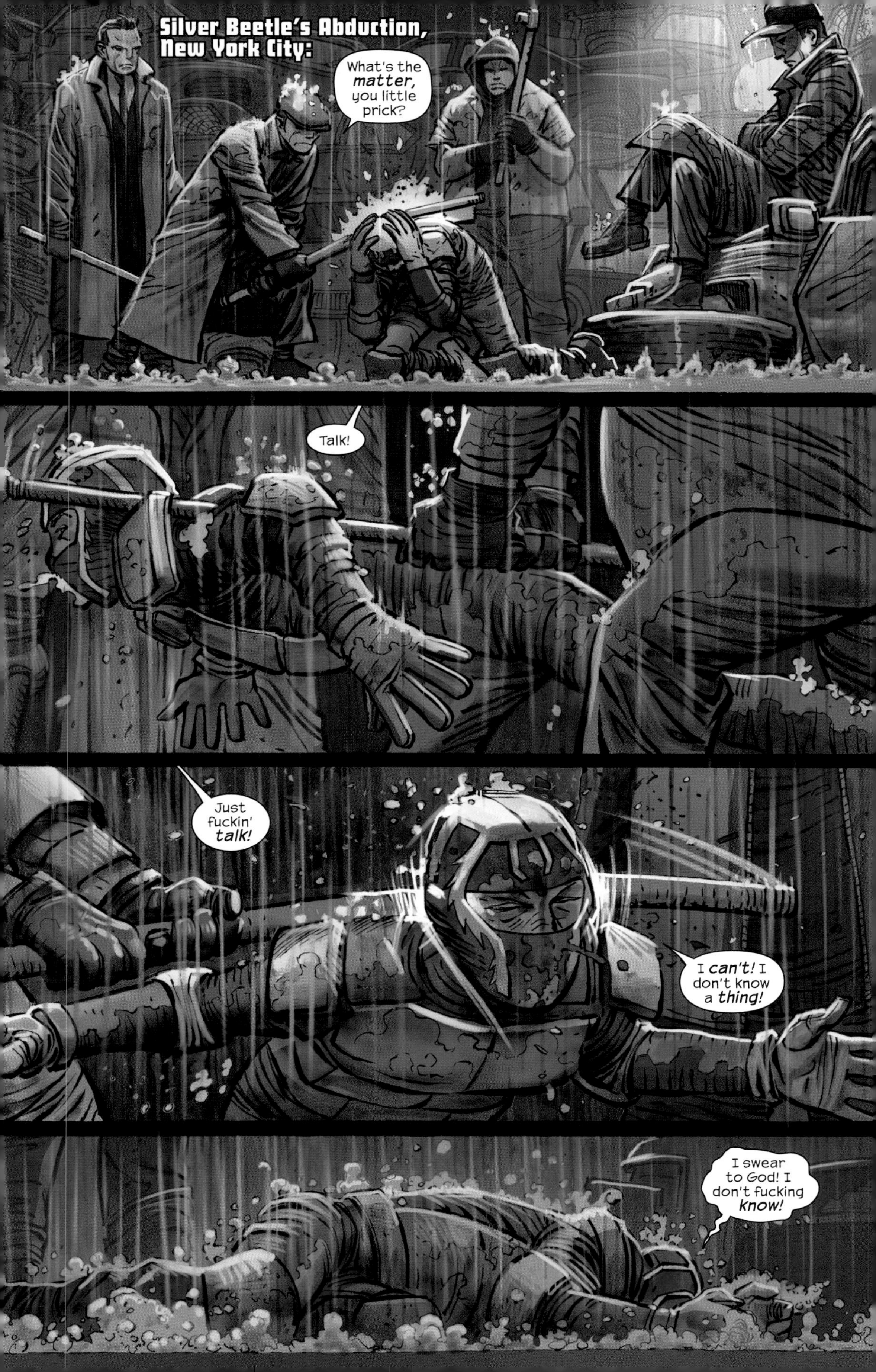
Silver Beetle's Abduction, New York City:
What's the matter, you little prick?
Talk!
Just fuckin' talk!
I can't! I don't know a thing!
I swear to God! I don't fucking know!

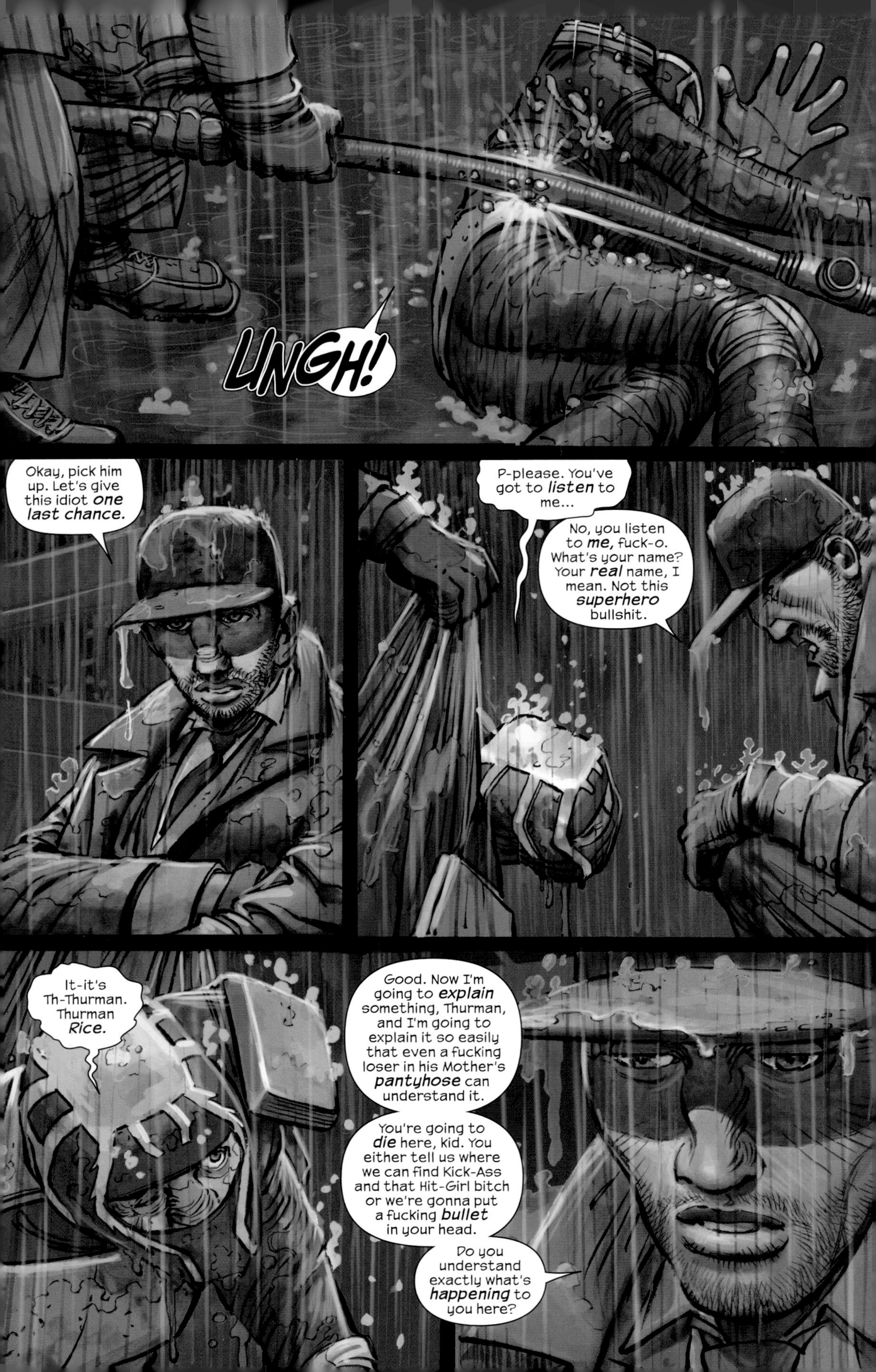
UNGH!
Okay, pick him up. Let's give this idiot one last chance.
P-please. You've got to listen to me...
No, you listen to me, fuck-o. What's your name? Your real name, I mean. Not this superhero bullshit.
It-it's Th-Thurman. Thurman Rice.
Good. Now I'm going to explain something, Thurman, and I'm going to explain it so easily that even a fucking loser in his Mother's pantyhose can understand it.
You're going to die here, kid. You either tell us where we can find Kick-Ass and that Hit-Girl bitch or we're gonna put a fucking bullet in your head.
Do you understand exactly what's happening to you here?

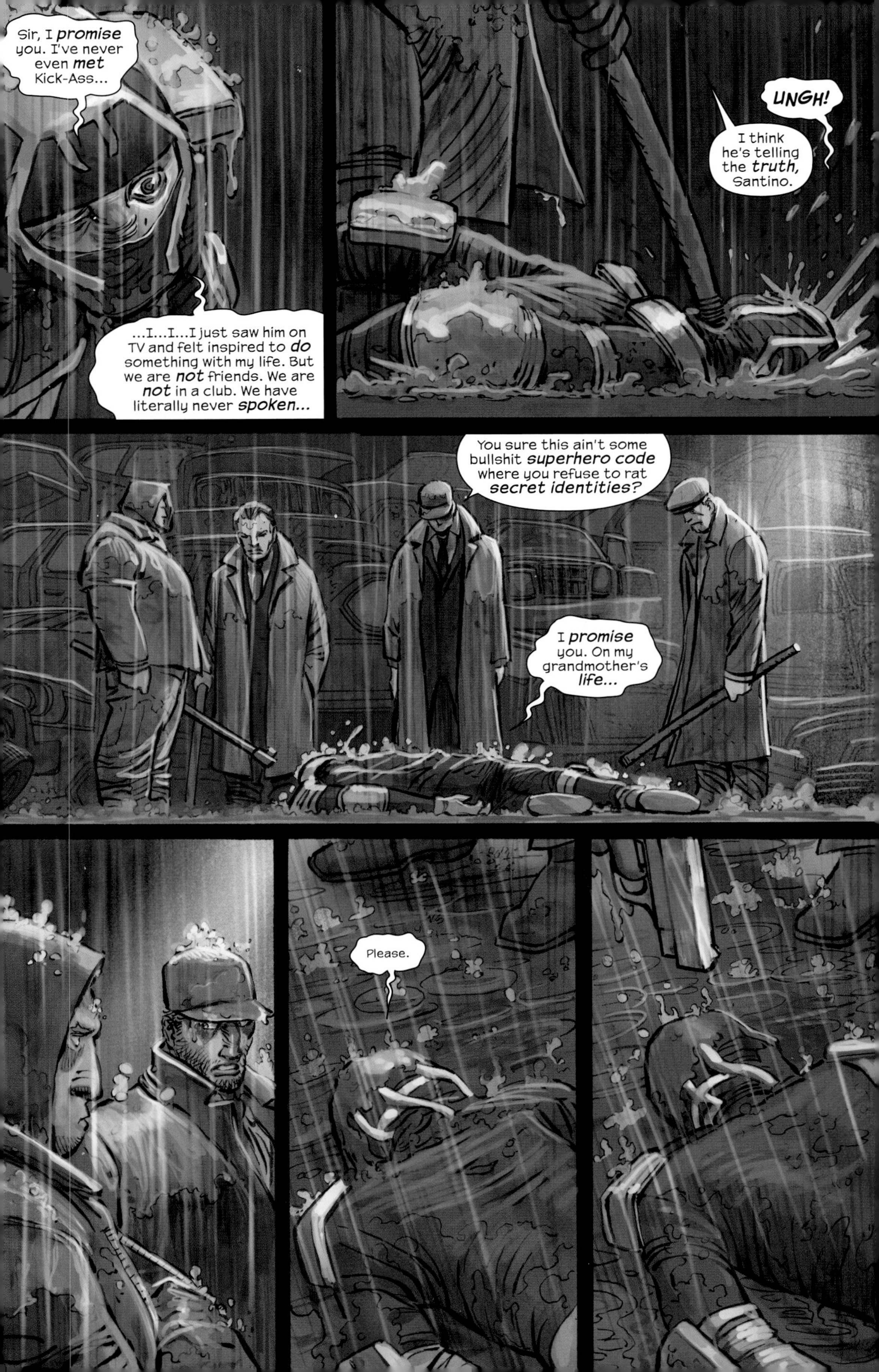
Sir, I promise you. I've never even met Kick-Ass...
...I...I...I just saw him on TV and felt inspired to do something with my life. But we are not friends. We are not in a club. We have literally never spoken...
UNGH!
I think he's telling the truth, Santino.
You sure this ain't some bullshit superhero code where you refuse to rat secret identities?
I promise you. On my grandmother's life...
Please.

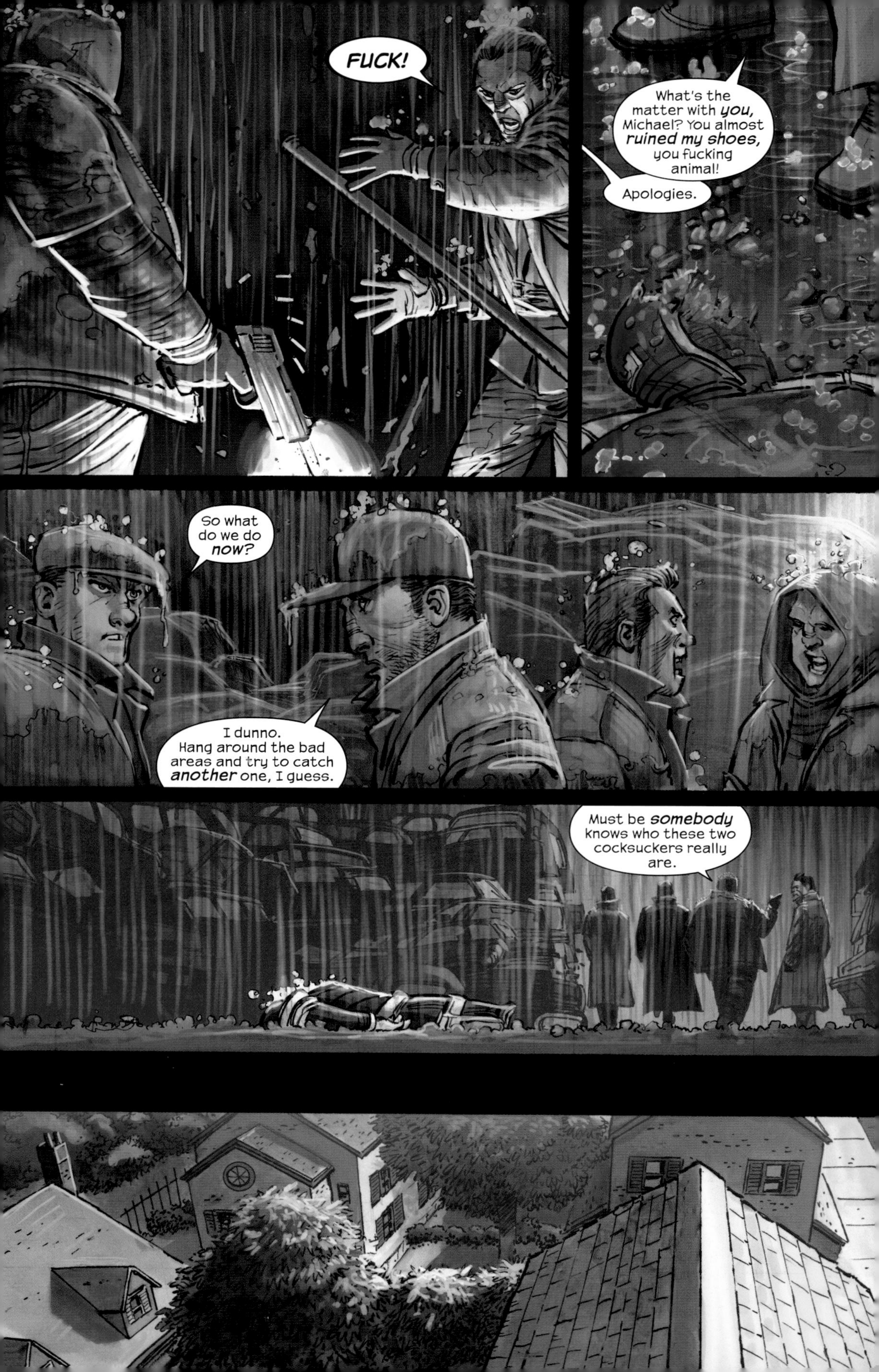
FUCK!
What's the matter with you, Michael? You almost ruined my shoes, you fucking animal!
Apologies.
So what do we do now?
I dunno. Hang around the bad areas and try to catch another one, I guess.
Must be somebody knows who these two cocksuckers really are.

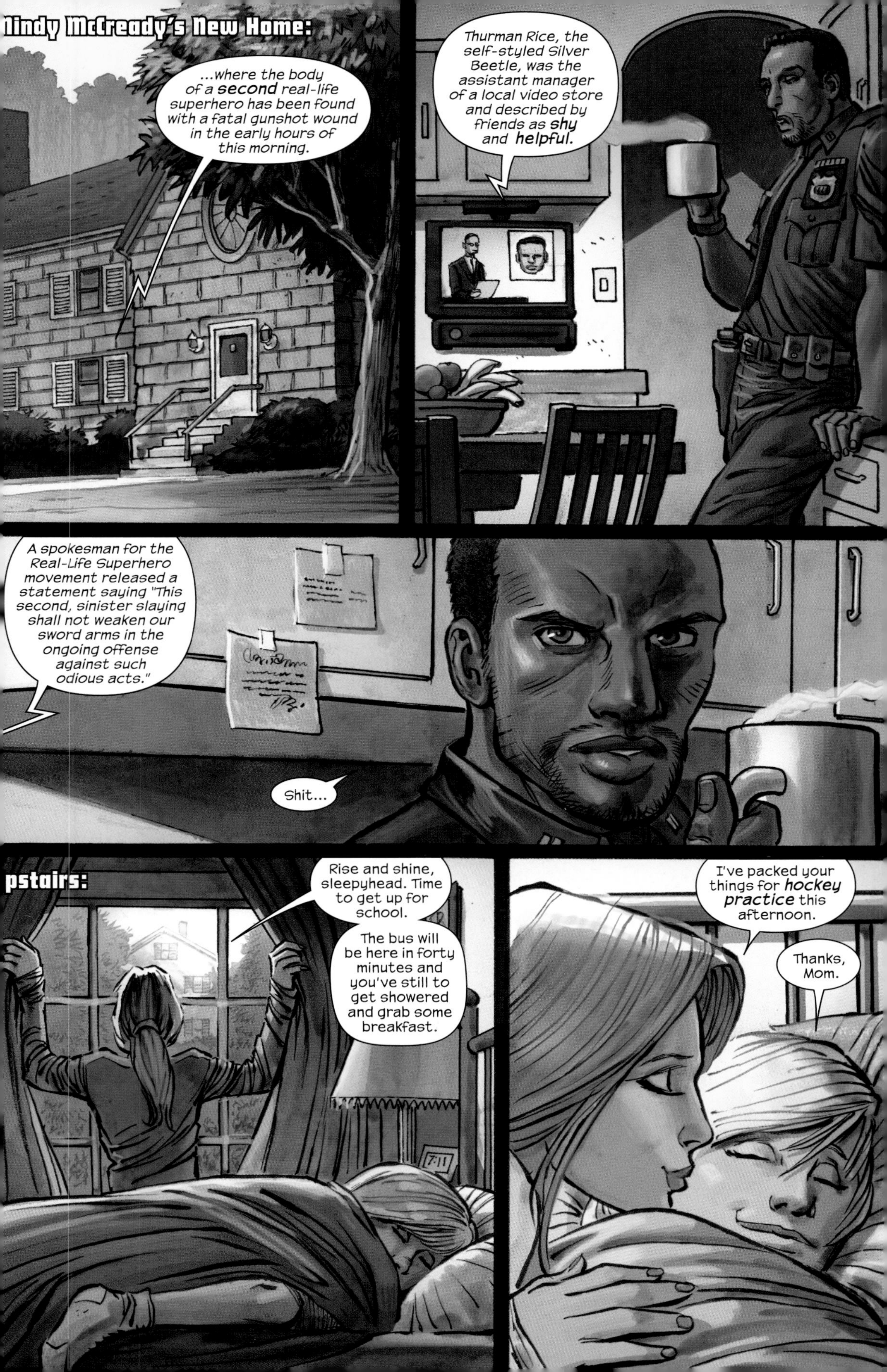

lindy McCready's New Home:
...where the body of a **second** real-life superhero has been found with a fatal gunshot wound in the early hours of this morning.
Thurman Rice, the self-styled Silver Beetle, was the assistant manager of a local video store and described by friends as **shy** and **helpful**.
A spokesman for the Real-Life Superhero movement released a statement saying "This second, sinister slaying shall not weaken our sword arms in the ongoing offense against such odious acts."
Shit...
pstairs:
Rise and shine, sleepyhead. Time to get up for school.
The bus will be here in forty minutes and you've still to get showered and grab some breakfast.
7:11
I've packed your things for ***hockey practice*** this afternoon.
Thanks, Mom.

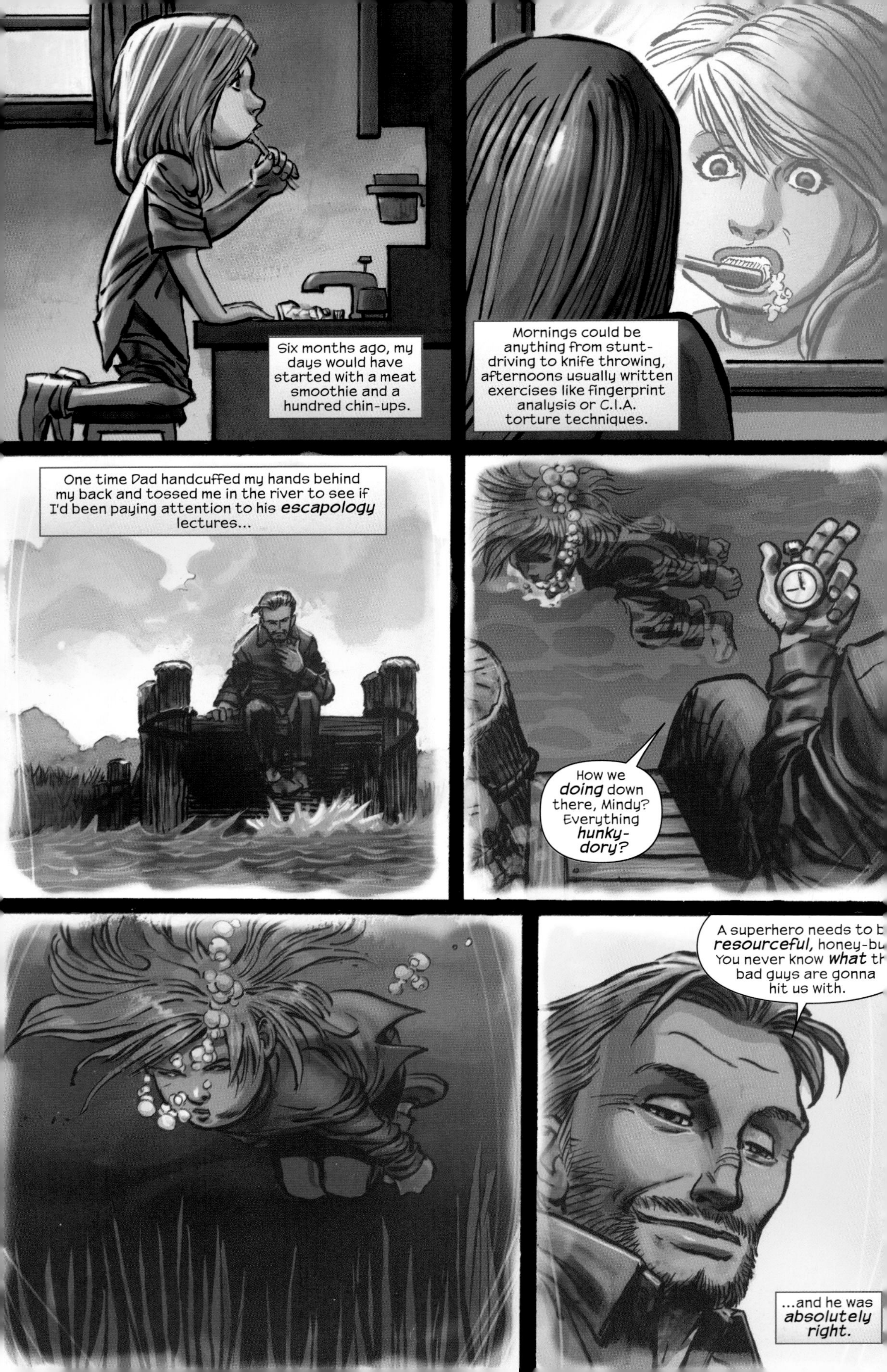

Six months ago, my days would have started with a meat smoothie and a hundred chin-ups.
Mornings could be anything from stunt-driving to knife throwing, afternoons usually written exercises like fingerprint analysis or C.I.A. torture techniques.
One time Dad handcuffed my hands behind my back and tossed me in the river to see if I'd been paying attention to his *escapology* lectures...
How we *doing* down there, Mindy? Everything *hunky-dory?*
A superhero needs to b *resourceful,* honey-bu You never know *what* th bad guys are gonna hit us with.
...and he was *absolutely right.*

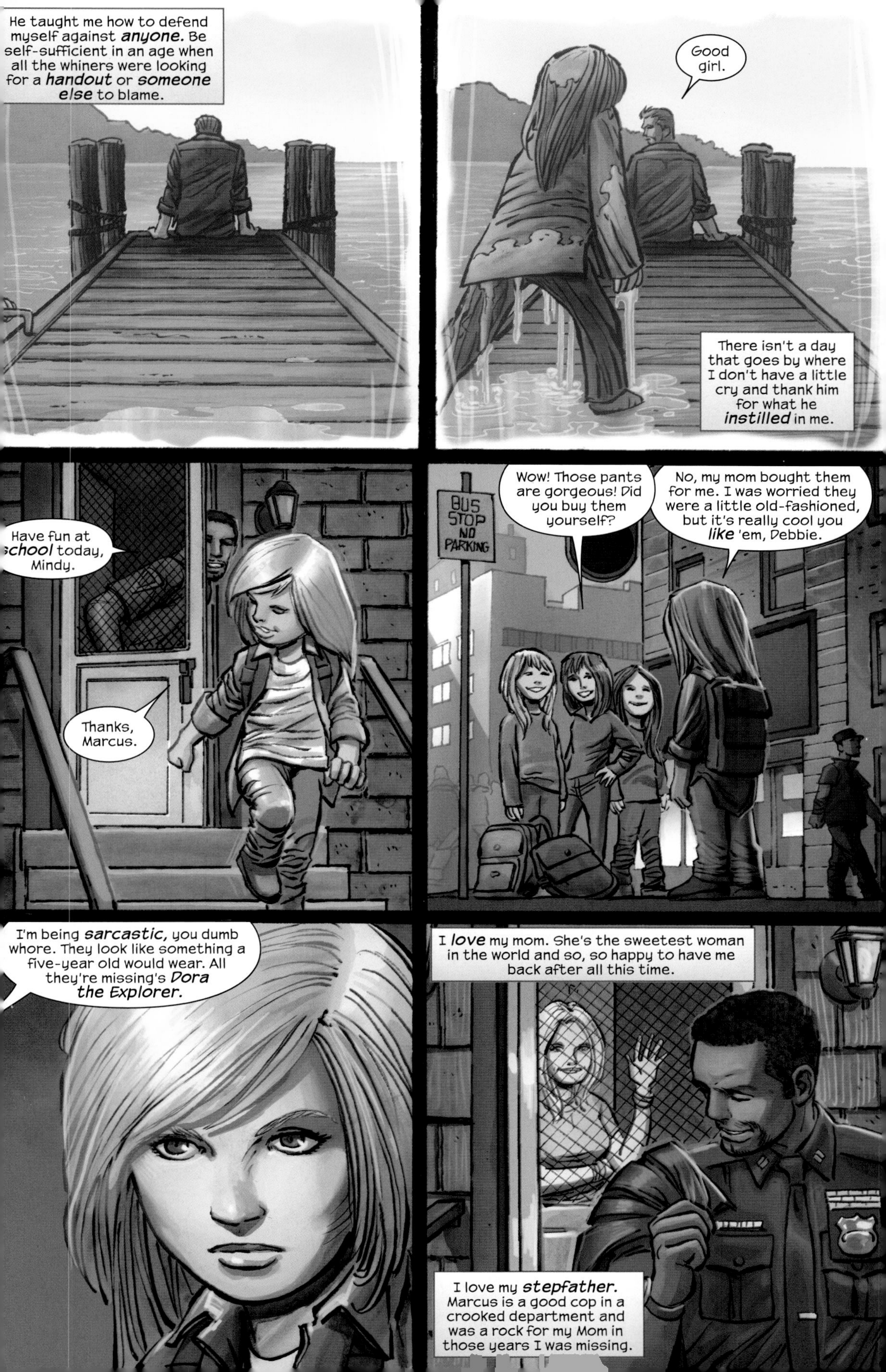
He taught me how to defend myself against anyone. Be self-sufficient in an age when all the whiners were looking for a handout or someone else to blame.
Good girl.
There isn't a day that goes by where I don't have a little cry and thank him for what he instilled in me.
Have fun at school today, Mindy.
Thanks, Marcus.
BUS STOP NO PARKING
Wow! Those pants are gorgeous! Did you buy them yourself?
No, my mom bought them for me. I was worried they were a little old-fashioned, but it's really cool you like 'em, Debbie.
I'm being sarcastic, you dumb whore. They look like something a five-year old would wear. All they're missing's Dora the Explorer.
I love my mom. She's the sweetest woman in the world and so, so happy to have me back after all this time.
I love my stepfather. Marcus is a good cop in a crooked department and was a rock for my Mom in those years I was missing.

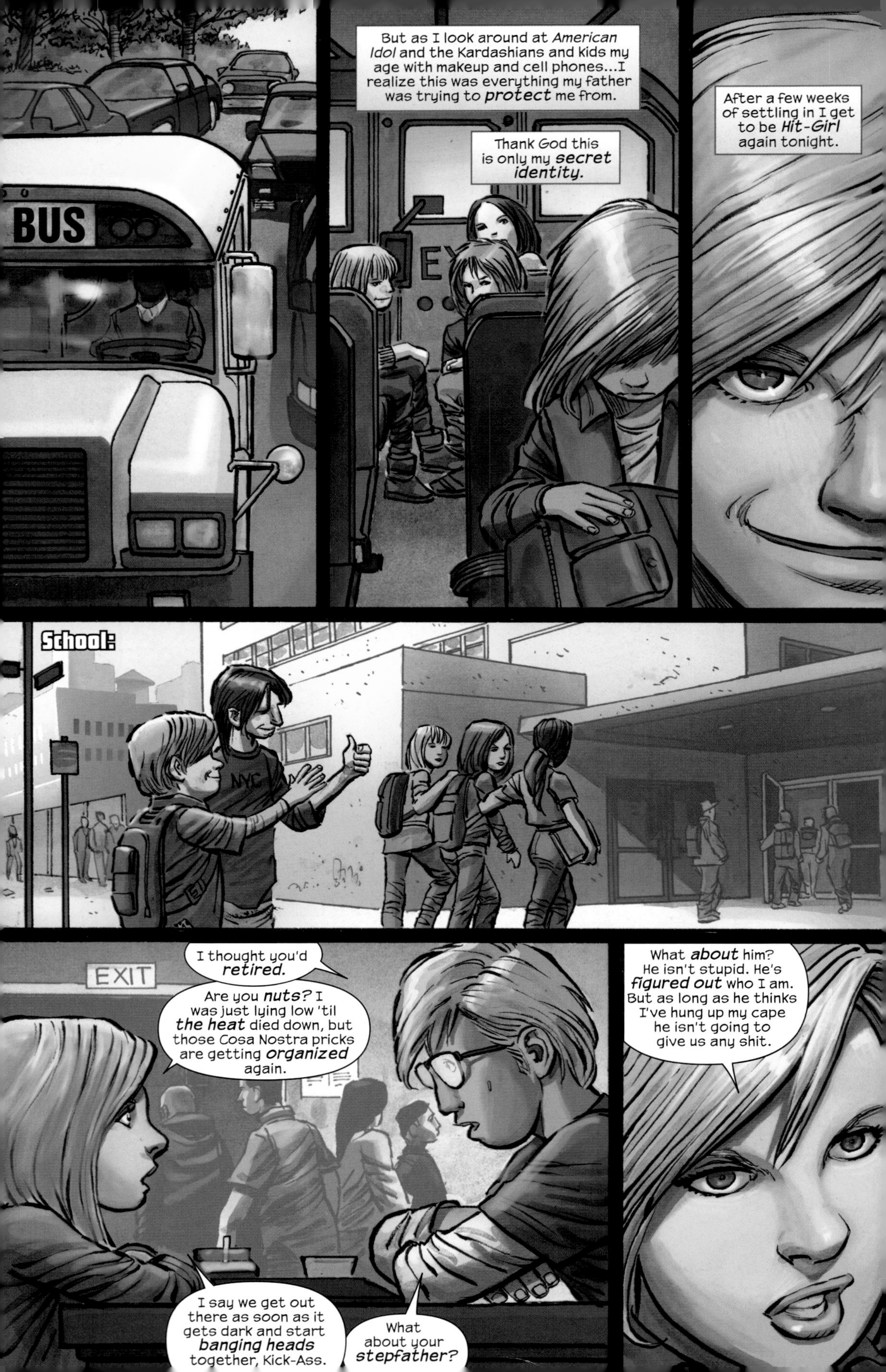
BUS
But as I look around at American Idol and the Kardashians and kids my age with makeup and cell phones...I realize this was everything my father was trying to protect me from.
Thank God this is only my secret identity.
After a few weeks of settling in I get to be Hit-Girl again tonight.
School:
NYC
EXIT
I thought you'd retired.
Are you nuts? I was just lying low 'til the heat died down, but those Cosa Nostra pricks are getting organized again.
I say we get out there as soon as it gets dark and start banging heads together, Kick-Ass.
What about your stepfather?
What about him? He isn't stupid. He's figured out who I am. But as long as he thinks I've hung up my cape he isn't going to give us any shit.

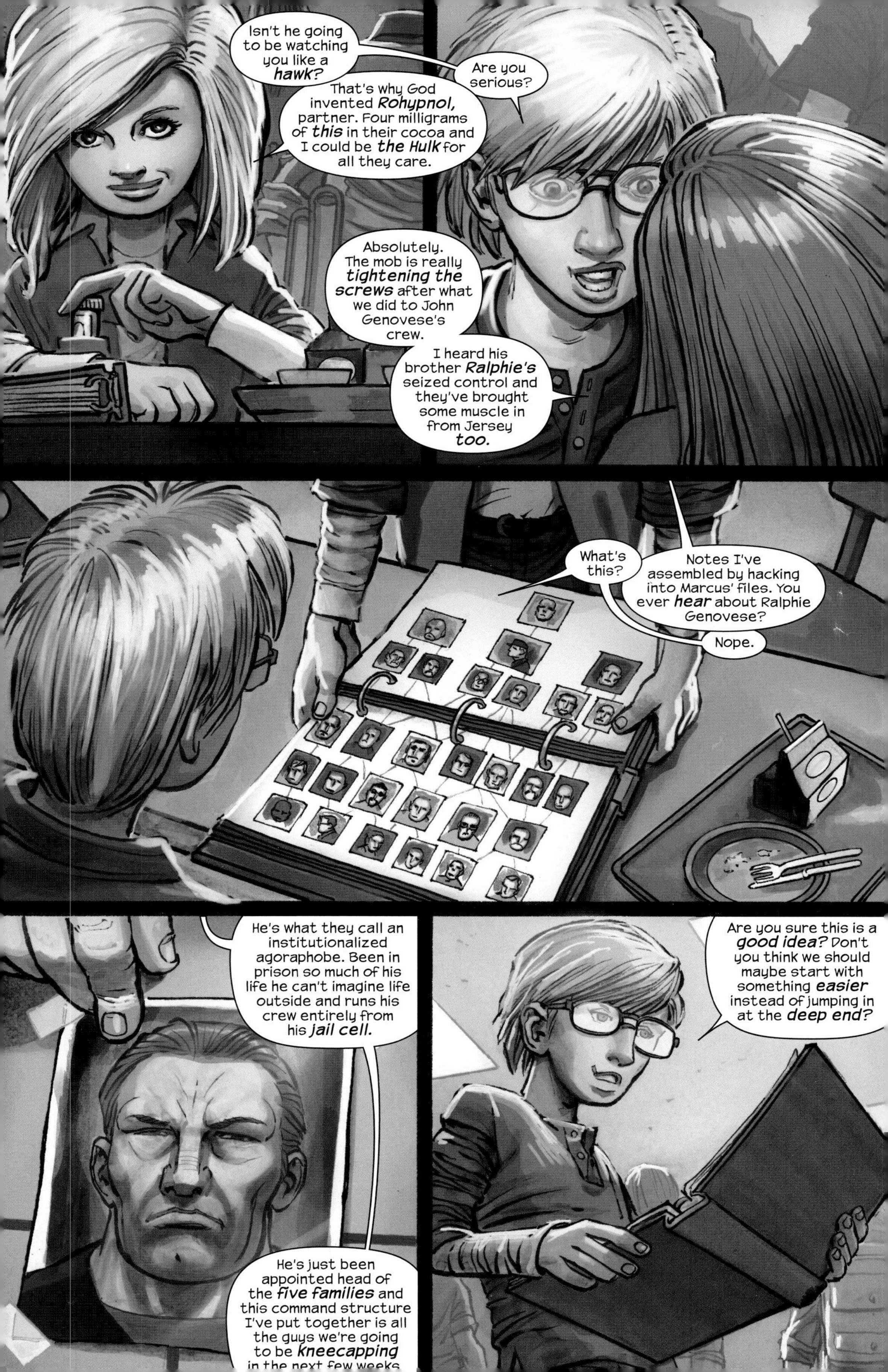
Isn't he going to be watching you like a hawk?
Are you serious?
That's why God invented Rohypnol, partner. Four milligrams of this in their cocoa and I could be the Hulk for all they care.
Absolutely. The mob is really tightening the screws after what we did to John Genovese's crew.
I heard his brother Ralphie's seized control and they've brought some muscle in from Jersey too.
What's this?
Notes I've assembled by hacking into Marcus' files. You ever hear about Ralphie Genovese?
Nope.
He's what they call an institutionalized agoraphobe. Been in prison so much of his life he can't imagine life outside and runs his crew entirely from his jail cell.
He's just been appointed head of the five families and this command structure I've put together is all the guys we're going to be kneecapping
Are you sure this is a good idea? Don't you think we should maybe start with something easier instead of jumping in at the deep end?

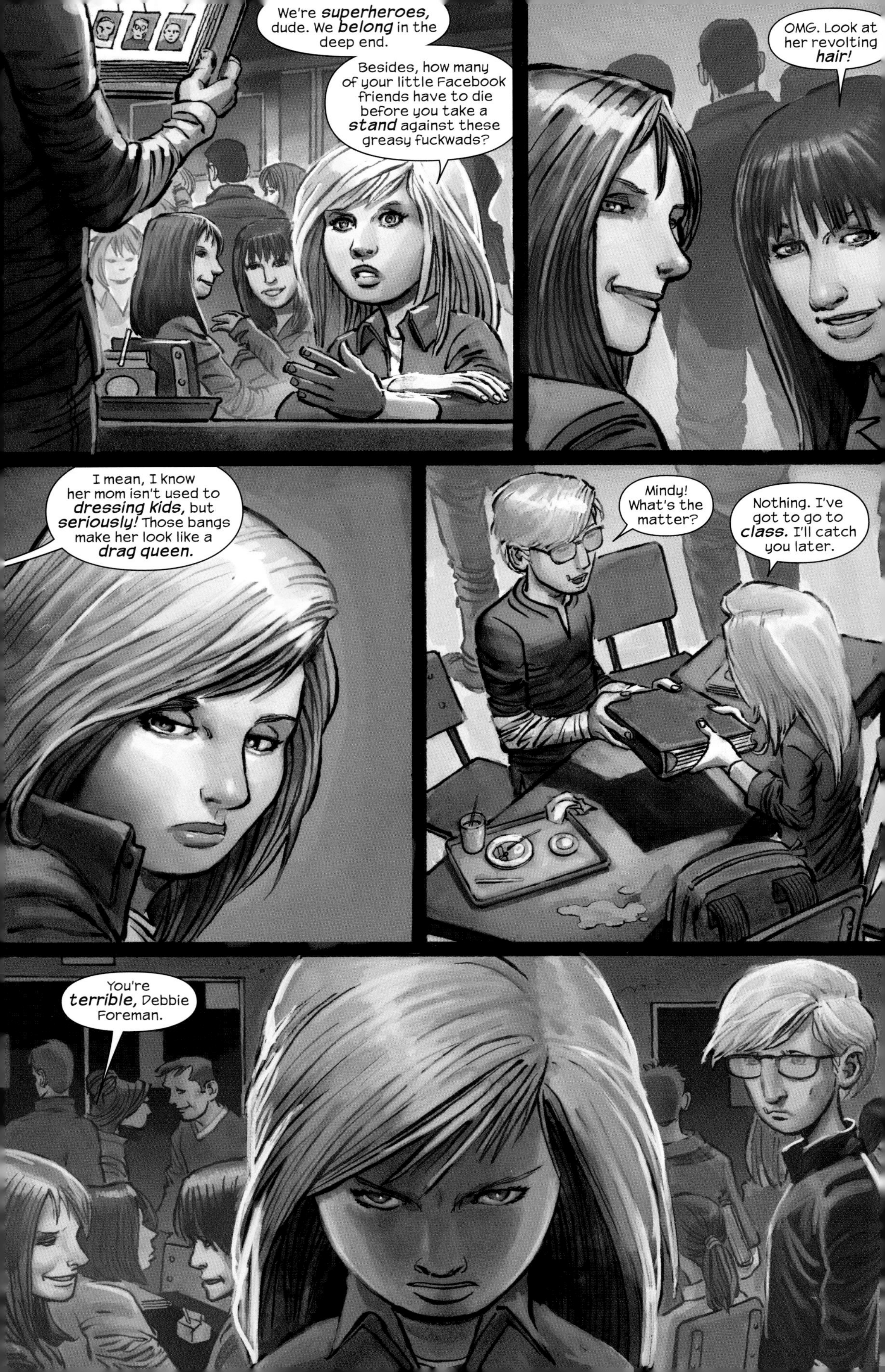
We're superheroes, dude. We belong in the deep end.
Besides, how many of your little Facebook friends have to die before you take a stand against these greasy fuckwads?
OMG. Look at her revolting hair!
I mean, I know her mom isn't used to dressing kids, but seriously! Those bangs make her look like a drag queen.
Mindy! What's the matter?
Nothing. I've got to go to class. I'll catch you later.
You're terrible, Debbie Foreman.

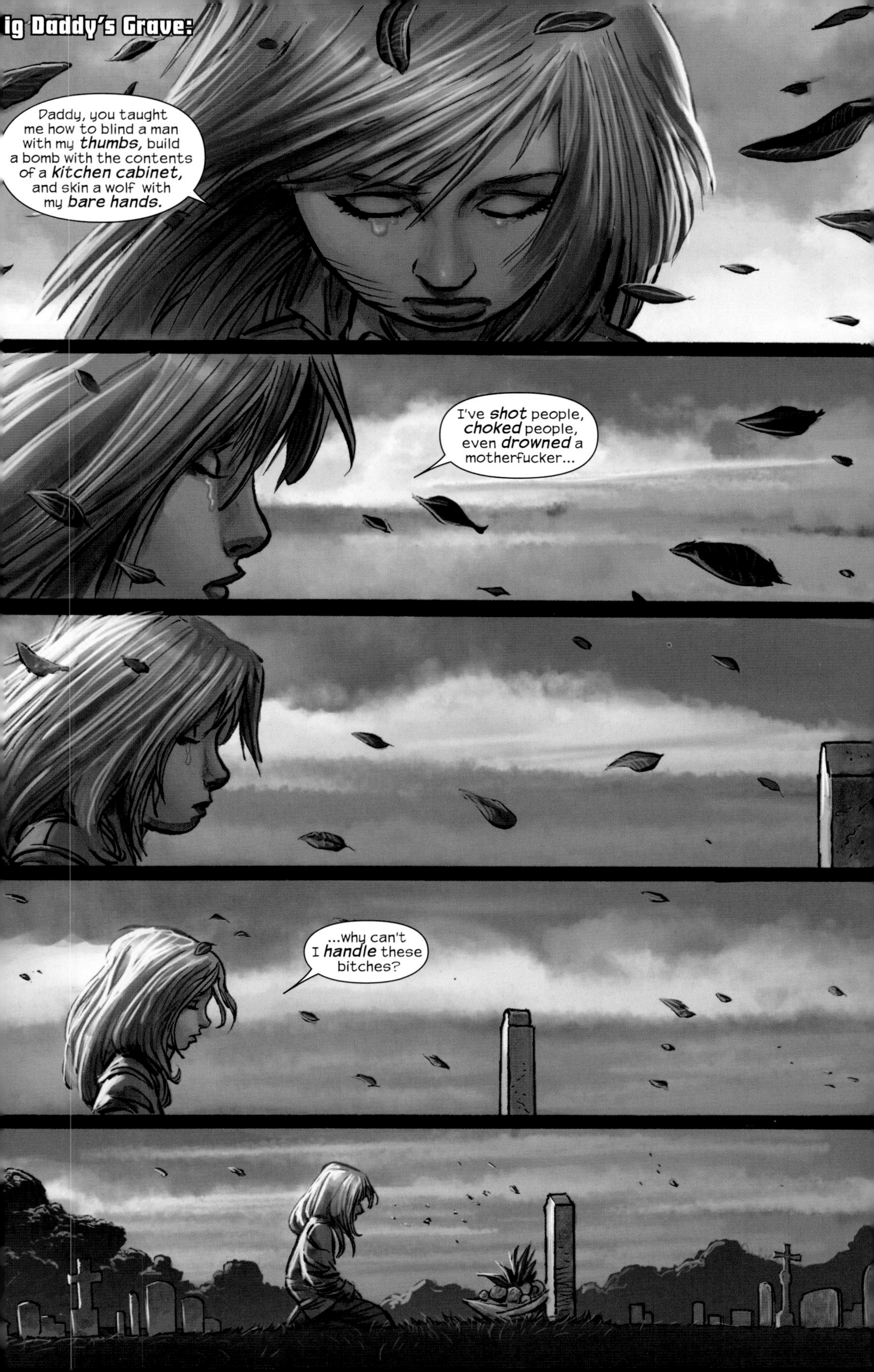
ig Daddy's Grave:
Daddy, you taught me how to blind a man with my *thumbs,* build a bomb with the contents of a *kitchen cabinet,* and skin a wolf with my *bare hands.*
I've *shot* people, *choked* people, even *drowned* a motherfucker...
...why can't I *handle* these bitches?

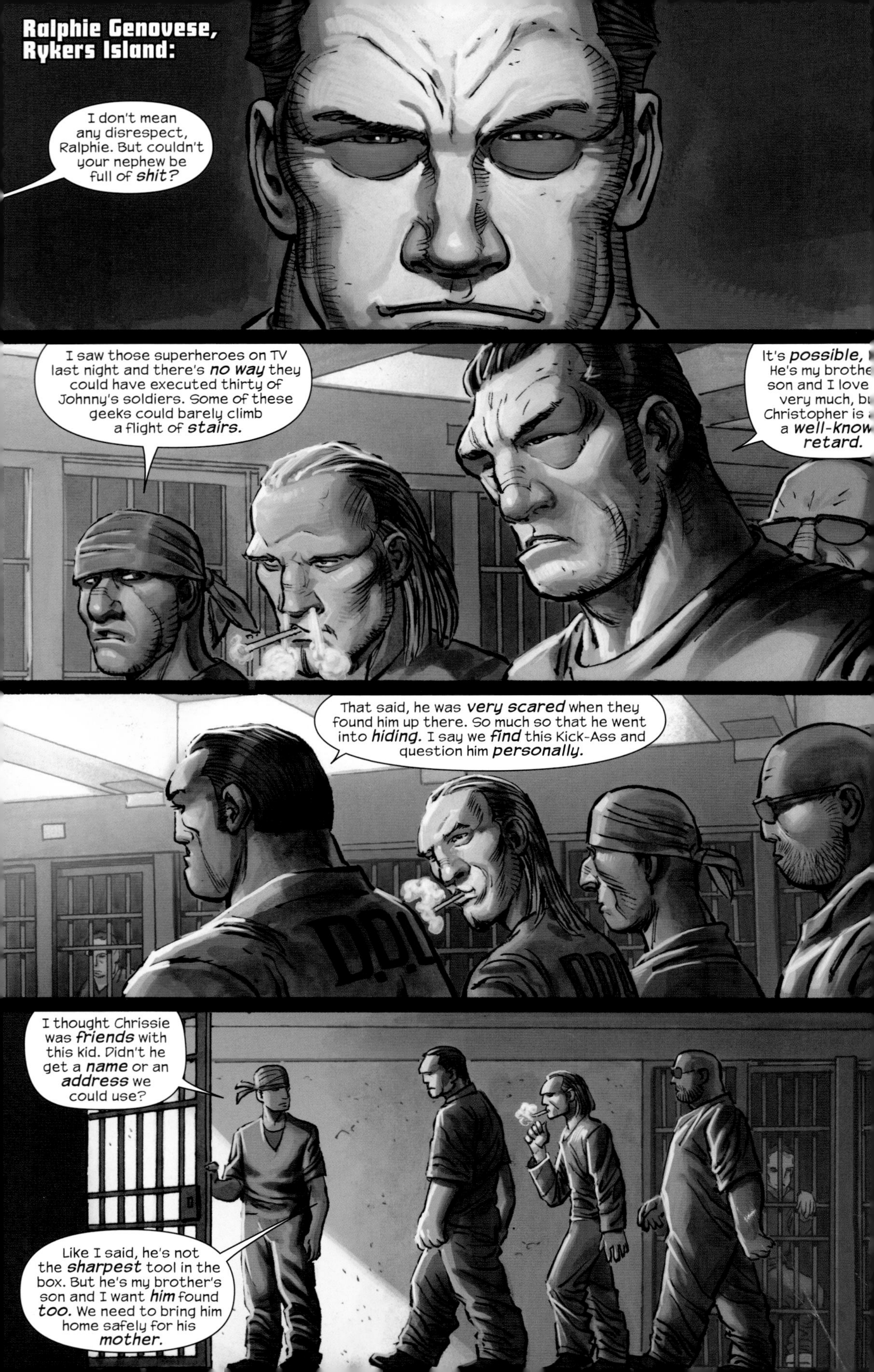

Ralphie Genovese, Rykers Island:
I don't mean any disrespect, Ralphie. But couldn't your nephew be full of shit?
I saw those superheroes on TV last night and there's no way they could have executed thirty of Johnny's soldiers. Some of these geeks could barely climb a flight of stairs.
It's possible, He's my brothe son and I love very much, bu Christopher is a well-know retard.
That said, he was very scared when they found him up there. So much so that he went into hiding. I say we find this Kick-Ass and question him personally.
D.O.
I thought Chrissie was friends with this kid. Didn't he get a name or an address we could use?
Like I said, he's not the sharpest tool in the box. But he's my brother's son and I want him found too. We need to bring him home safely for his mother.

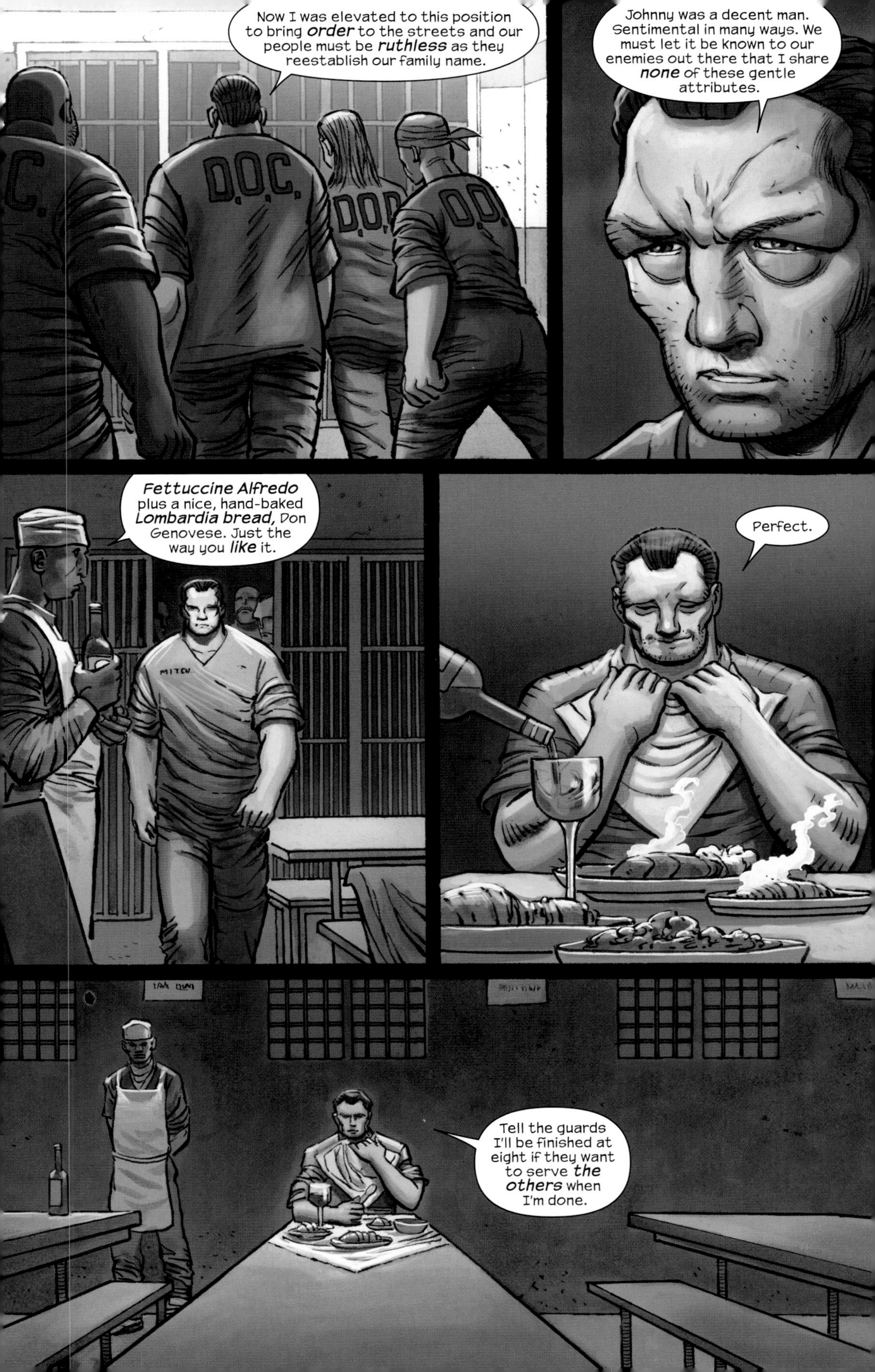

Now I was elevated to this position to bring *order* to the streets and our people must be *ruthless* as they reestablish our family name.
D.O.C.
Johnny was a decent man. Sentimental in many ways. We must let it be known to our enemies out there that I share *none* of these gentle attributes.
Fettuccine Alfredo plus a nice, hand-baked *Lombardia bread,* Don Genovese. Just the way you *like* it.
Perfect.
Tell the guards I'll be finished at eight if they want to serve *the others* when I'm done.

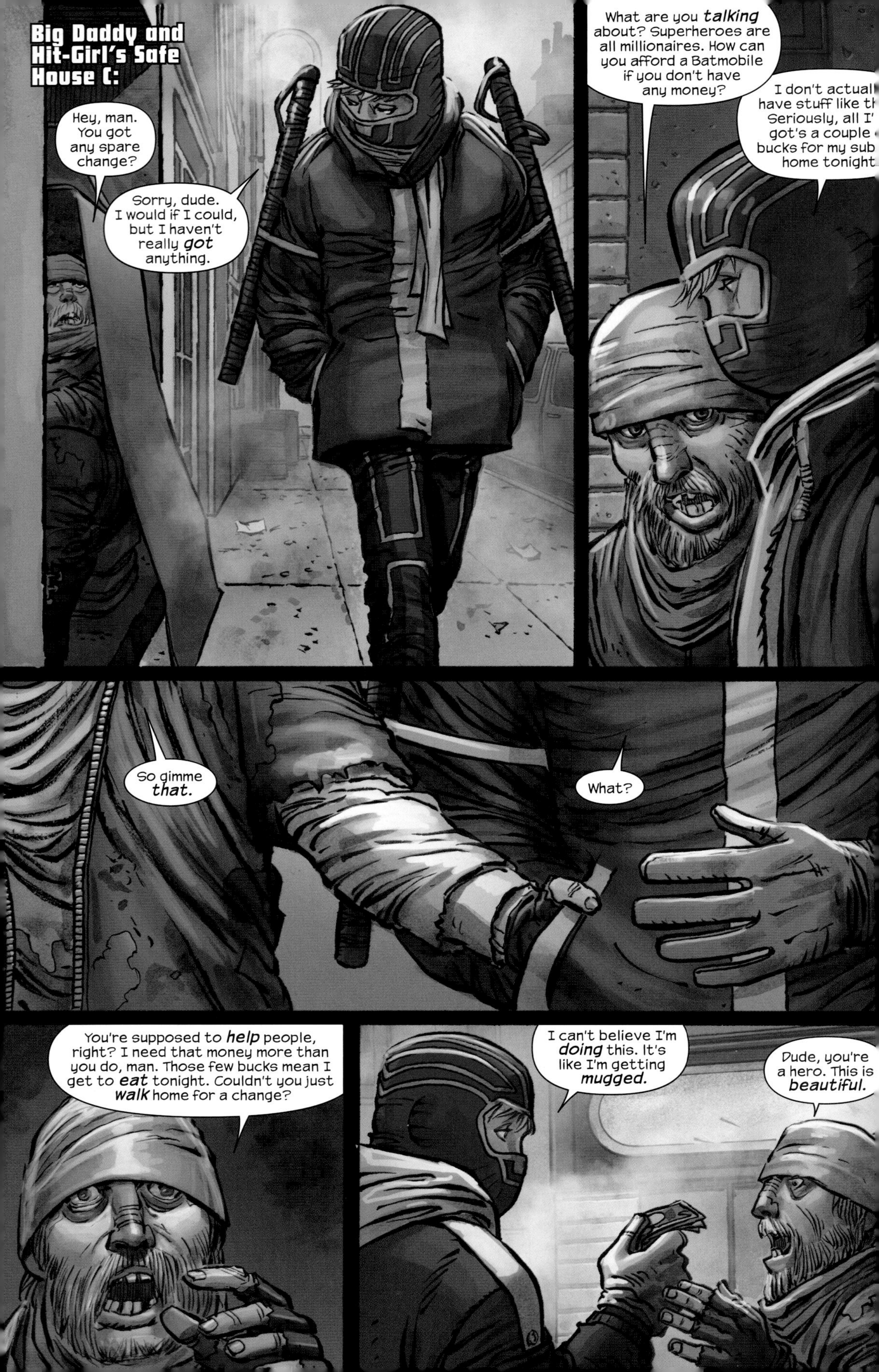
Big Daddy and Hit-Girl's Safe House C:
Hey, man. You got any spare change?
Sorry, dude. I would if I could, but I haven't really *got* anything.
What are you *talking* about? Superheroes are all millionaires. How can you afford a Batmobile if you don't have any money?
I don't actual have stuff like th Seriously, all I' got's a couple bucks for my sub home tonight
So gimme *that.*
What?
You're supposed to *help* people, right? I need that money more than you do, man. Those few bucks mean I get to *eat* tonight. Couldn't you just *walk* home for a change?
I can't believe I'm *doing* this. It's like I'm getting *mugged.*
Dude, you're a hero. This is *beautiful.*

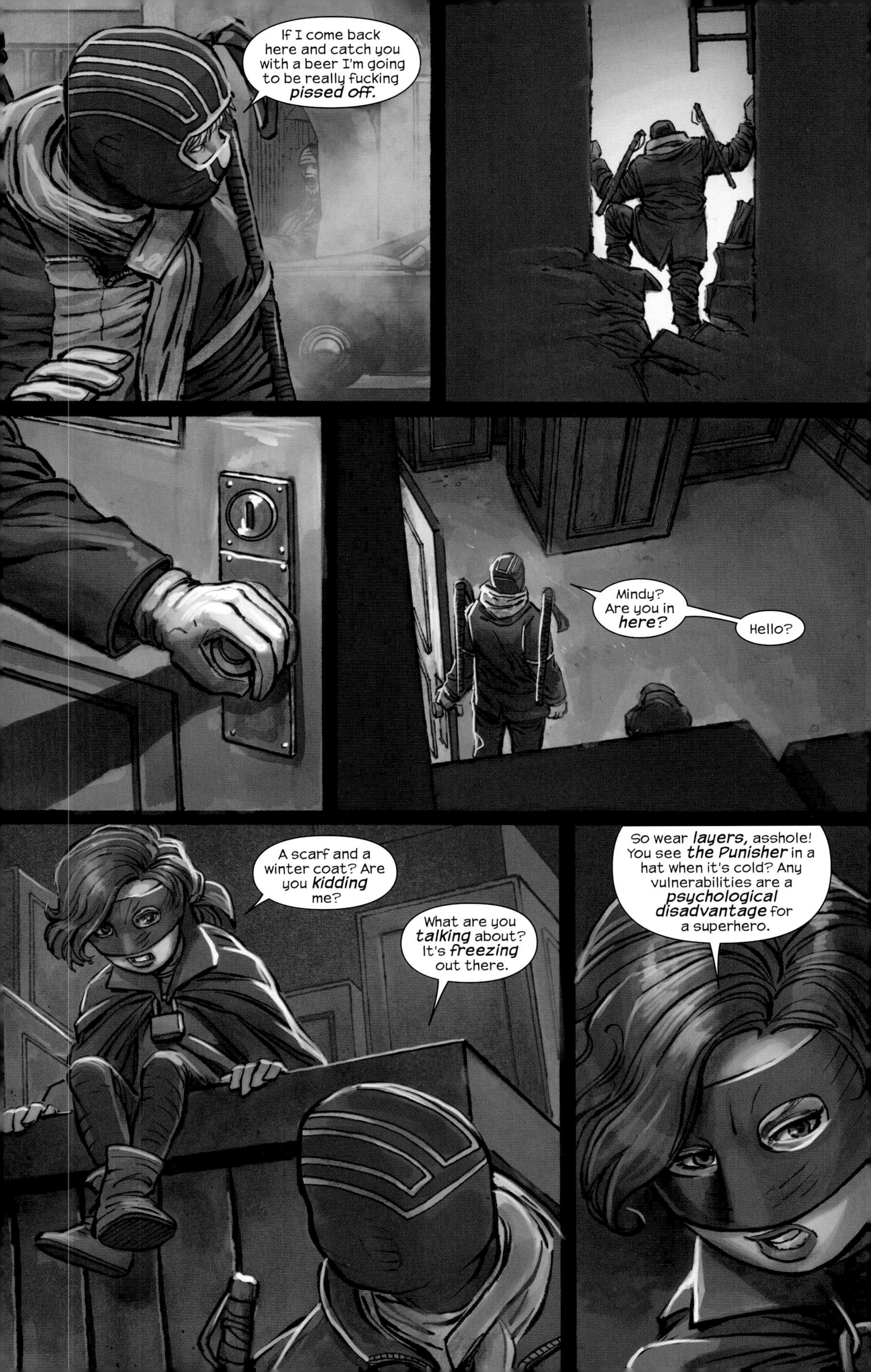
If I come back here and catch you with a beer I'm going to be really fucking pissed off.
Mindy? Are you in here?
Hello?
A scarf and a winter coat? Are you kidding me?
What are you talking about? It's freezing out there.
So wear layers, asshole! You see the Punisher in a hat when it's cold? Any vulnerabilities are a psychological disadvantage for a superhero.

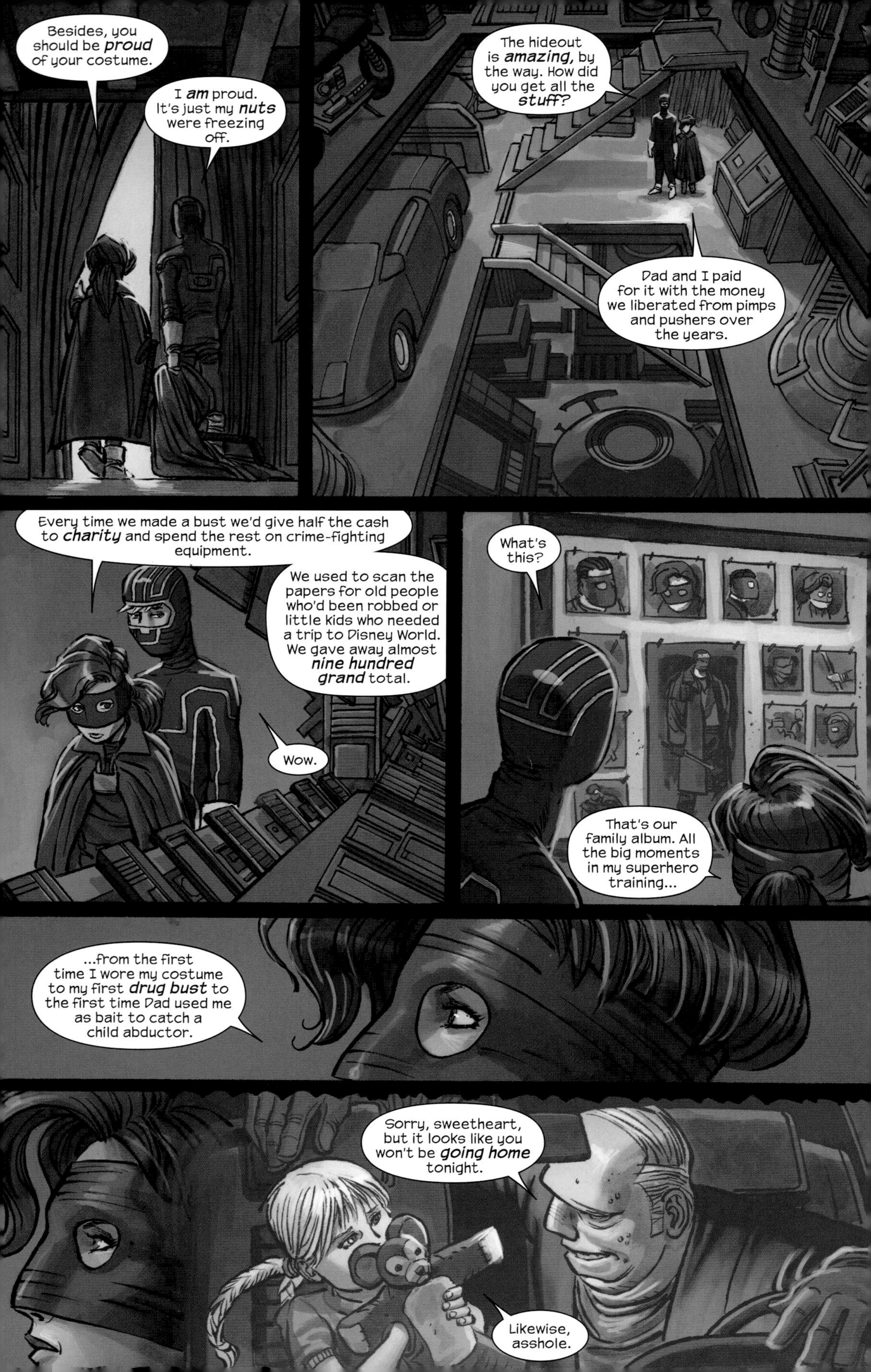
Besides, you should be *proud* of your costume.
I *am* proud. It's just my *nuts* were freezing off.
The hideout is *amazing,* by the way. How did you get all the *stuff?*
Dad and I paid for it with the money we liberated from pimps and pushers over the years.
Every time we made a bust we'd give half the cash to *charity* and spend the rest on crime-fighting equipment.
We used to scan the papers for old people who'd been robbed or little kids who needed a trip to Disney World. We gave away almost *nine hundred grand* total.
Wow.
What's this?
That's our family album. All the big moments in my superhero training...
...from the first time I wore my costume to my first *drug bust* to the first time Dad used me as bait to catch a child abductor.
Sorry, sweetheart, but it looks like you won't be *going home* tonight.
Likewise, asshole.

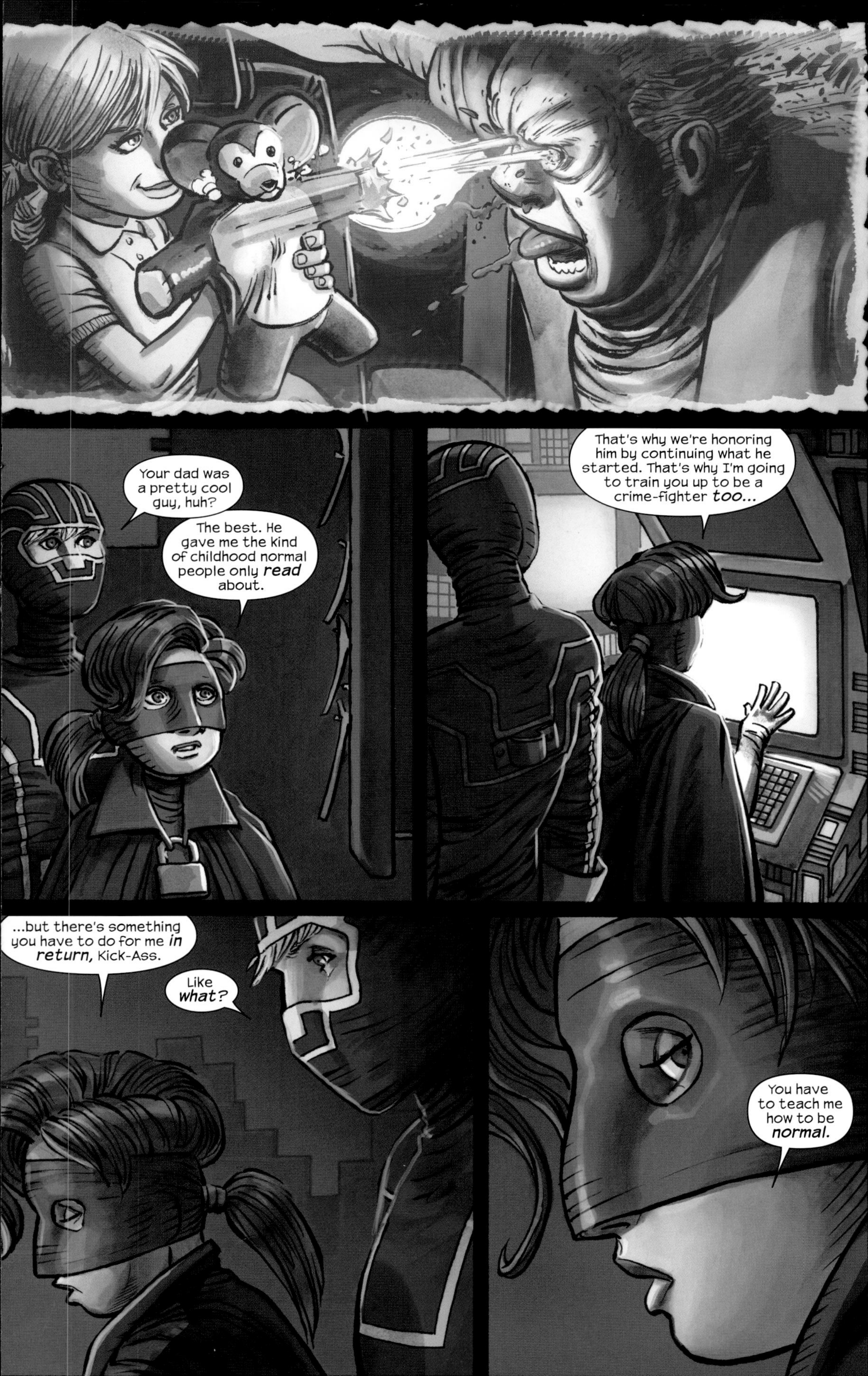
Your dad was a pretty cool guy, huh?
The best. He gave me the kind of childhood normal people only *read* about.
That's why we're honoring him by continuing what he started. That's why I'm going to train you up to be a crime-fighter *too...*
...but there's something you have to do for me *in return,* Kick-Ass.
Like *what?*
You have to teach me how to be *normal.*

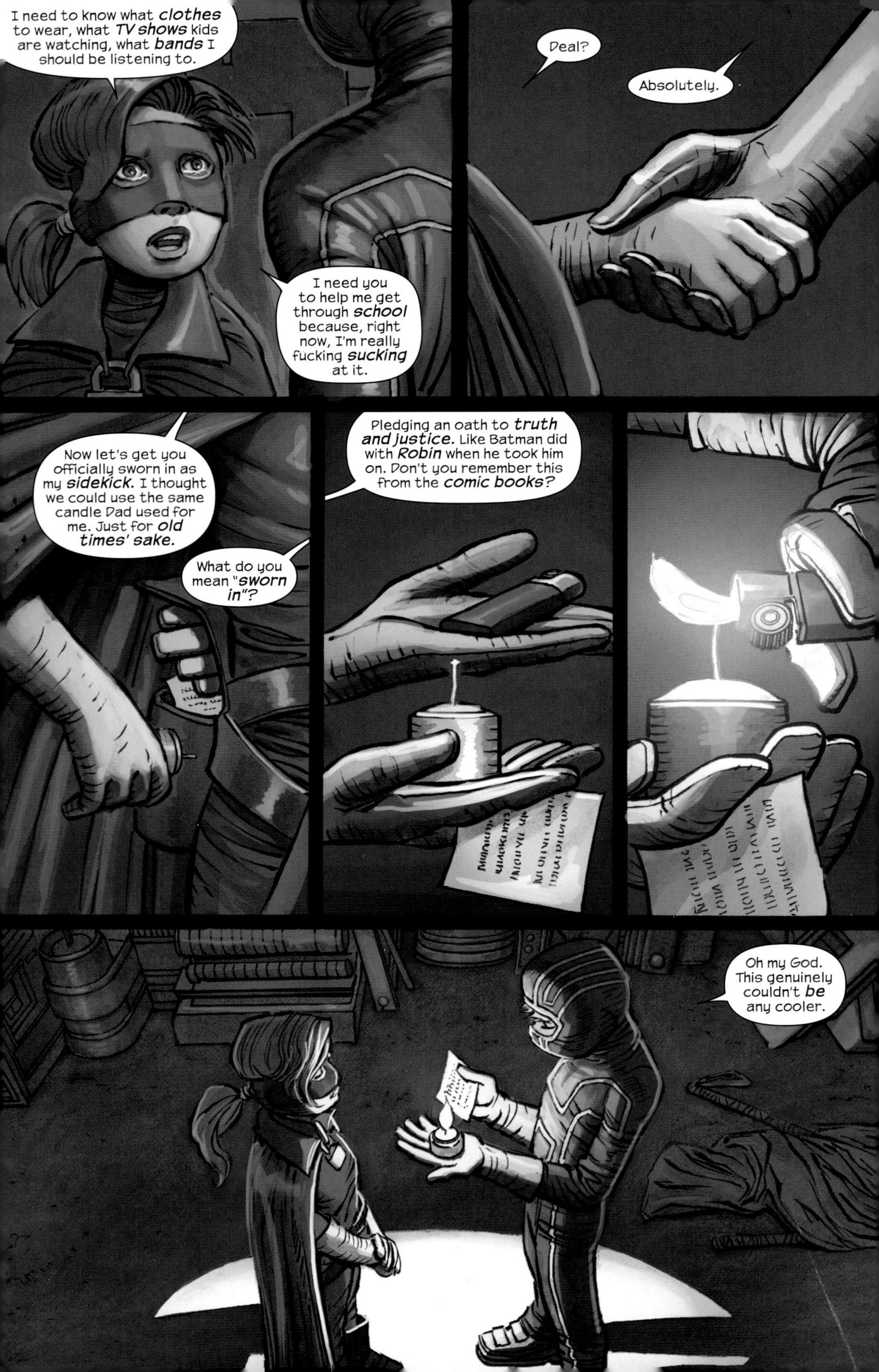
I need to know what *clothes* to wear, what *TV shows* kids are watching, what *bands* I should be listening to.
I need you to help me get through *school* because, right now, I'm really fucking *sucking* at it.
Deal?
Absolutely.
Now let's get you officially sworn in as my *sidekick.* I thought we could use the same candle Dad used for me. Just for *old times' sake.*
What do you mean "*sworn in*"?
Pledging an oath to *truth and justice.* Like Batman did with *Robin* when he took him on. Don't you remember this from the *comic books*?
Oh my God. This genuinely couldn't *be* any cooler.

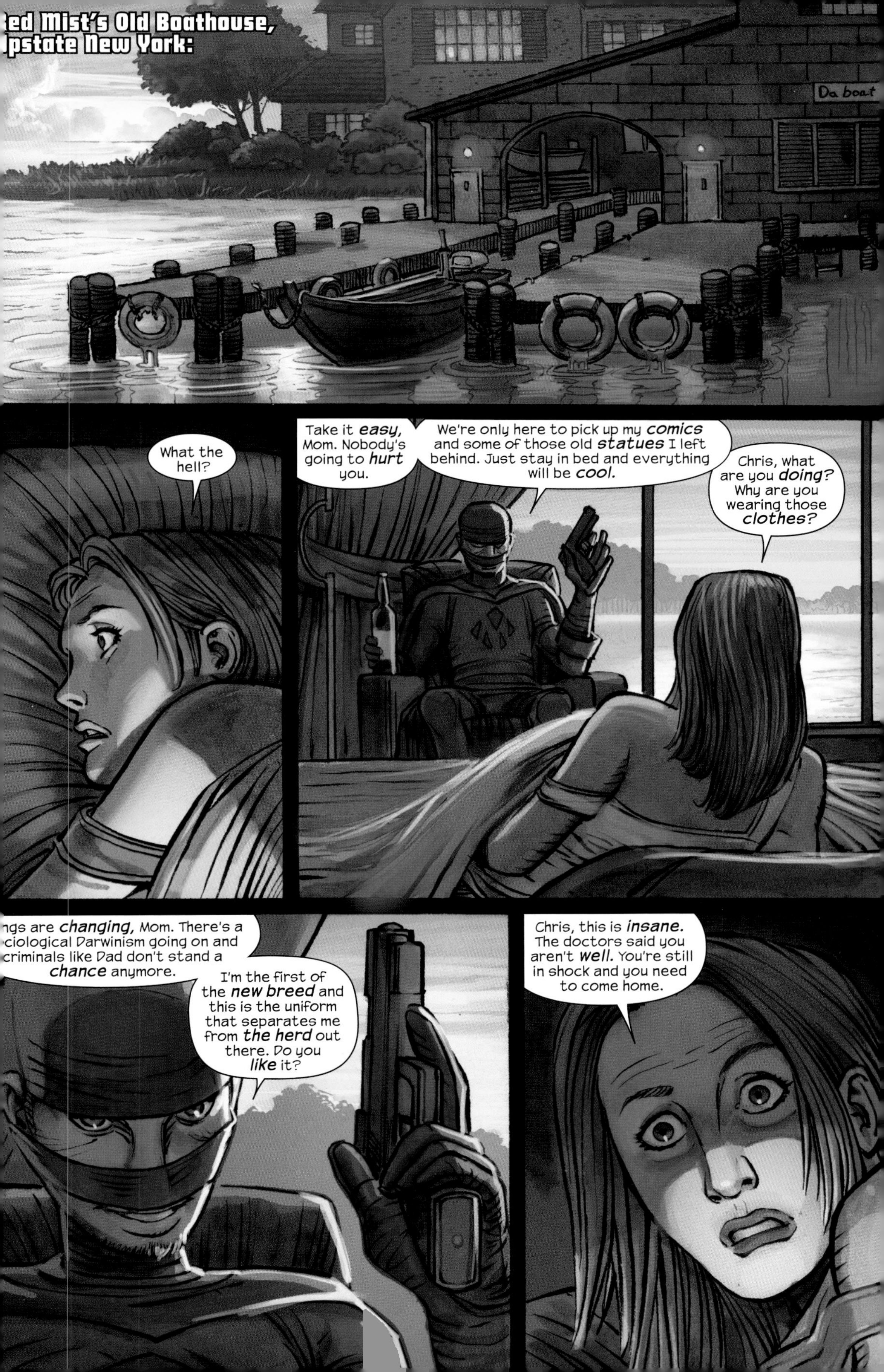
ed Mist's Old Boathouse, pstate New York:
Da boat
What the hell?
Take it easy, Mom. Nobody's going to hurt you.
We're only here to pick up my comics and some of those old statues I left behind. Just stay in bed and everything will be cool.
Chris, what are you doing? Why are you wearing those clothes?
ngs are changing, Mom. There's a ciological Darwinism going on and criminals like Dad don't stand a chance anymore.
I'm the first of the new breed and this is the uniform that separates me from the herd out there. Do you like it?
Chris, this is insane. The doctors said you aren't well. You're still in shock and you need to come home.

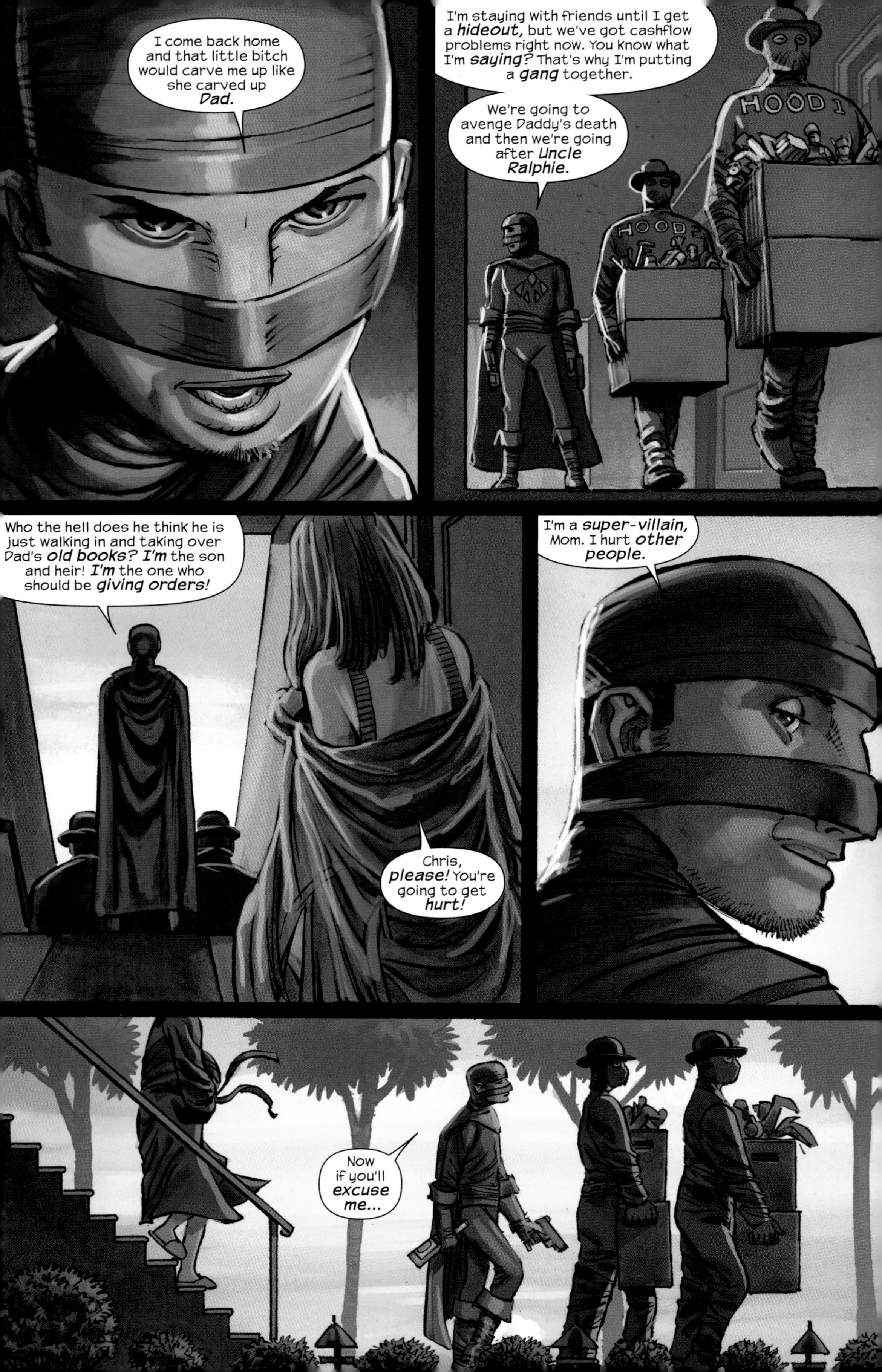
I come back home and that little bitch would carve me up like she carved up Dad.
I'm staying with friends until I get a hideout, but we've got cashflow problems right now. You know what I'm saying? That's why I'm putting a gang together.
We're going to avenge Daddy's death and then we're going after Uncle Ralphie.
HOOD 1
HOOD 2
Who the hell does he think he is just walking in and taking over Dad's old books? I'm the son and heir! I'm the one who should be giving orders!
Chris, please! You're going to get hurt!
I'm a super-villain, Mom. I hurt other people.
Now if you'll excuse me...

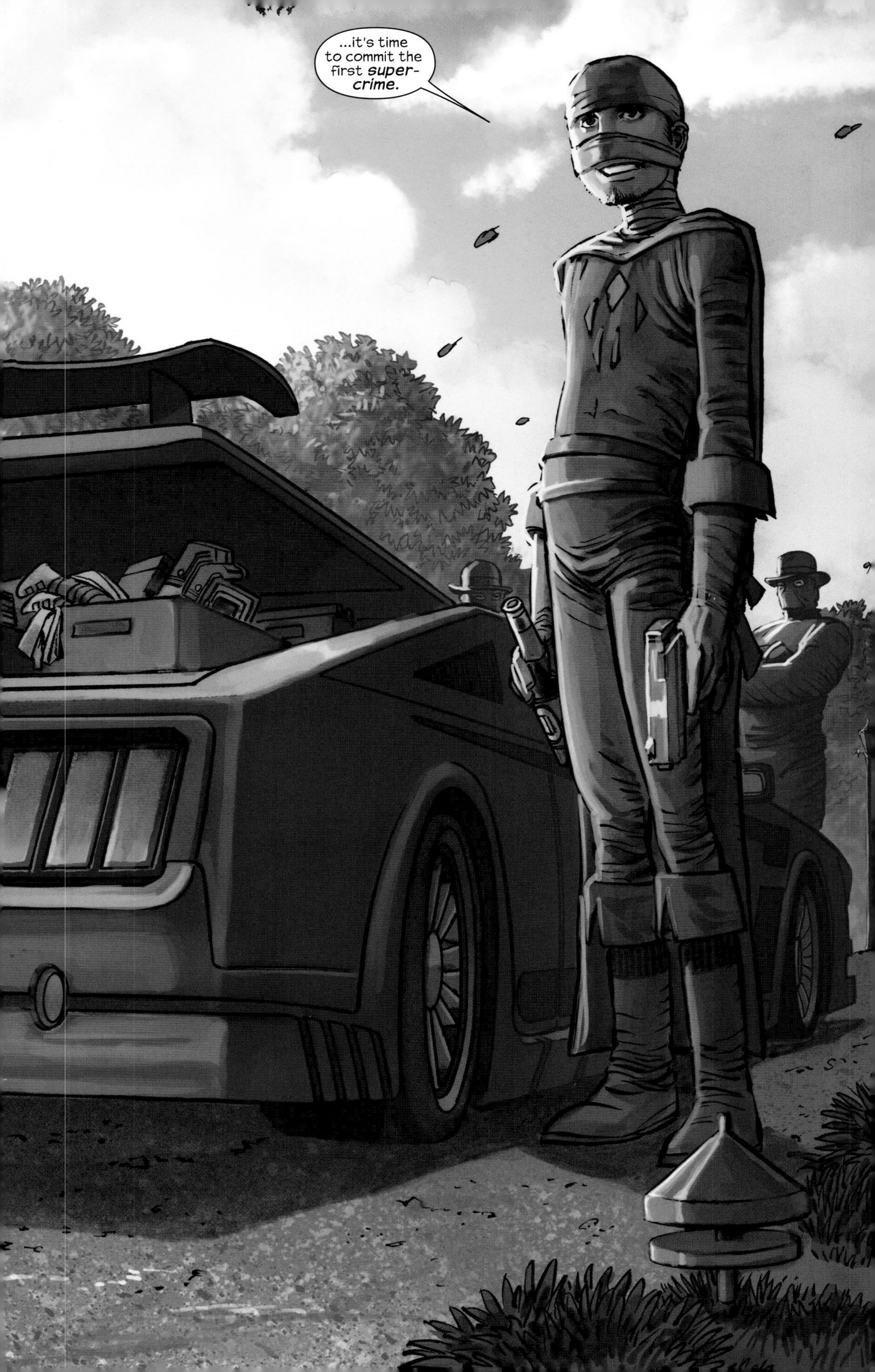
...it's time to commit the first *super-crime.*

TWO

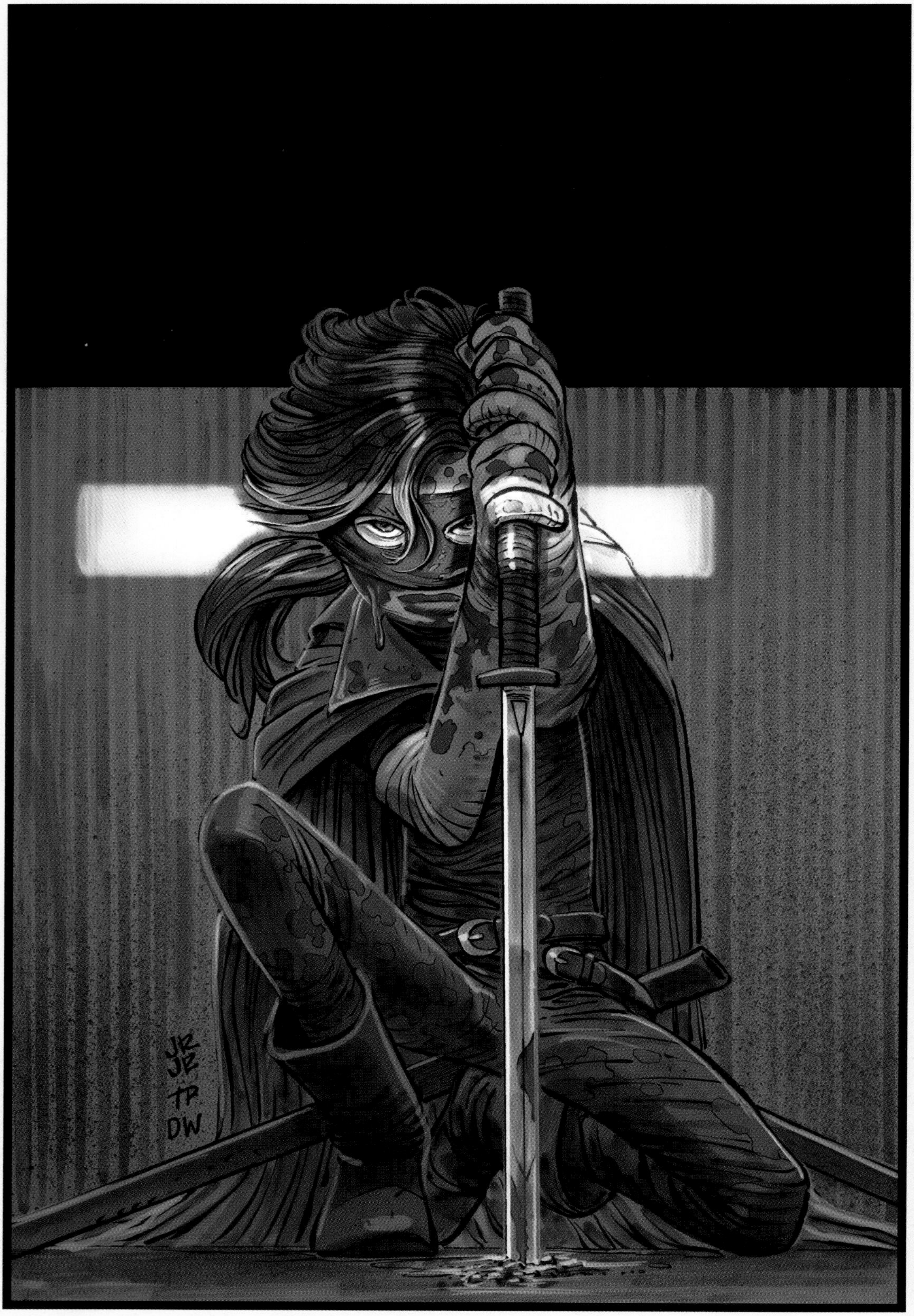
JR JR
TP
DW.

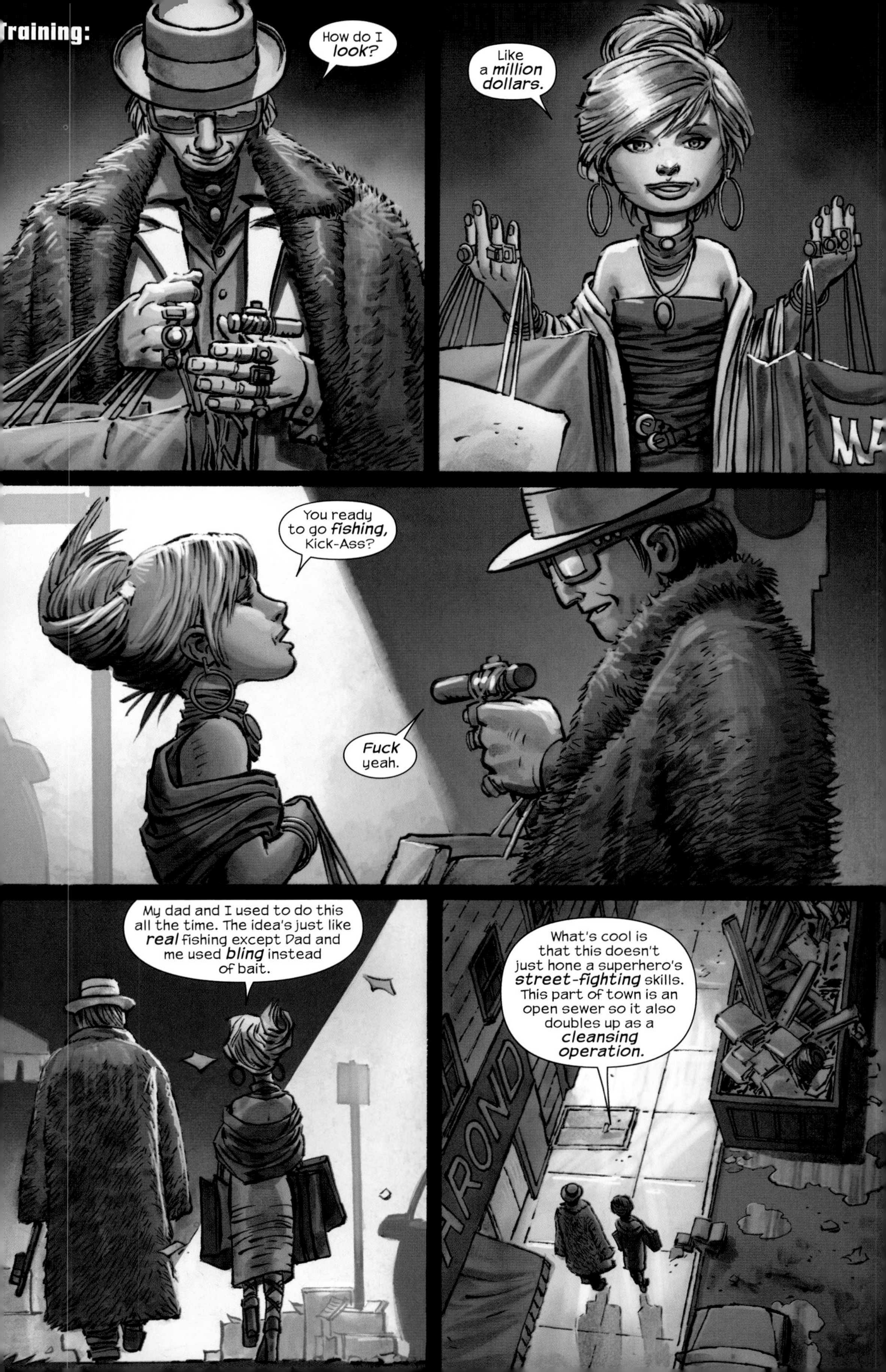
Training:
How do I look?
Like a million dollars.
You ready to go fishing, Kick-Ass?
Fuck yeah.
My dad and I used to do this all the time. The idea's just like real fishing except Dad and me used bling instead of bait.
What's cool is that this doesn't just hone a superhero's street-fighting skills. This part of town is an open sewer so it also doubles up as a cleansing operation.

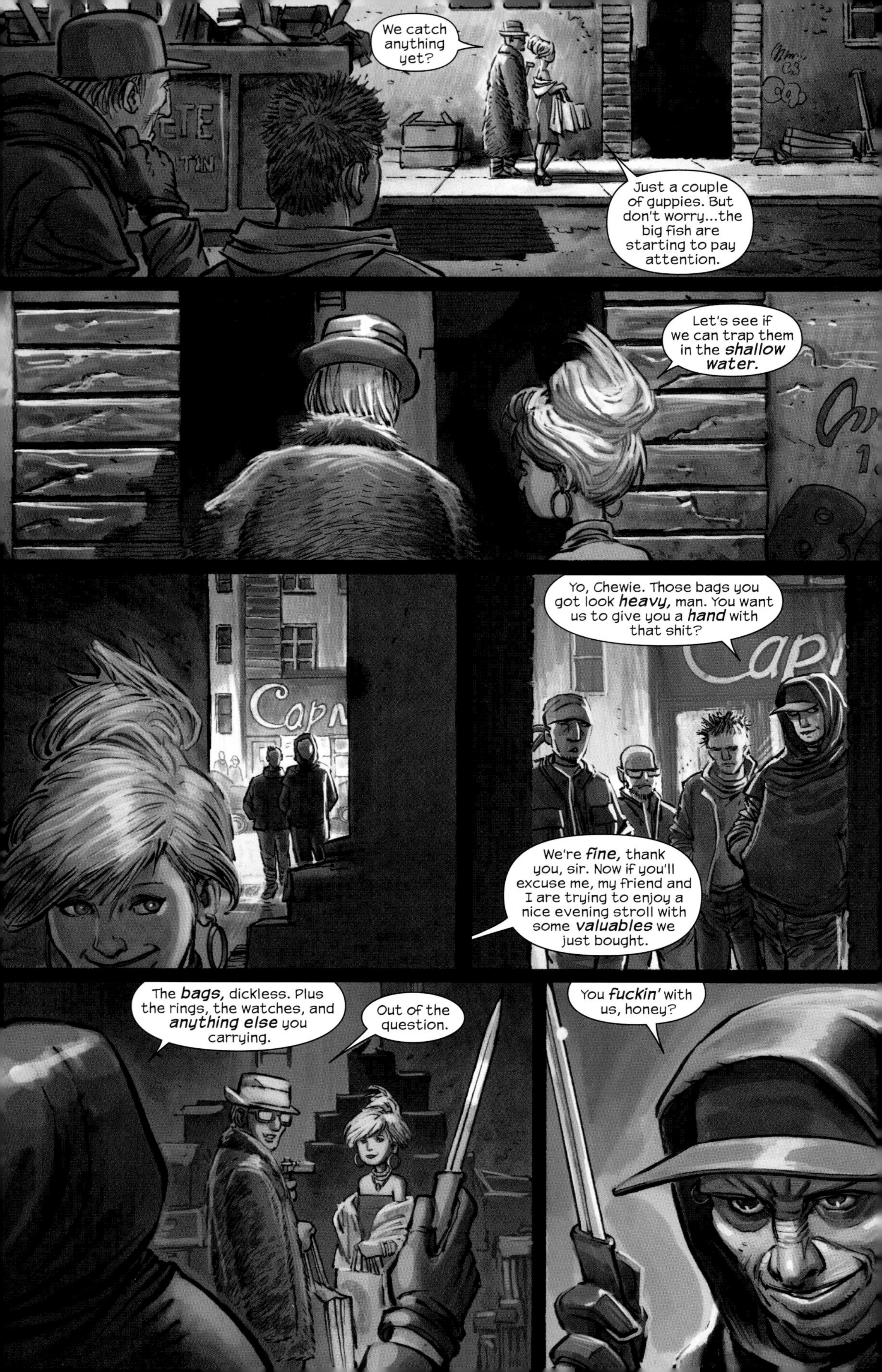
We catch anything yet?
Just a couple of guppies. But don't worry...the big fish are starting to pay attention.
Let's see if we can trap them in the *shallow water.*
Capri
Yo, Chewie. Those bags you got look *heavy,* man. You want us to give you a *hand* with that shit?
We're *fine,* thank you, sir. Now if you'll excuse me, my friend and I are trying to enjoy a nice evening stroll with some *valuables* we just bought.
The *bags,* dickless. Plus the rings, the watches, and *anything else* you carrying.
Out of the question.
You *fuckin'* with us, honey?

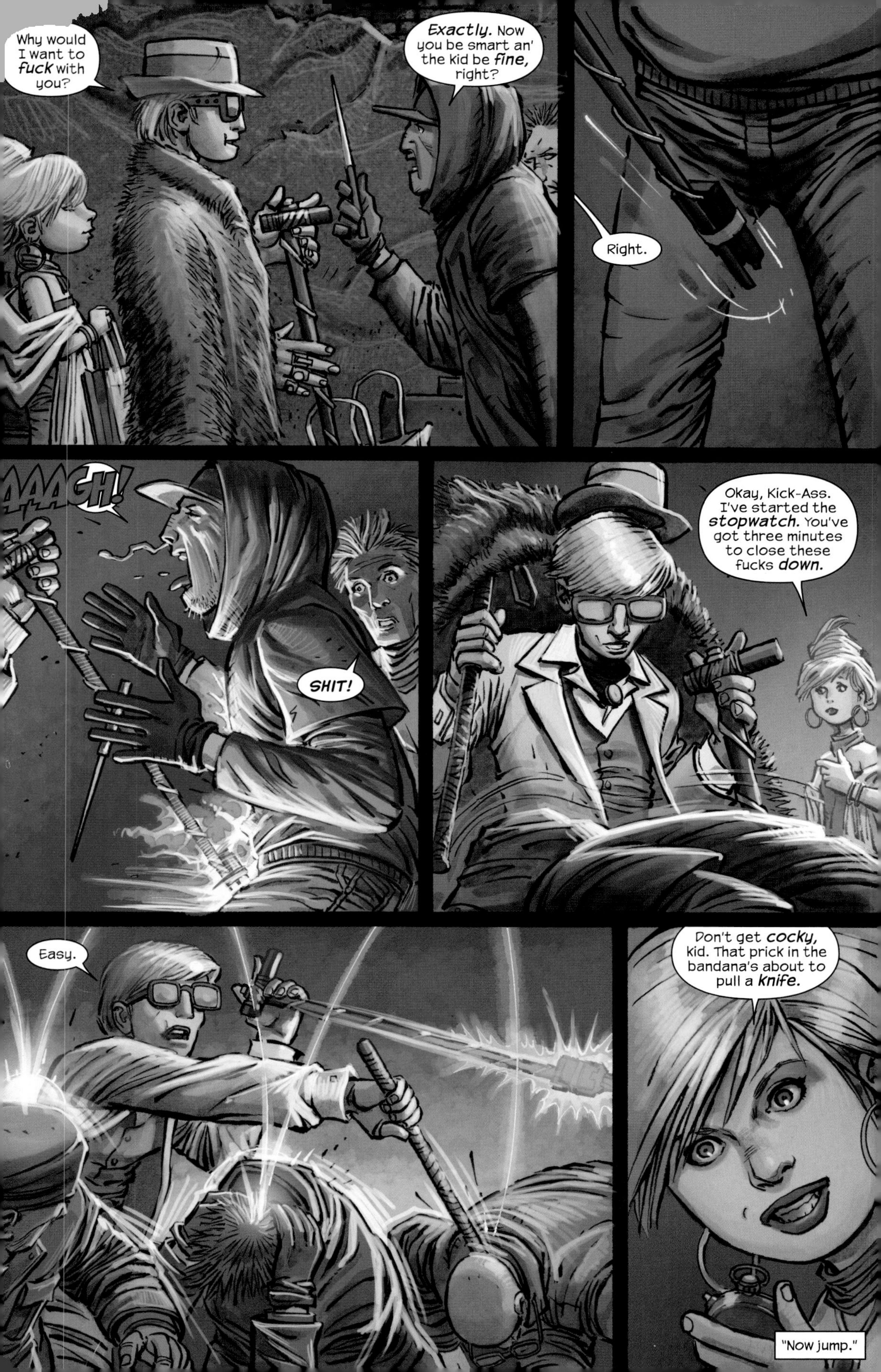
Why would I want to fuck with you?
Exactly. Now you be smart an' the kid be fine, right?
Right.
AAAGH!
SHIT!
Okay, Kick-Ass. I've started the stopwatch. You've got three minutes to close these fucks down.
Easy.
Don't get cocky, kid. That prick in the bandana's about to pull a knife.
"Now jump."

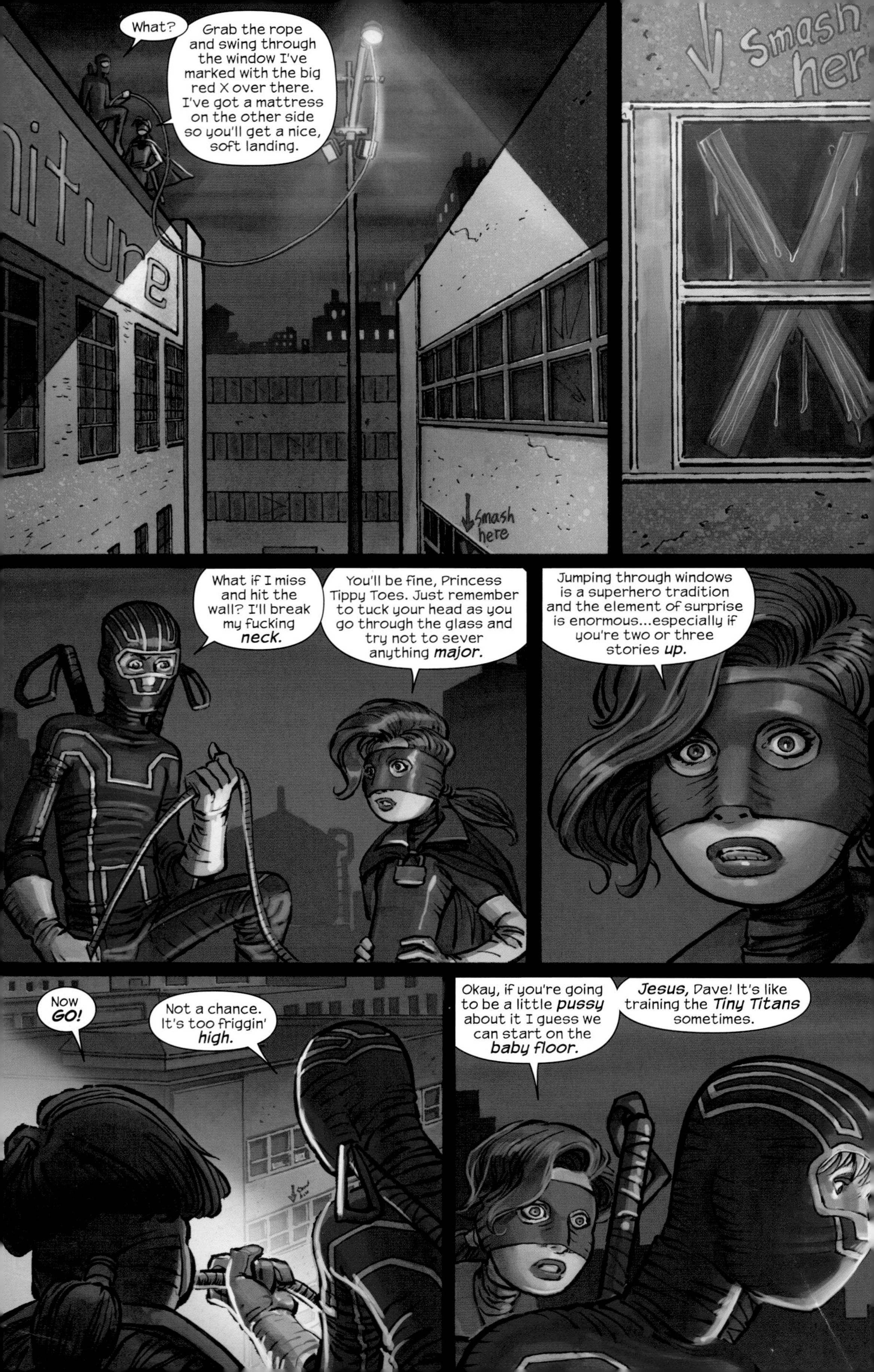
What?
Grab the rope and swing through the window I've marked with the big red X over there. I've got a mattress on the other side so you'll get a nice, soft landing.
Smash here
Smash here
What if I miss and hit the wall? I'll break my fucking *neck.*
You'll be fine, Princess Tippy Toes. Just remember to tuck your head as you go through the glass and try not to sever anything *major.*
Jumping through windows is a superhero tradition and the element of surprise is enormous...especially if you're two or three stories *up.*
Now *GO!*
Not a chance. It's too friggin' *high.*
Okay, if you're going to be a little *pussy* about it I guess we can start on the *baby floor.*
Jesus, Dave! It's like training the *Tiny Titans* sometimes.

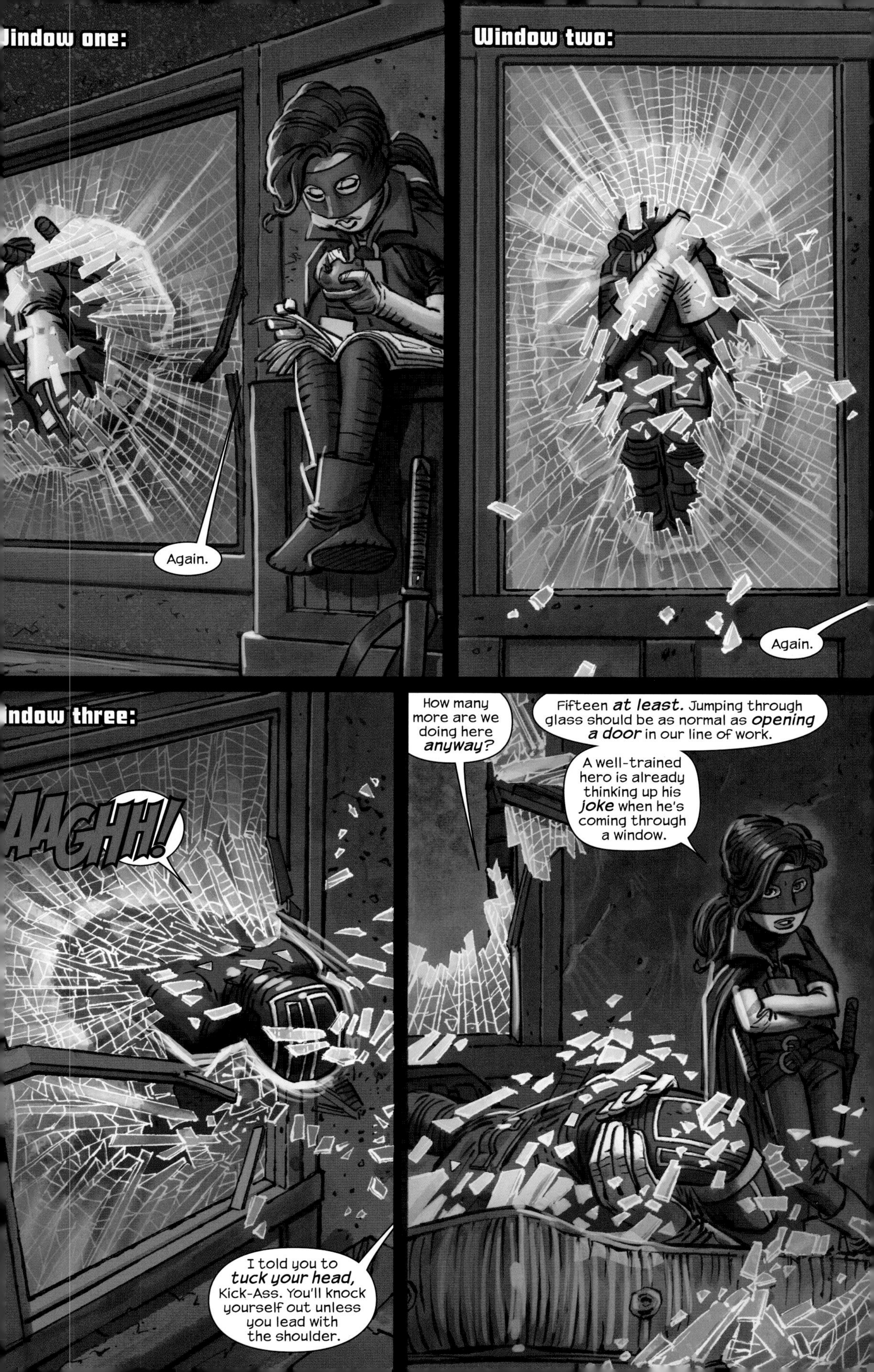

Window one:
Again.
Window two:
Again.
Window three:
AAGHH!
I told you to tuck your head, Kick-Ass. You'll knock yourself out unless you lead with the shoulder.
How many more are we doing here anyway?
Fifteen at least. Jumping through glass should be as normal as opening a door in our line of work.
A well-trained hero is already thinking up his joke when he's coming through a window.

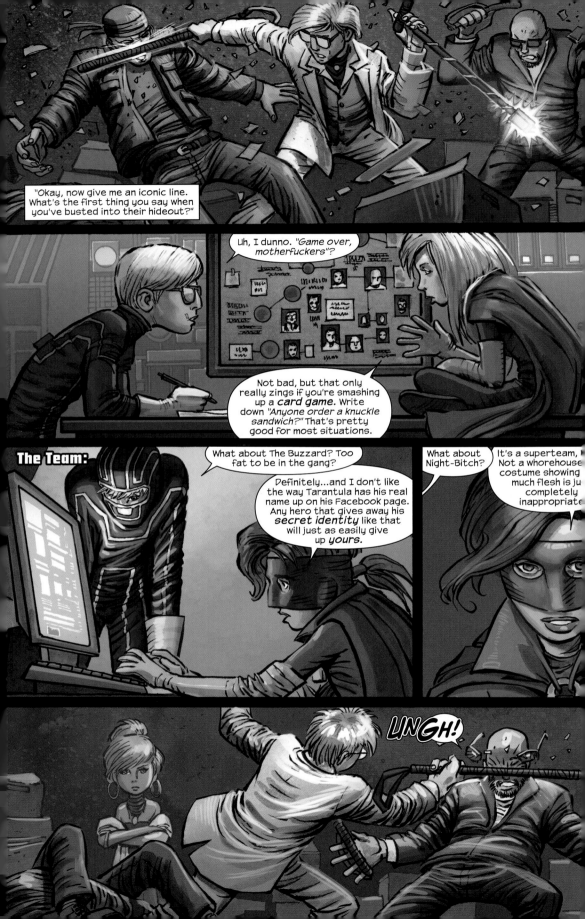

"Okay, now give me an iconic line. What's the first thing you say when you've busted into their hideout?"

Uh, I dunno. "Game over, motherfuckers"?

Not bad, but that only really zings if you're smashing up a *card game*. Write down "*Anyone order a knuckle sandwich?*" That's pretty good for most situations.

The Team:

What about The Buzzard? Too fat to be in the gang?

Definitely...and I don't like the way Tarantula has his real name up on his Facebook page. Any hero that gives away his *secret identity* like that will just as easily give up *yours*.

What about Night-Bitch?

It's a superteam. Not a whorehouse. A costume showing much flesh is ju completely inappropriate

UNGH!

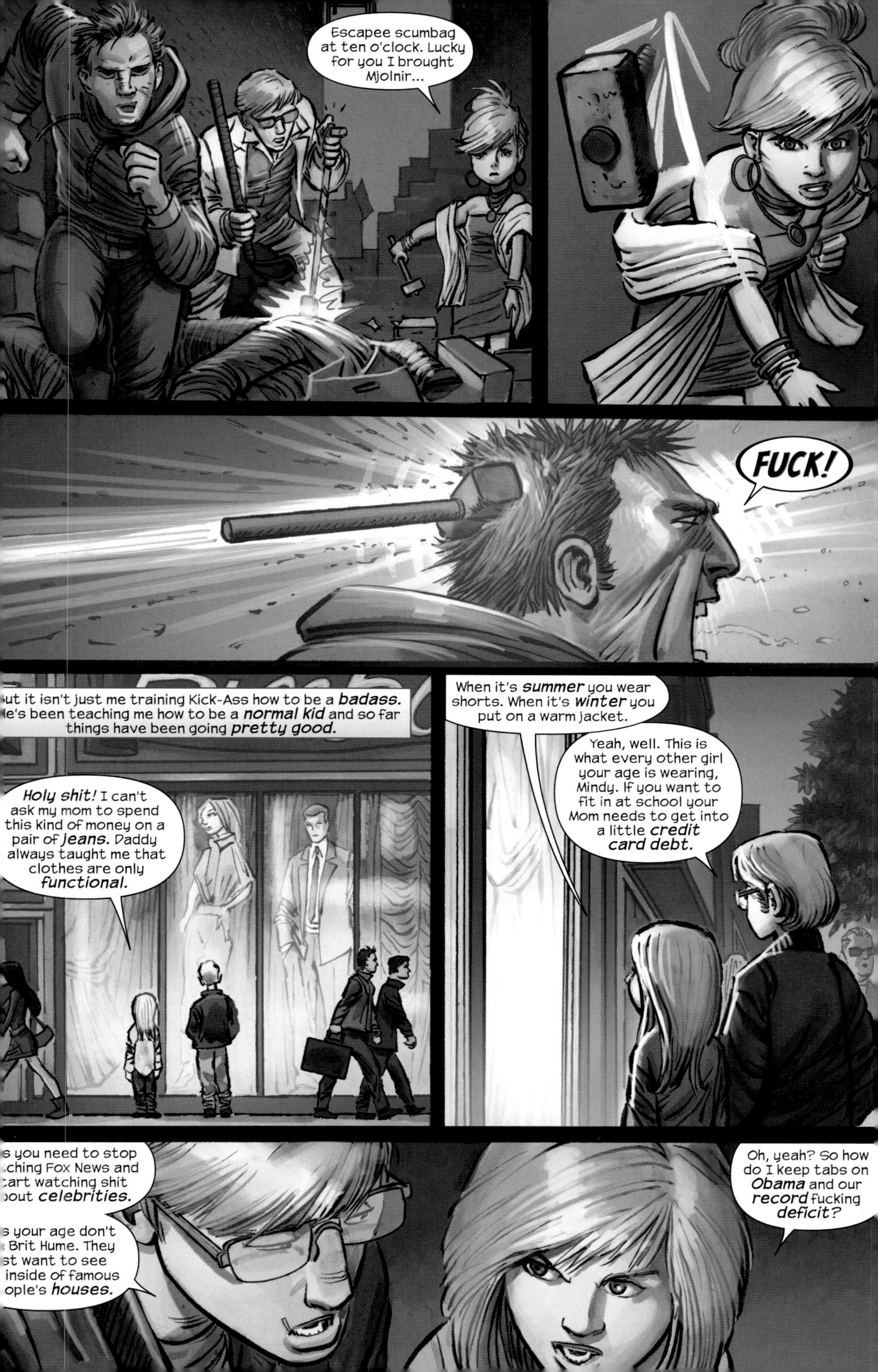

Escapee scumbag at ten o'clock. Lucky for you I brought Mjolnir...
FUCK!
ut it isn't just me training Kick-Ass how to be a badass. le's been teaching me how to be a normal kid and so far things have been going pretty good.
Holy shit! I can't ask my mom to spend this kind of money on a pair of jeans. Daddy always taught me that clothes are only functional.
When it's summer you wear shorts. When it's winter you put on a warm jacket.
Yeah, well. This is what every other girl your age is wearing, Mindy. If you want to fit in at school your Mom needs to get into a little credit card debt.
s you need to stop ching Fox News and tart watching shit bout celebrities.
s your age don't Brit Hume. They st want to see inside of famous ople's houses.
Oh, yeah? So how do I keep tabs on Obama and our record fucking deficit?

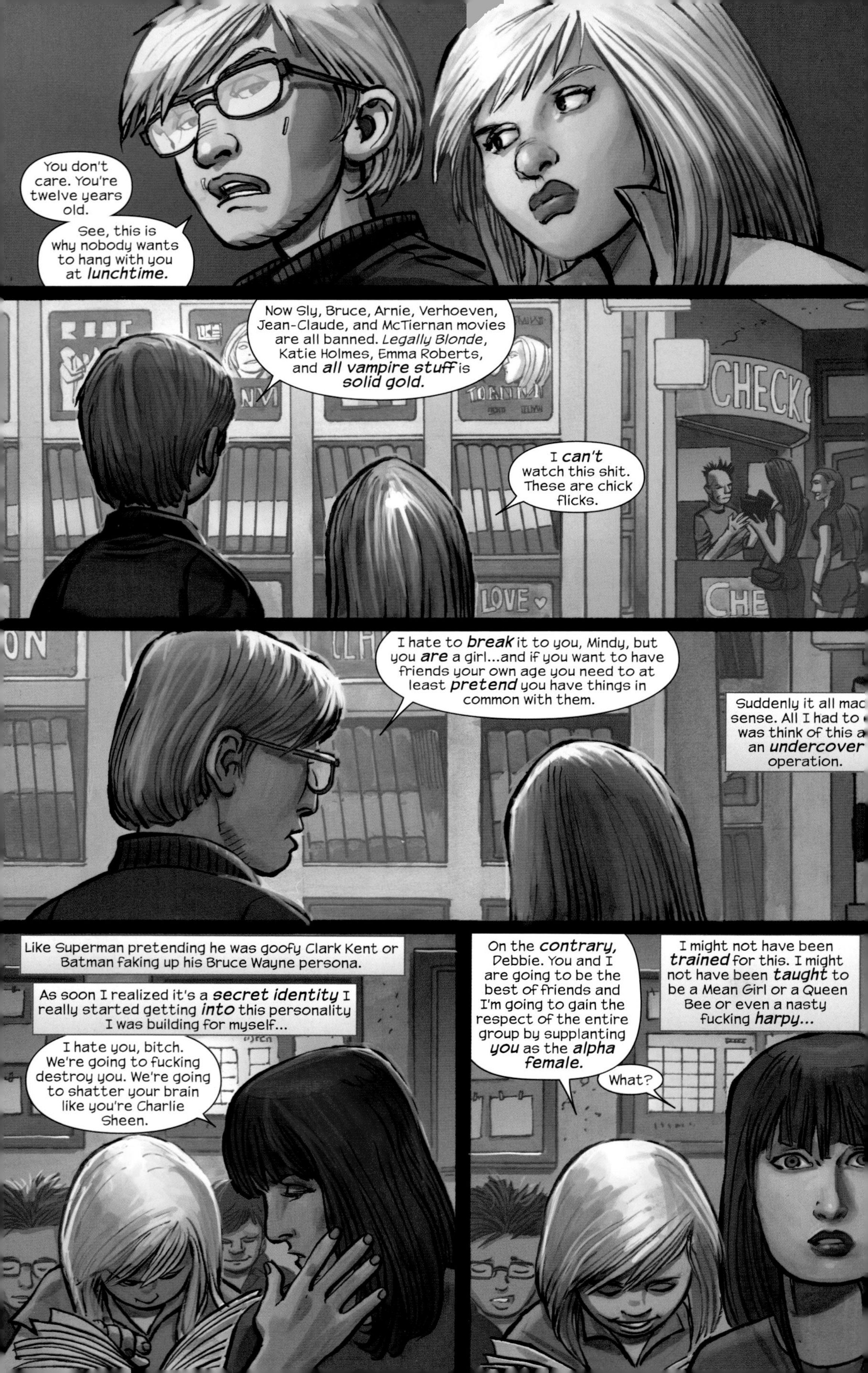

You don't care. You're twelve years old.
See, this is why nobody wants to hang with you at *lunchtime.*
Now Sly, Bruce, Arnie, Verhoeven, Jean-Claude, and McTiernan movies are all banned. *Legally Blonde*, Katie Holmes, Emma Roberts, and ***all vampire stuff*** is ***solid gold.***
I ***can't*** watch this shit. These are chick flicks.
CHECK
LOVE
I hate to ***break*** it to you, Mindy, but you ***are*** a girl...and if you want to have friends your own age you need to at least ***pretend*** you have things in common with them.
Like Superman pretending he was goofy Clark Kent or Batman faking up his Bruce Wayne persona.
As soon I realized it's a ***secret identity*** I really started getting ***into*** this personality I was building for myself...
I hate you, bitch. We're going to fucking destroy you. We're going to shatter your brain like you're Charlie Sheen.
On the ***contrary,*** Debbie. You and I are going to be the best of friends and I'm going to gain the respect of the entire group by supplanting ***you*** as the ***alpha female.***
What?
I might not have been ***trained*** for this. I might not have been ***taught*** to be a Mean Girl or a Queen Bee or even a nasty fucking ***harpy...***

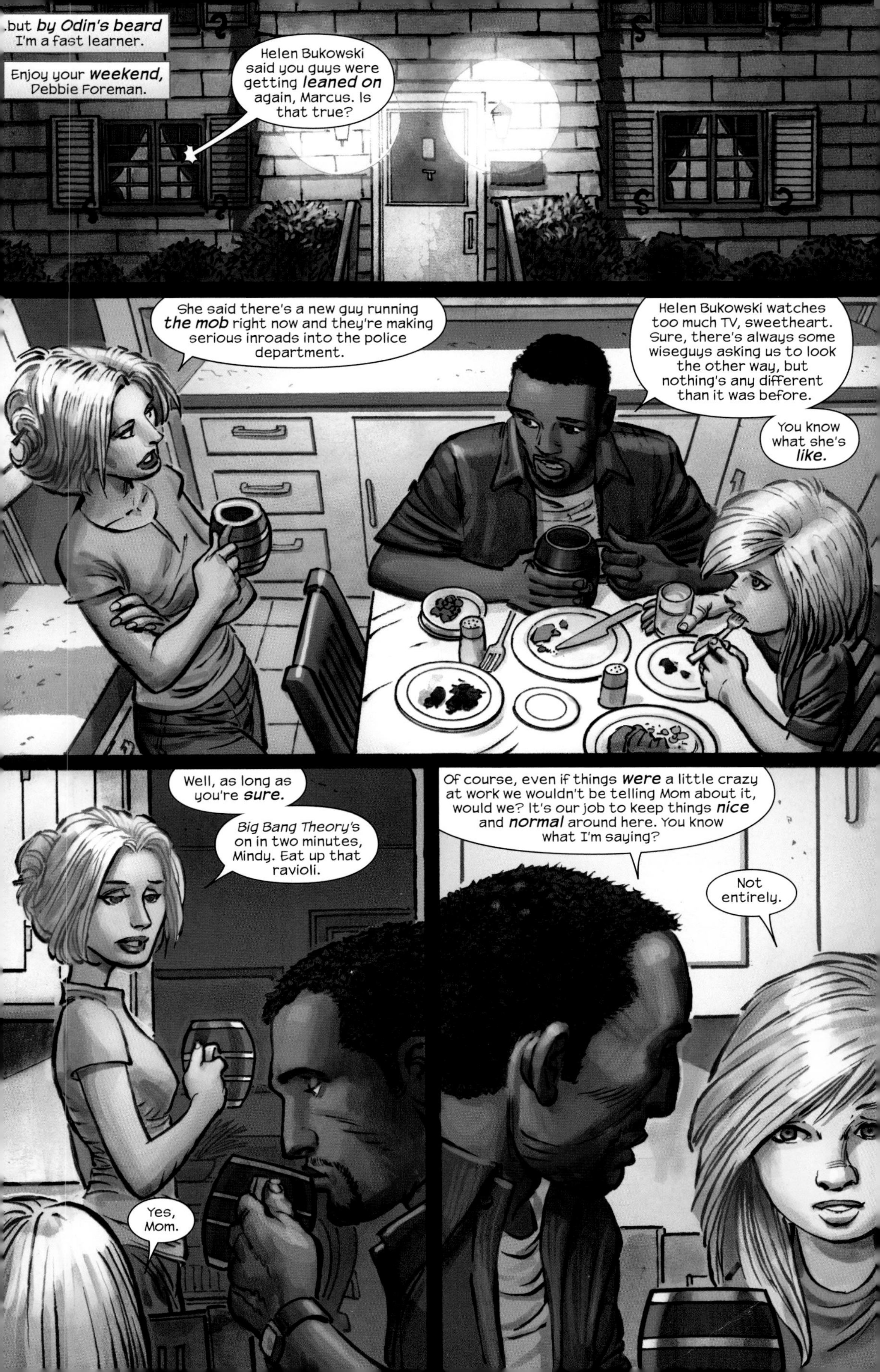
...but by Odin's beard I'm a fast learner.
Enjoy your weekend, Debbie Foreman.
Helen Bukowski said you guys were getting leaned on again, Marcus. Is that true?
She said there's a new guy running the mob right now and they're making serious inroads into the police department.
Helen Bukowski watches too much TV, sweetheart. Sure, there's always some wiseguys asking us to look the other way, but nothing's any different than it was before.
You know what she's like.
Well, as long as you're sure.
Big Bang Theory's on in two minutes, Mindy. Eat up that ravioli.
Yes, Mom.
Of course, even if things were a little crazy at work we wouldn't be telling Mom about it, would we? It's our job to keep things nice and normal around here. You know what I'm saying?
Not entirely.

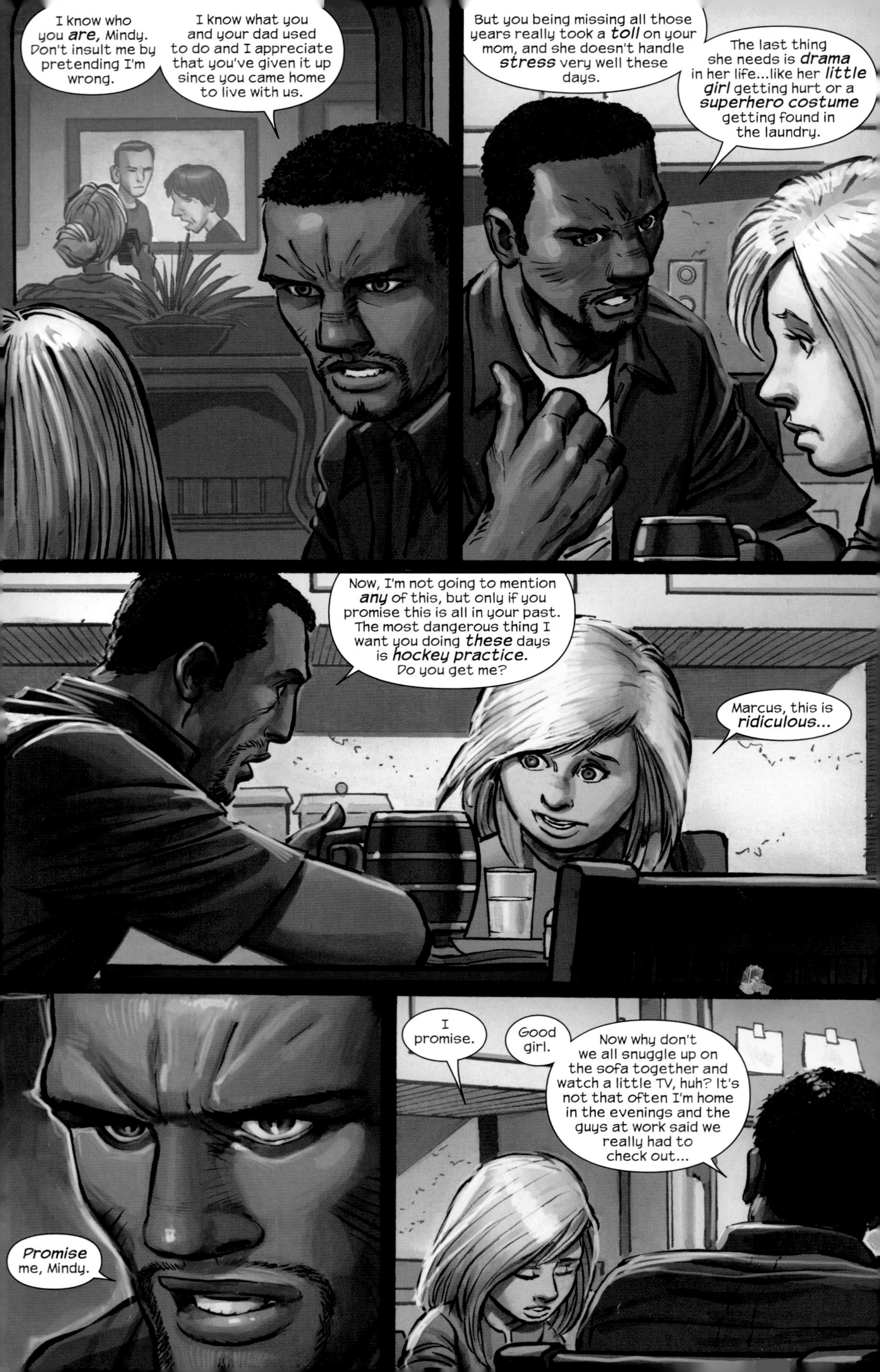
I know who you *are,* Mindy. Don't insult me by pretending I'm wrong.
I know what you and your dad used to do and I appreciate that you've given it up since you came home to live with us.
But you being missing all those years really took a *toll* on your mom, and she doesn't handle *stress* very well these days.
The last thing she needs is *drama* in her life...like her *little girl* getting hurt or a *superhero costume* getting found in the laundry.
Now, I'm not going to mention *any* of this, but only if you promise this is all in your past. The most dangerous thing I want you doing *these* days is *hockey practice.* Do you get me?
Marcus, this is *ridiculous...*
Promise me, Mindy.
I promise.
Good girl.
Now why don't we all snuggle up on the sofa together and watch a little TV, huh? It's not that often I'm home in the evenings and the guys at work said we really had to check out...

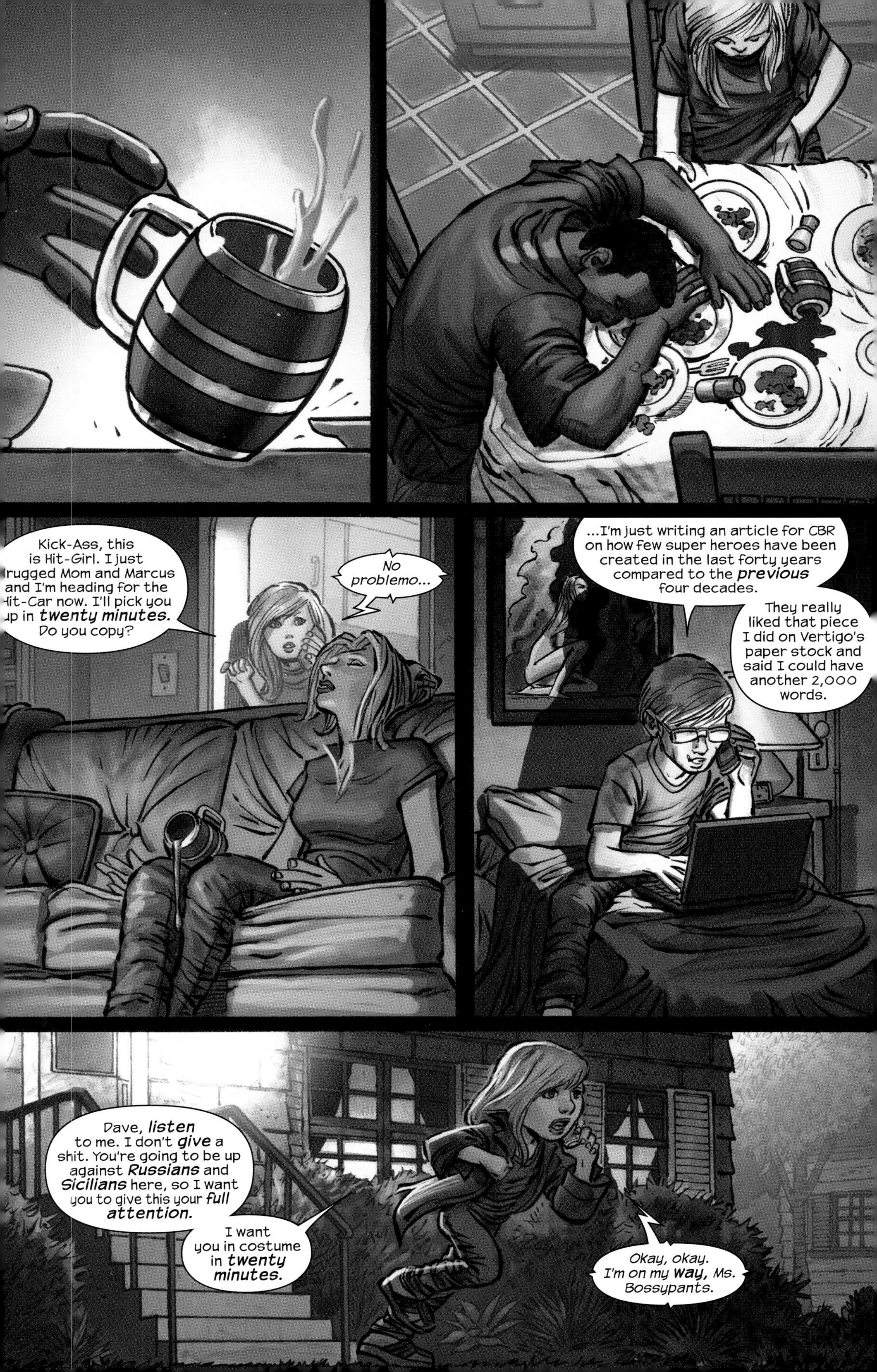
Kick-Ass, this is Hit-Girl. I just rugged Mom and Marcus and I'm heading for the it-Car now. I'll pick you p in twenty minutes. Do you copy?
No problemo...
...I'm just writing an article for CBR on how few super heroes have been created in the last forty years compared to the previous four decades.
They really liked that piece I did on Vertigo's paper stock and said I could have another 2,000 words.
Dave, listen to me. I don't give a shit. You're going to be up against Russians and Sicilians here, so I want you to give this your full attention.
I want you in costume in twenty minutes.
Okay, okay. I'm on my way, Ms. Bossypants.

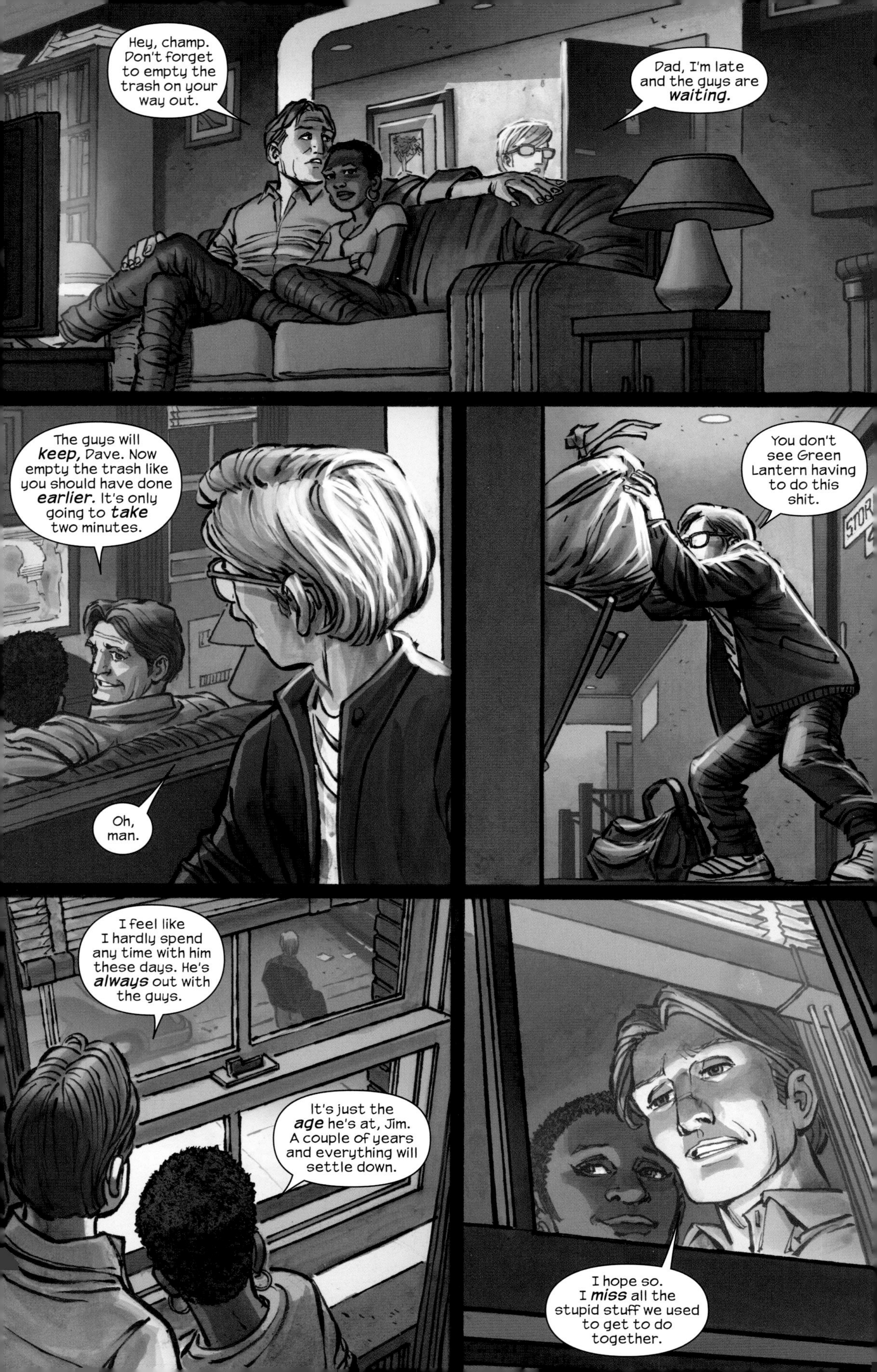
Hey, champ. Don't forget to empty the trash on your way out.
Dad, I'm late and the guys are *waiting.*
The guys will *keep,* Dave. Now empty the trash like you should have done *earlier.* It's only going to *take* two minutes.
Oh, man.
You don't see Green Lantern having to do this shit.
I feel like I hardly spend any time with him these days. He's *always* out with the guys.
It's just the *age* he's at, Jim. A couple of years and everything will settle down.
I hope so. I *miss* all the stupid stuff we used to get to do together.

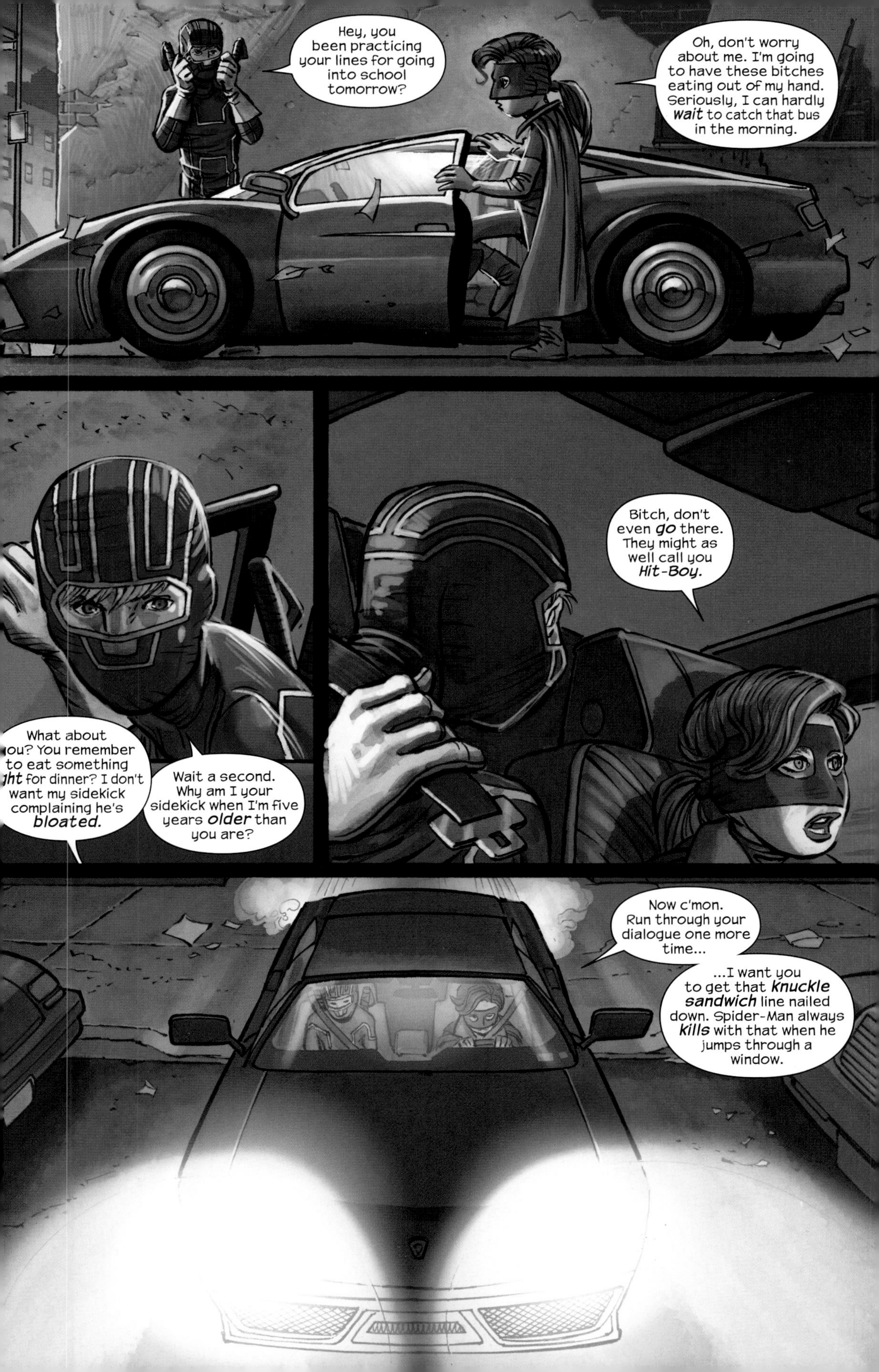
Hey, you been practicing your lines for going into school tomorrow?
Oh, don't worry about me. I'm going to have these bitches eating out of my hand. Seriously, I can hardly *wait* to catch that bus in the morning.
What about ou? You remember to eat something ght for dinner? I don't want my sidekick complaining he's *bloated.*
Wait a second. Why am I your sidekick when I'm five years *older* than you are?
Bitch, don't even *go* there. They might as well call you *Hit-Boy.*
Now c'mon. Run through your dialogue one more time...
...I want you to get that *knuckle sandwich* line nailed down. Spider-Man always *kills* with that when he jumps through a window.

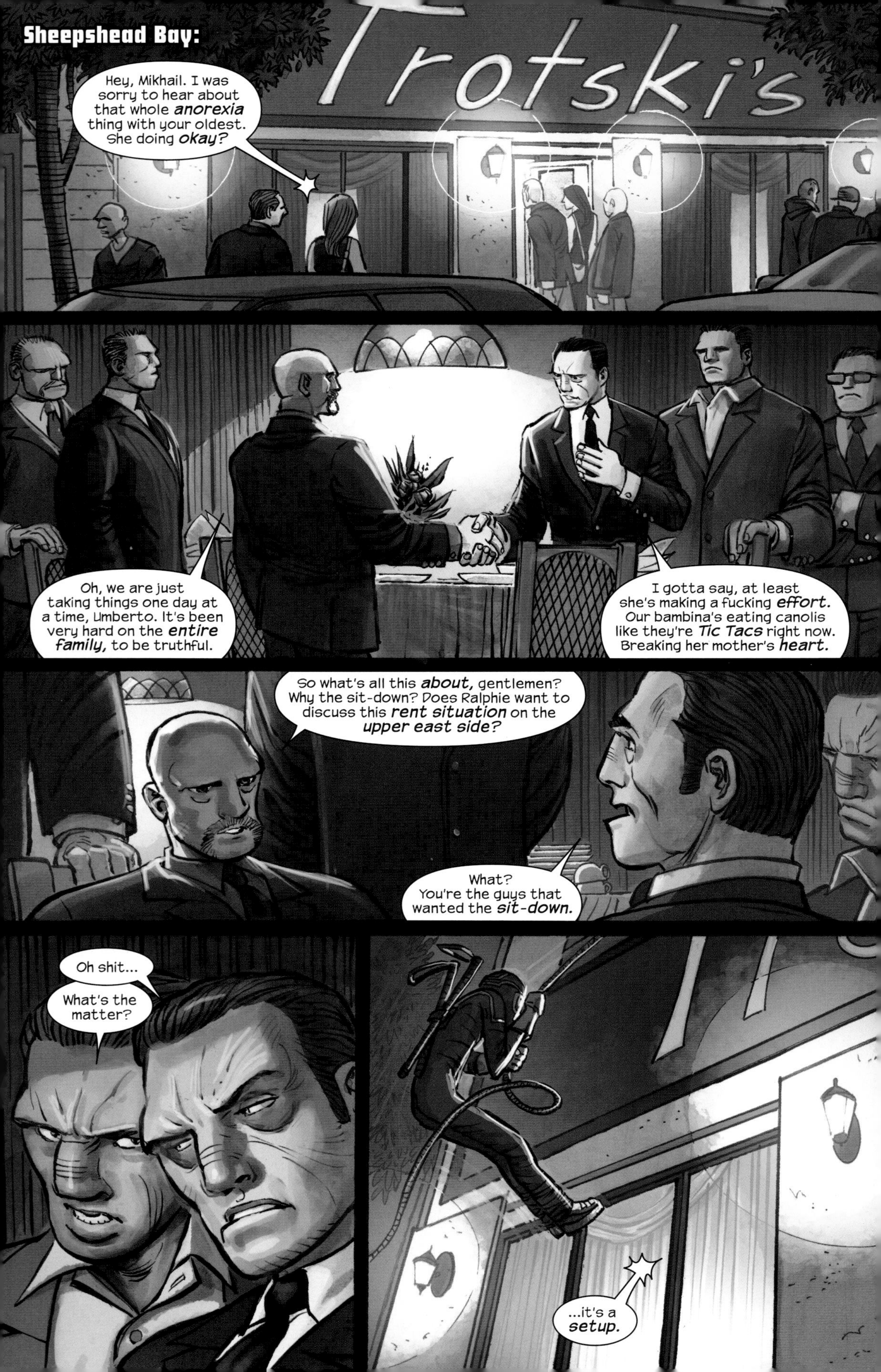
Sheepshead Bay:
Trotski's
Hey, Mikhail. I was sorry to hear about that whole anorexia thing with your oldest. She doing okay?
Oh, we are just taking things one day at a time, Umberto. It's been very hard on the entire family, to be truthful.
I gotta say, at least she's making a fucking effort. Our bambina's eating canolis like they're Tic Tacs right now. Breaking her mother's heart.
So what's all this about, gentlemen? Why the sit-down? Does Ralphie want to discuss this rent situation on the upper east side?
What? You're the guys that wanted the sit-down.
Oh shit...
What's the matter?
...it's a setup.

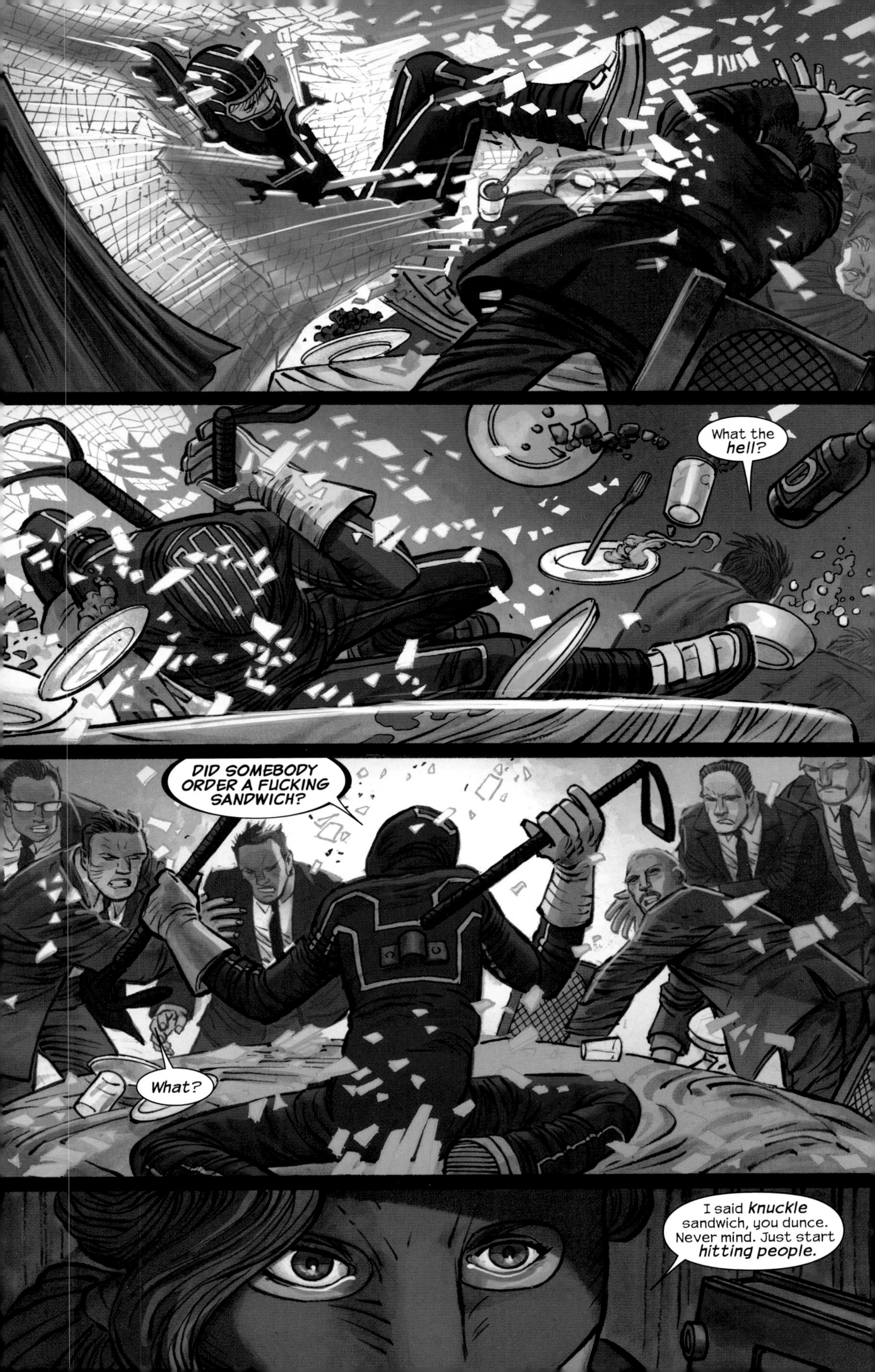
What the *hell?*
DID SOMEBODY ORDER A FUCKING SANDWICH?
What?
I said *knuckle* sandwich, you dunce. Never mind. Just start *hitting people.*

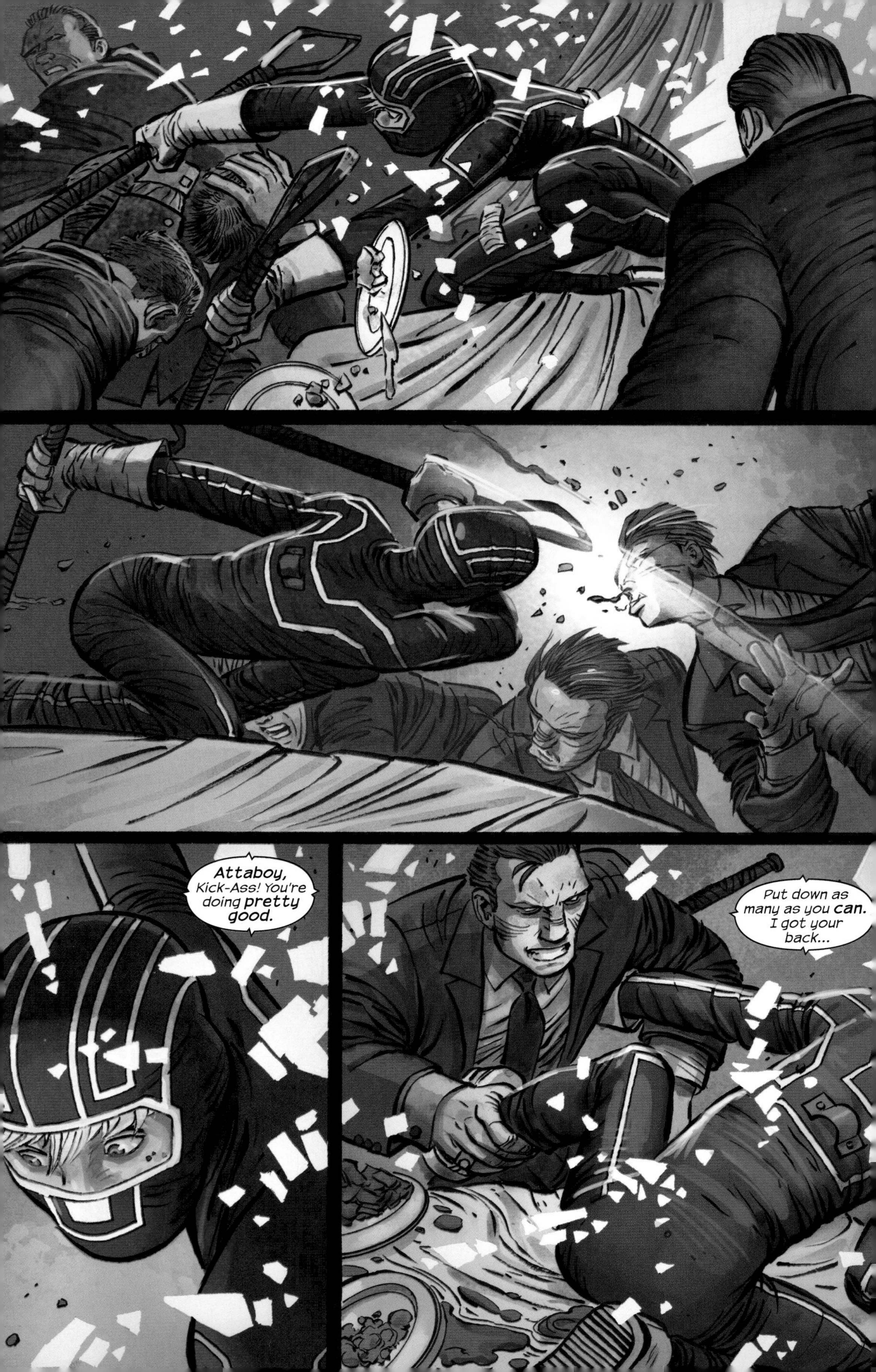
Attaboy, Kick-Ass! You're doing pretty good.
Put down as many as you can. I got your back...

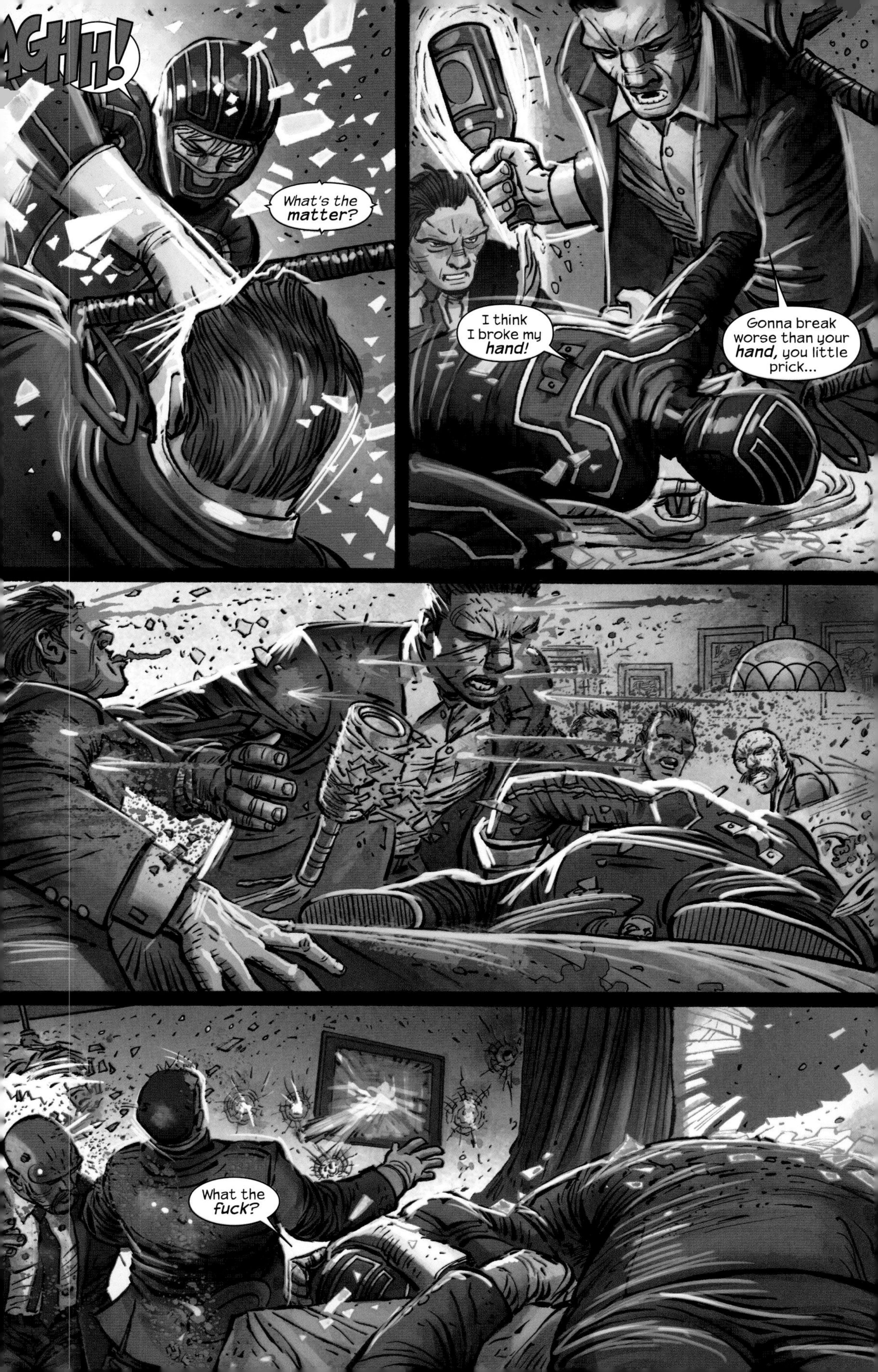
AGHH!
What's the matter?
I think I broke my hand!
Gonna break worse than your hand, you little prick...
What the fuck?

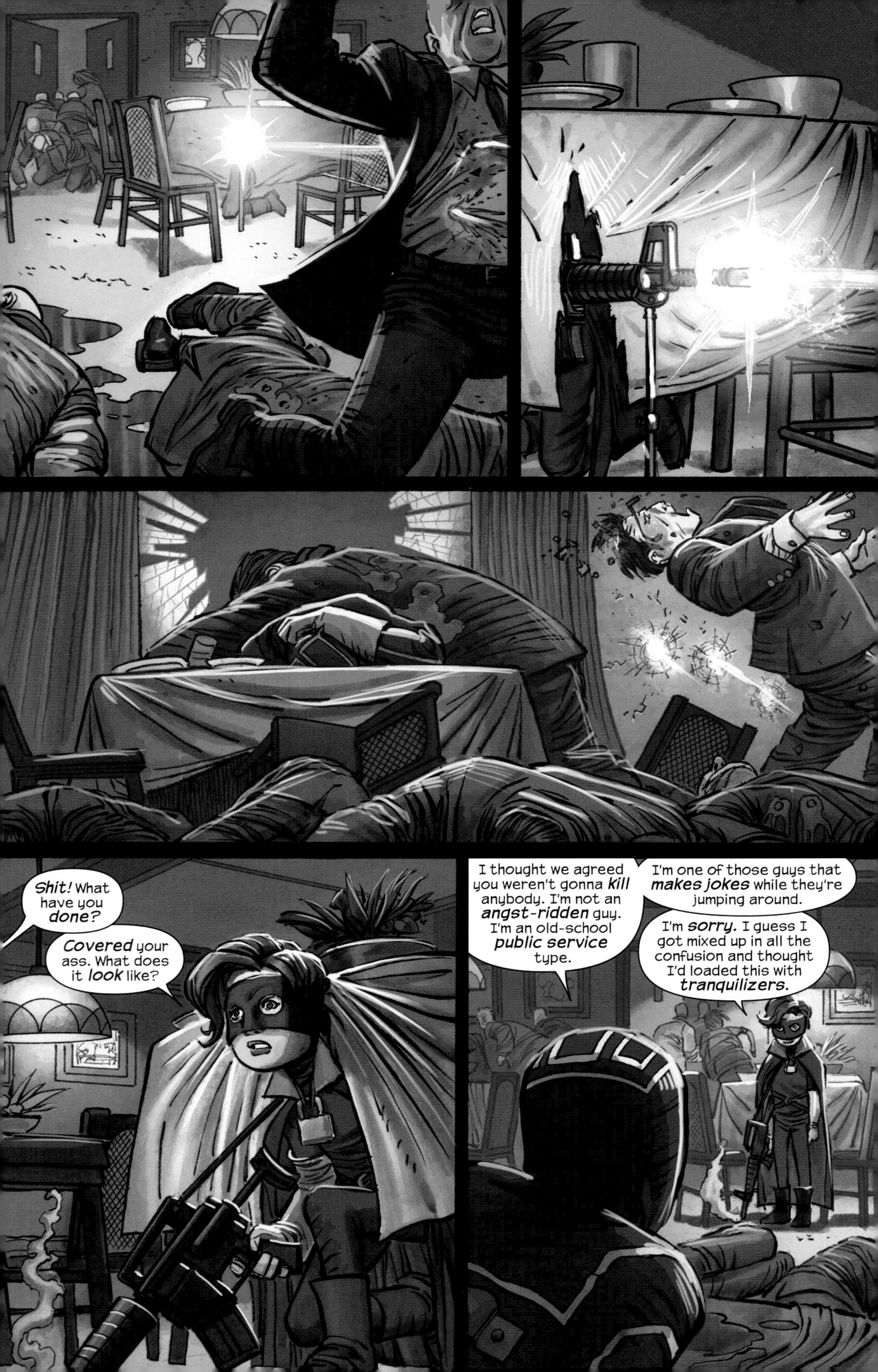
Shit! What have you done?
Covered your ass. What does it look like?
I thought we agreed you weren't gonna kill anybody. I'm not an angst-ridden guy. I'm an old-school public service type.
I'm one of those guys that makes jokes while they're jumping around.
I'm sorry. I guess I got mixed up in all the confusion and thought I'd loaded this with tranquilizers.

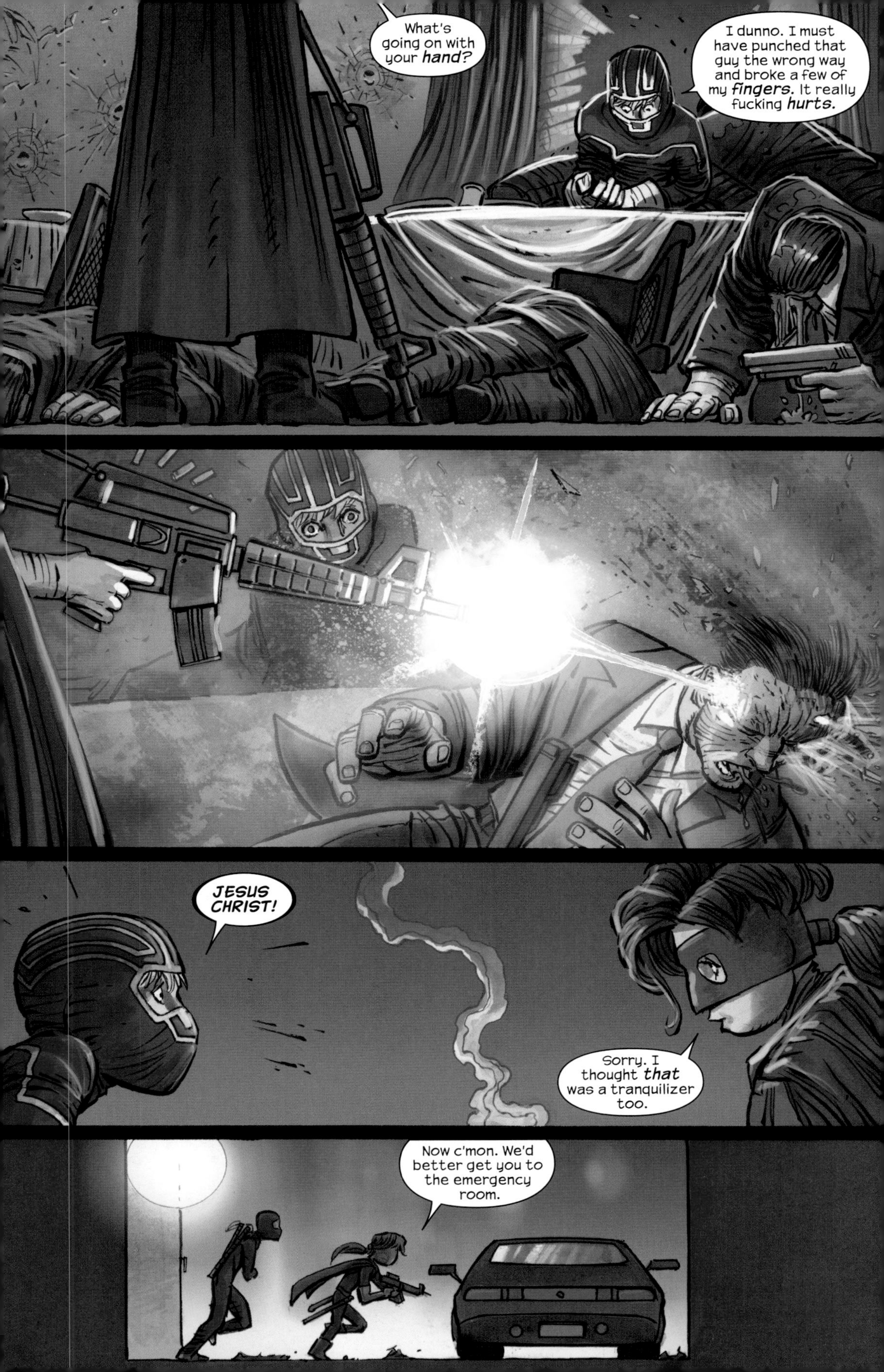
What's going on with your *hand*?
I dunno. I must have punched that guy the wrong way and broke a few of my *fingers*. It really fucking *hurts*.
JESUS CHRIST!
Sorry. I thought *that* was a tranquilizer too.
Now c'mon. We'd better get you to the emergency room.

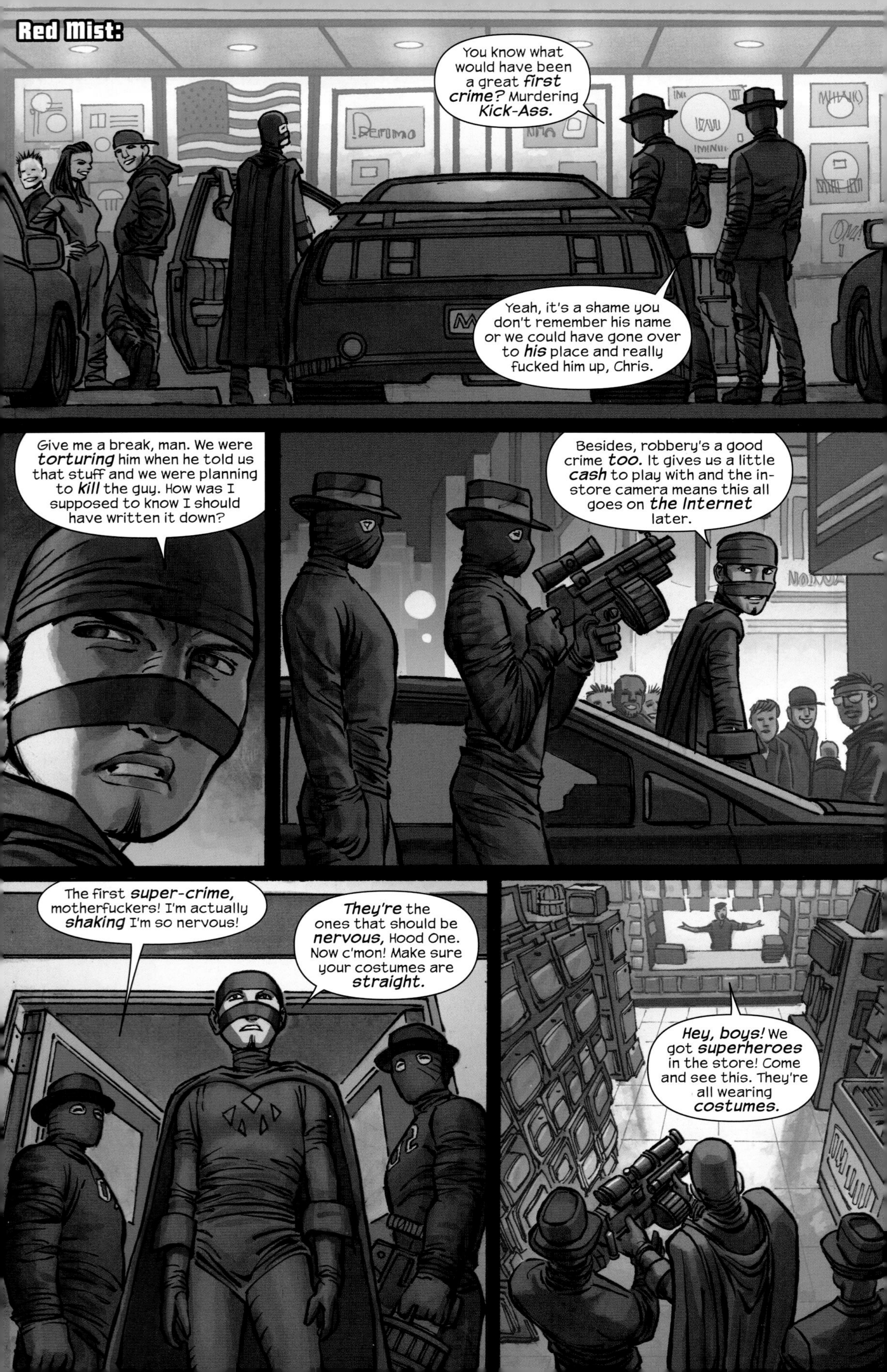
Red Mist:
You know what would have been a great first crime? Murdering Kick-Ass.
Yeah, it's a shame you don't remember his name or we could have gone over to his place and really fucked him up, Chris.
Give me a break, man. We were torturing him when he told us that stuff and we were planning to kill the guy. How was I supposed to know I should have written it down?
Besides, robbery's a good crime too. It gives us a little cash to play with and the in-store camera means this all goes on the Internet later.
The first super-crime, motherfuckers! I'm actually shaking I'm so nervous!
They're the ones that should be nervous, Hood One. Now c'mon! Make sure your costumes are straight.
Hey, boys! We got superheroes in the store! Come and see this. They're all wearing costumes.

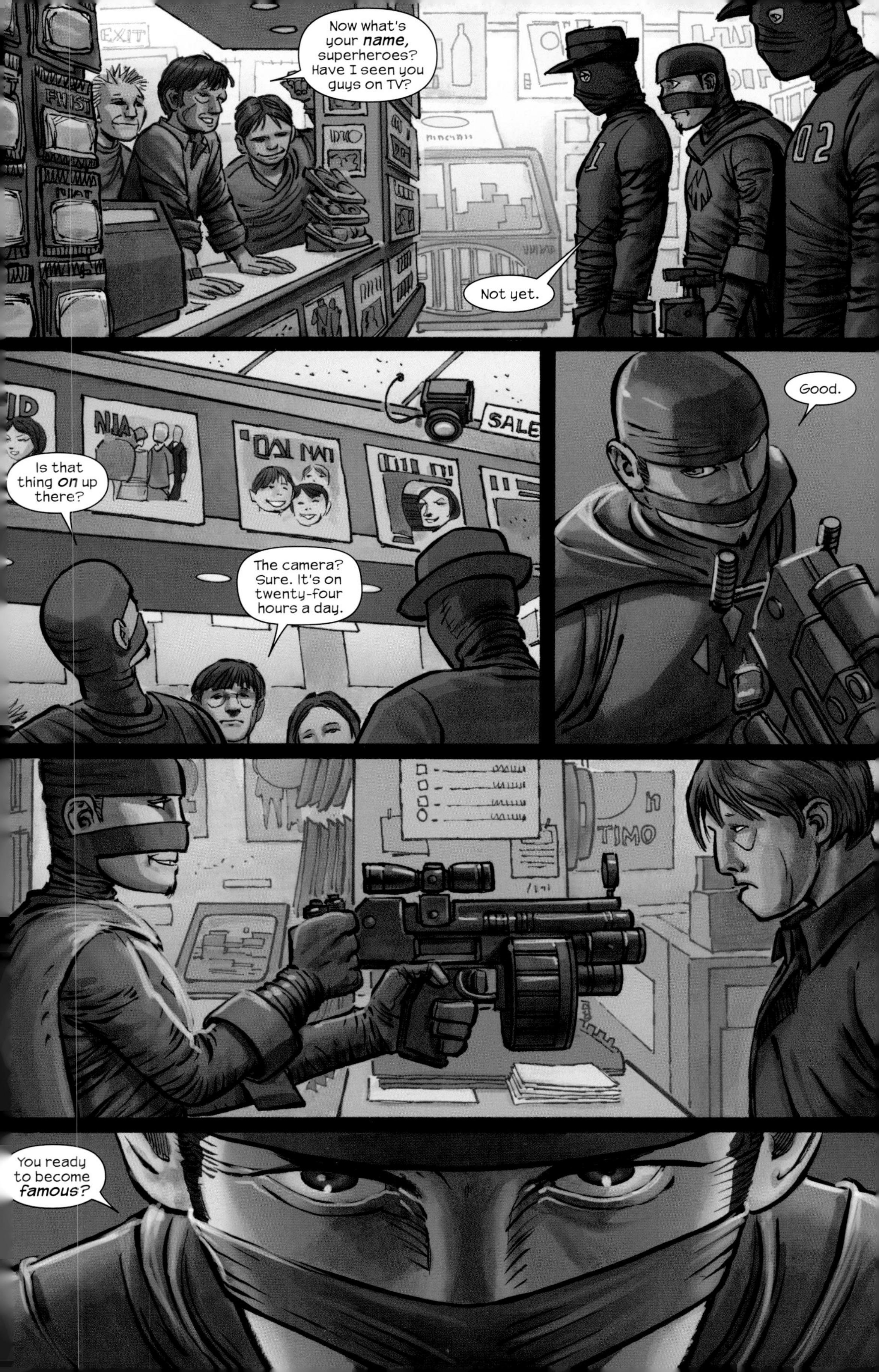
Now what's your *name,* superheroes? Have I seen you guys on TV?
Not yet.
Is that thing *on* up there?
The camera? Sure. It's on twenty-four hours a day.
Good.
You ready to become *famous?*

THREE

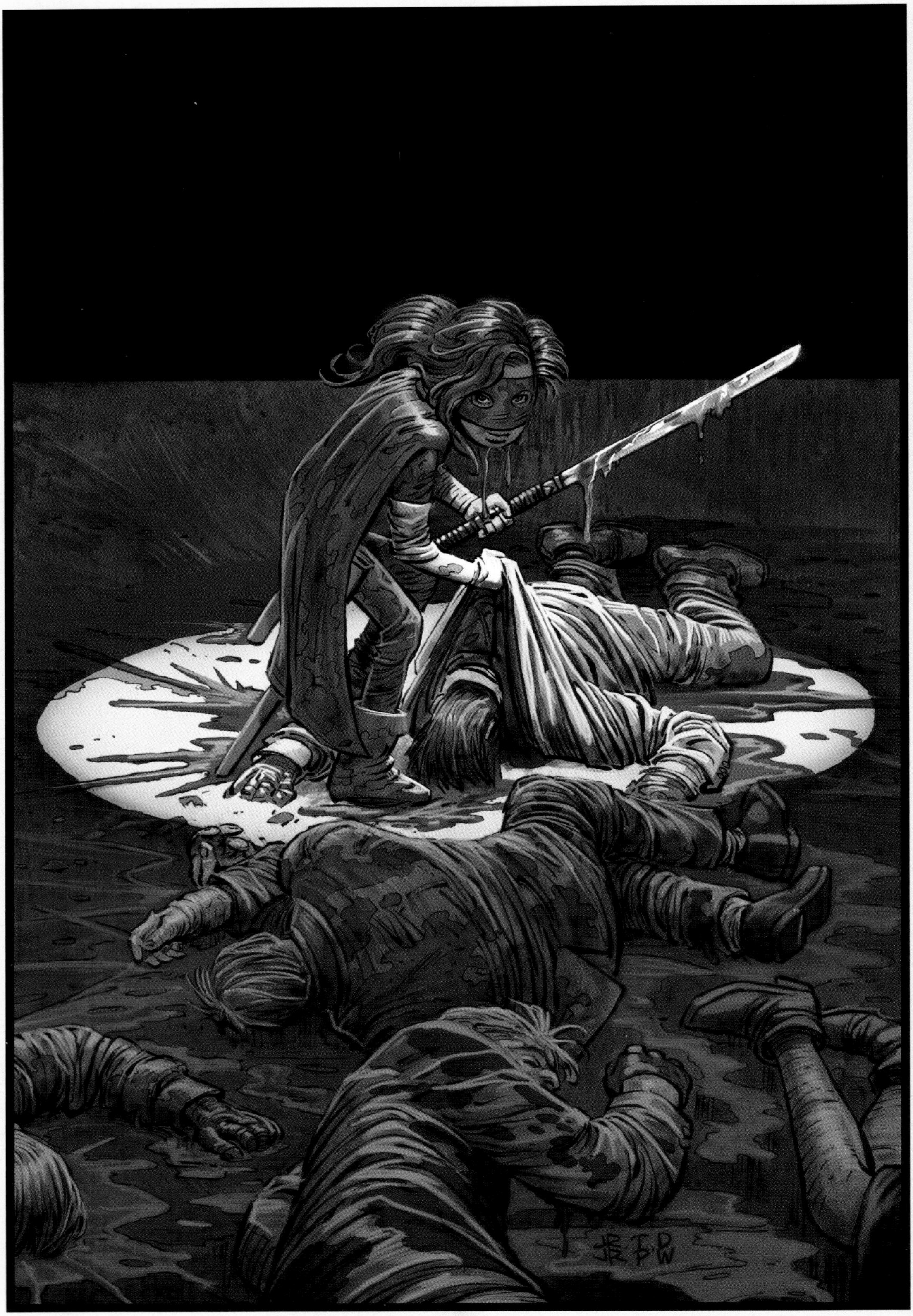

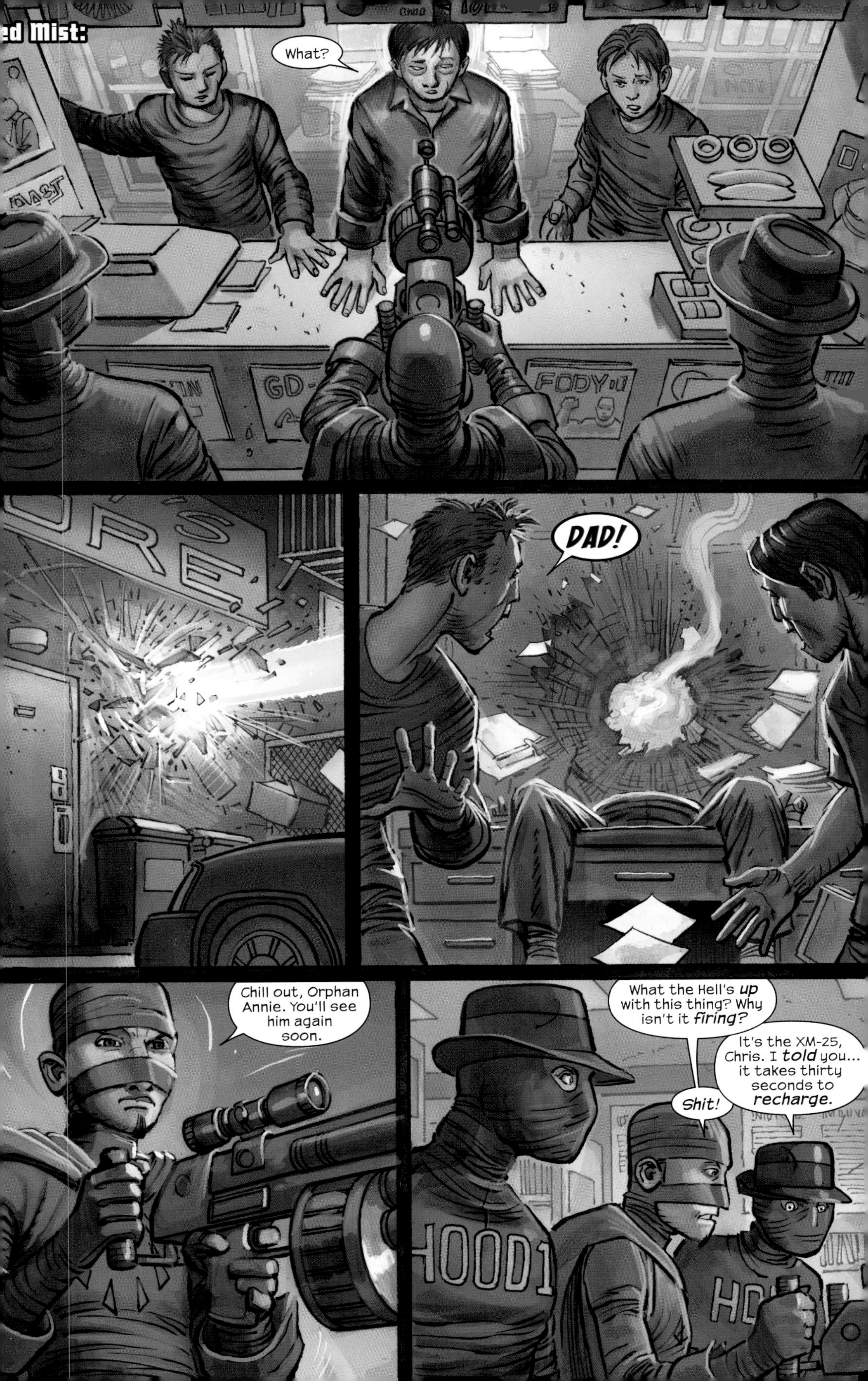
ed Mist:
What?
DAD!
Chill out, Orphan Annie. You'll see him again soon.
What the Hell's *up* with this thing? Why isn't it *firing?*
Shit!
It's the XM-25, Chris. I *told* you... it takes thirty seconds to *recharge.*
HOOD1

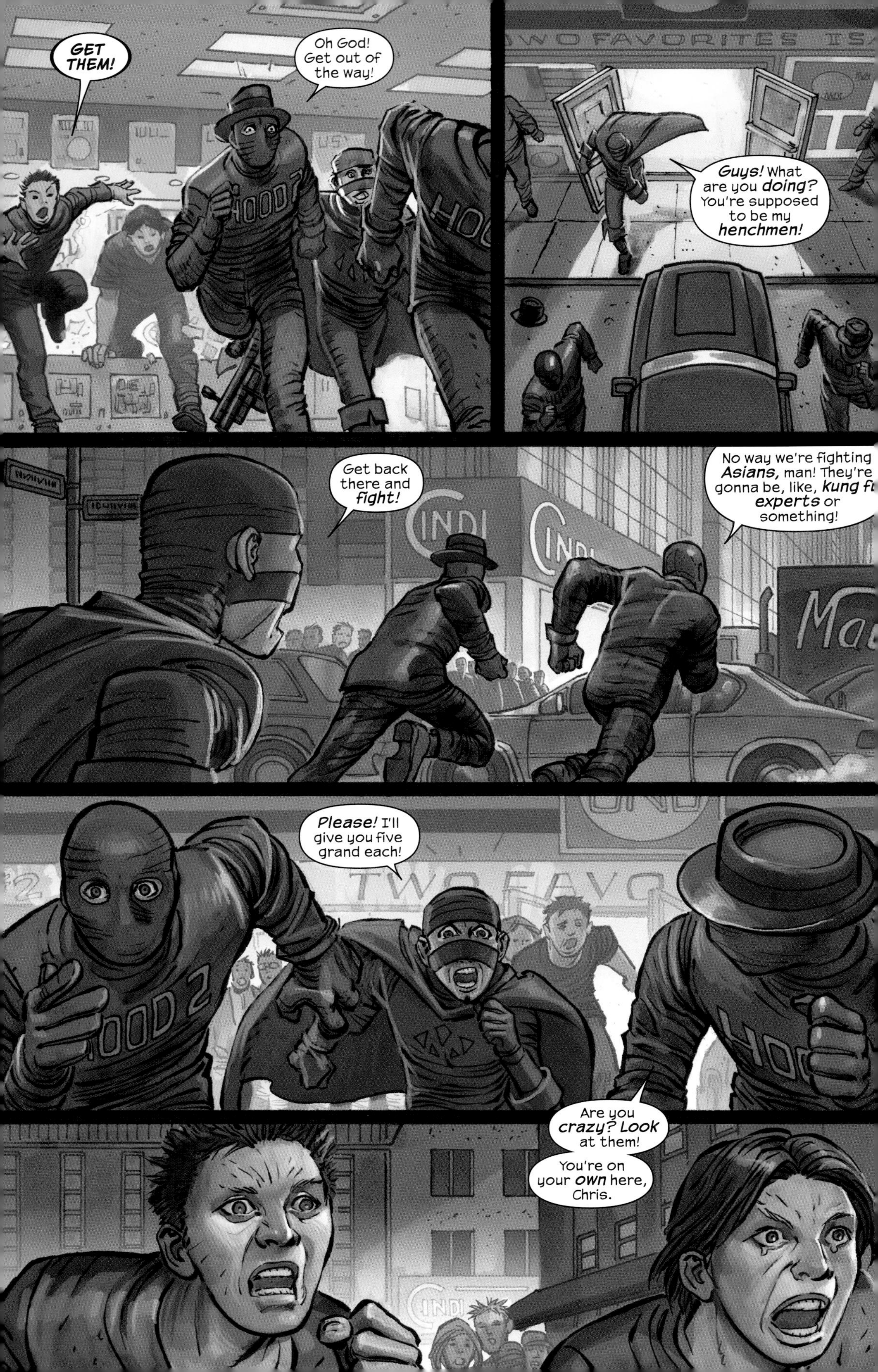
GET THEM!
Oh God! Get out of the way!
HOOD 2
TWO FAVORITES IS
Guys! What are you doing? You're supposed to be my henchmen!
Get back there and fight!
No way we're fighting Asians, man! They're gonna be, like, kung fu experts or something!
CINDI
Please! I'll give you five grand each!
TWO FAVO
HOOD 2
Are you crazy? Look at them!
You're on your own here, Chris.

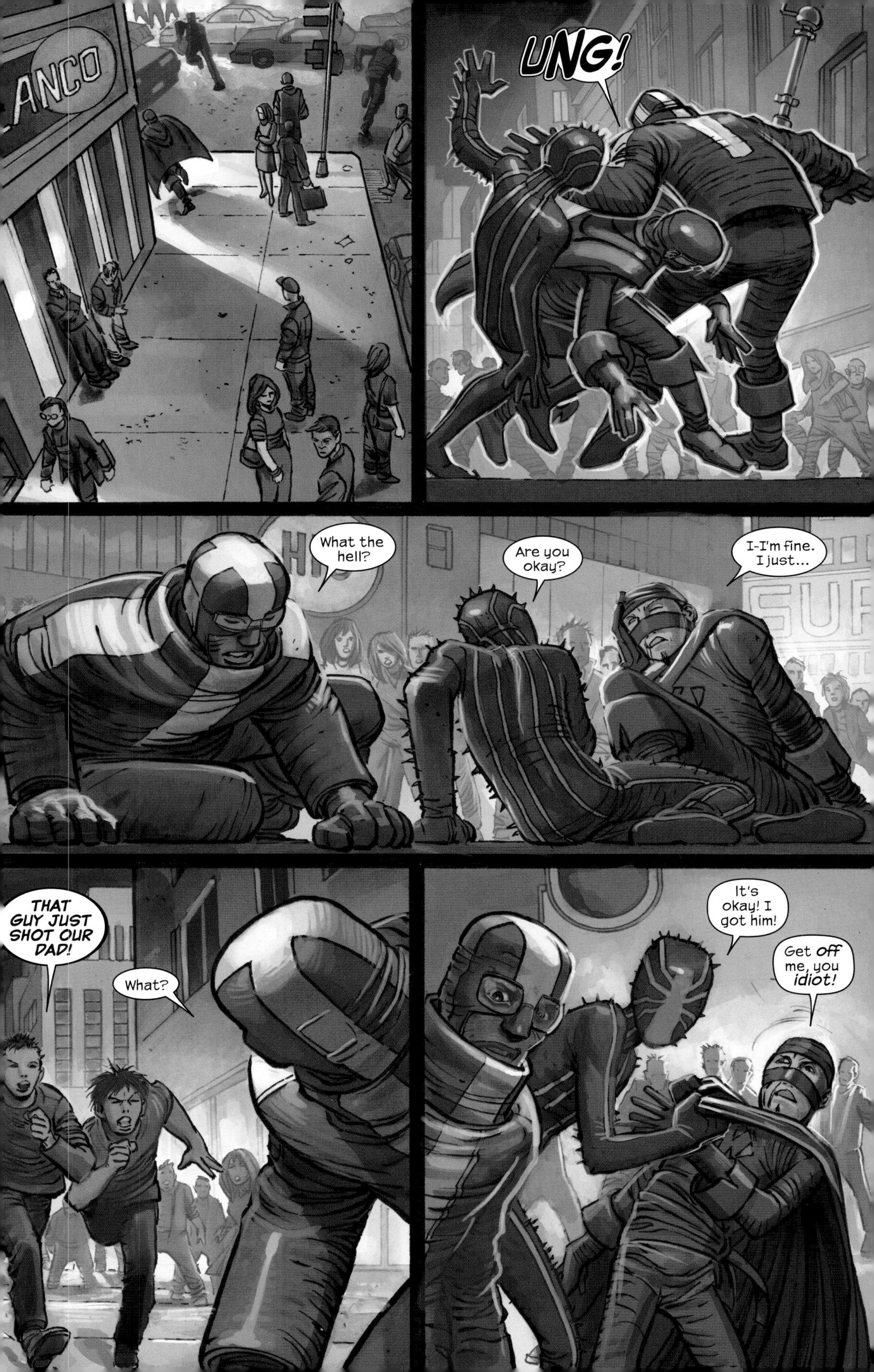
ANCO
UNG!
What the hell?
Are you okay?
I-I'm fine. I just...
SUP
THAT GUY JUST SHOT OUR DAD!
What?
It's okay! I got him!
Get *off* me, you *idiot!*

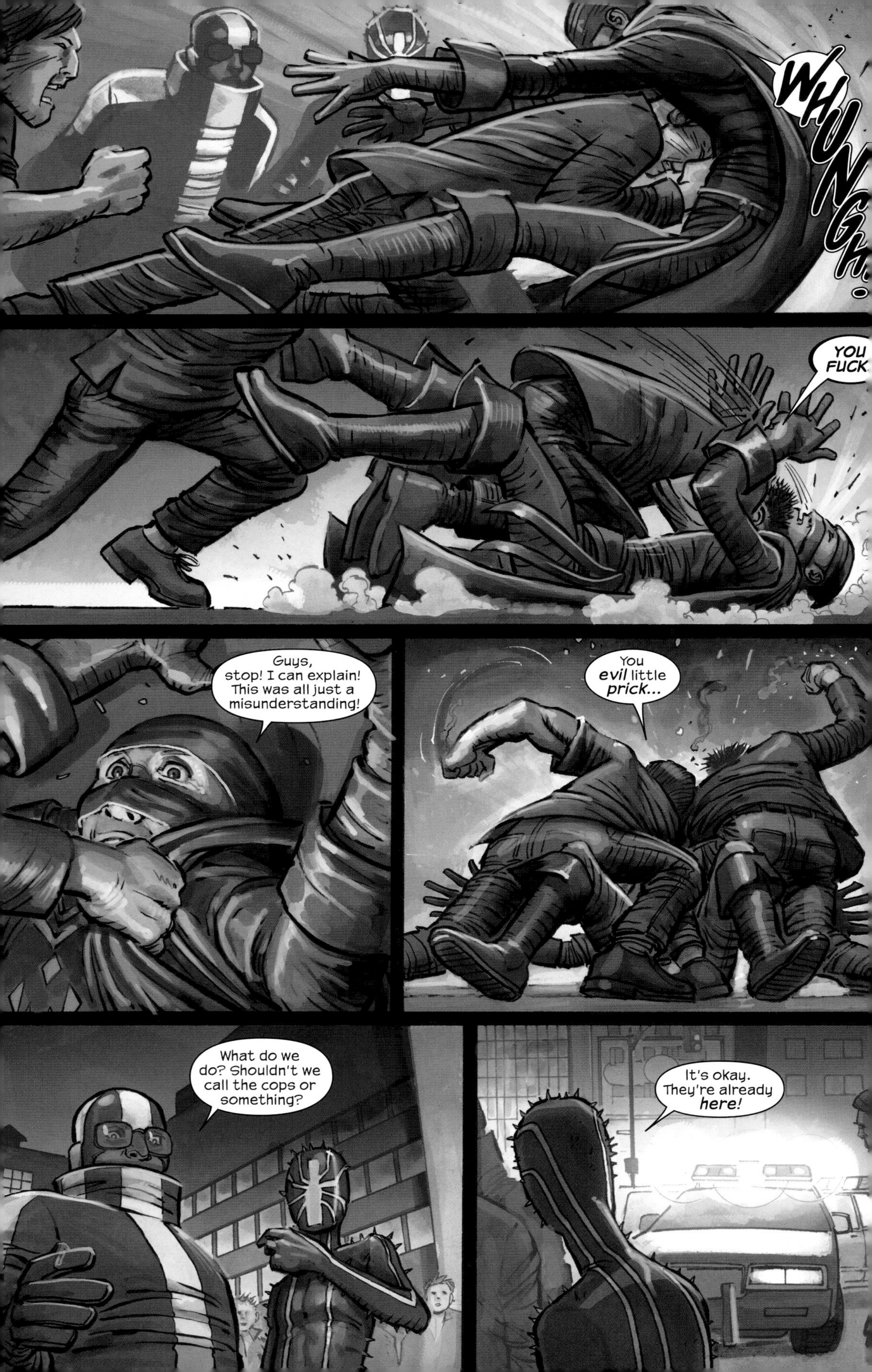
WHUNGH!
YOU FUCK
Guys, stop! I can explain! This was all just a misunderstanding!
You evil little prick...
What do we do? Shouldn't we call the cops or something?
It's okay. They're already here!

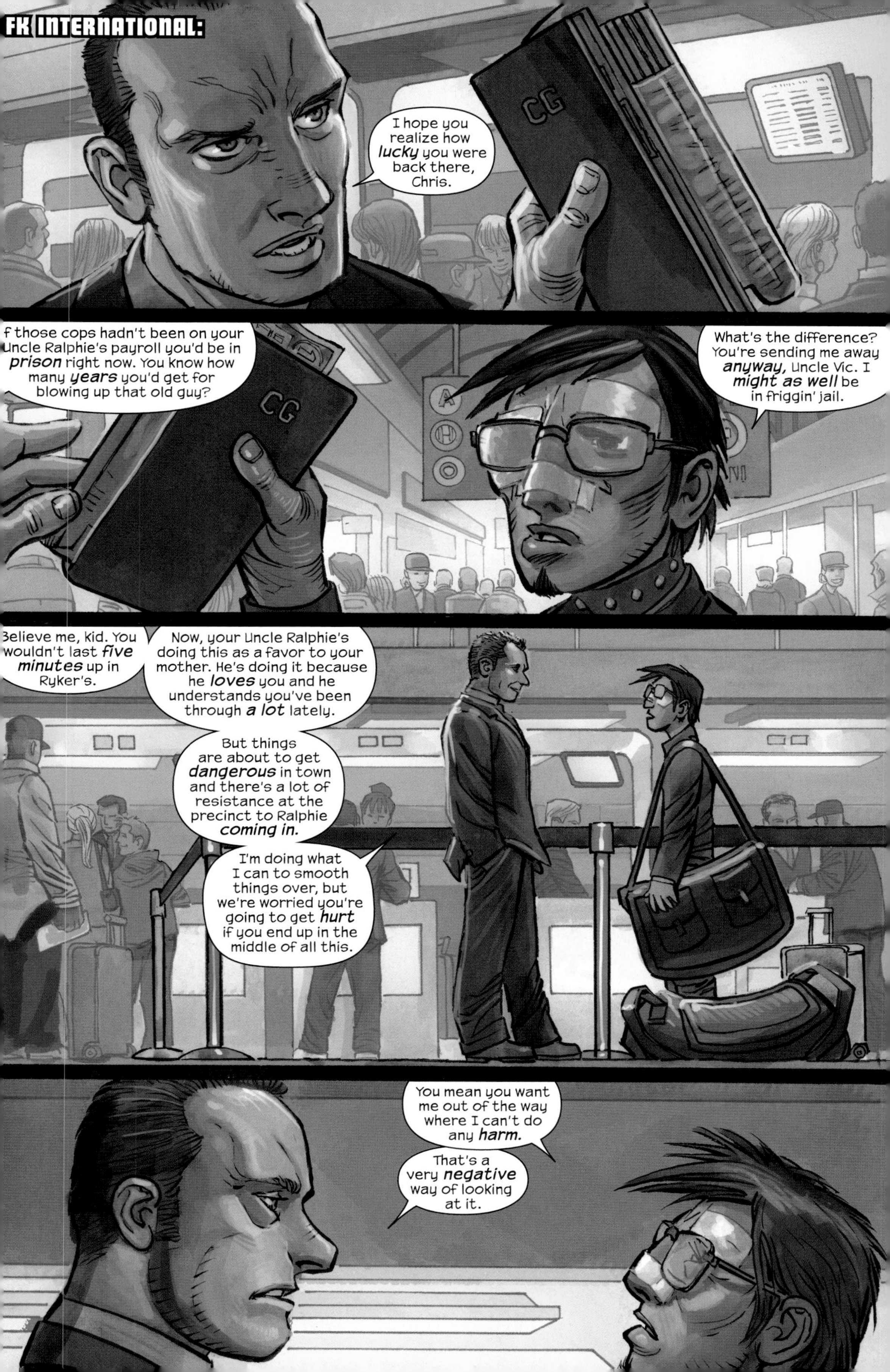
FK INTERNATIONAL:
I hope you realize how lucky you were back there, Chris.
f those cops hadn't been on your Uncle Ralphie's payroll you'd be in prison right now. You know how many years you'd get for blowing up that old guy?
What's the difference? You're sending me away anyway, Uncle Vic. I might as well be in friggin' jail.
Believe me, kid. You wouldn't last five minutes up in Ryker's.
Now, your Uncle Ralphie's doing this as a favor to your mother. He's doing it because he loves you and he understands you've been through a lot lately.
But things are about to get dangerous in town and there's a lot of resistance at the precinct to Ralphie coming in.
I'm doing what I can to smooth things over, but we're worried you're going to get hurt if you end up in the middle of all this.
You mean you want me out of the way where I can't do any harm.
That's a very negative way of looking at it.

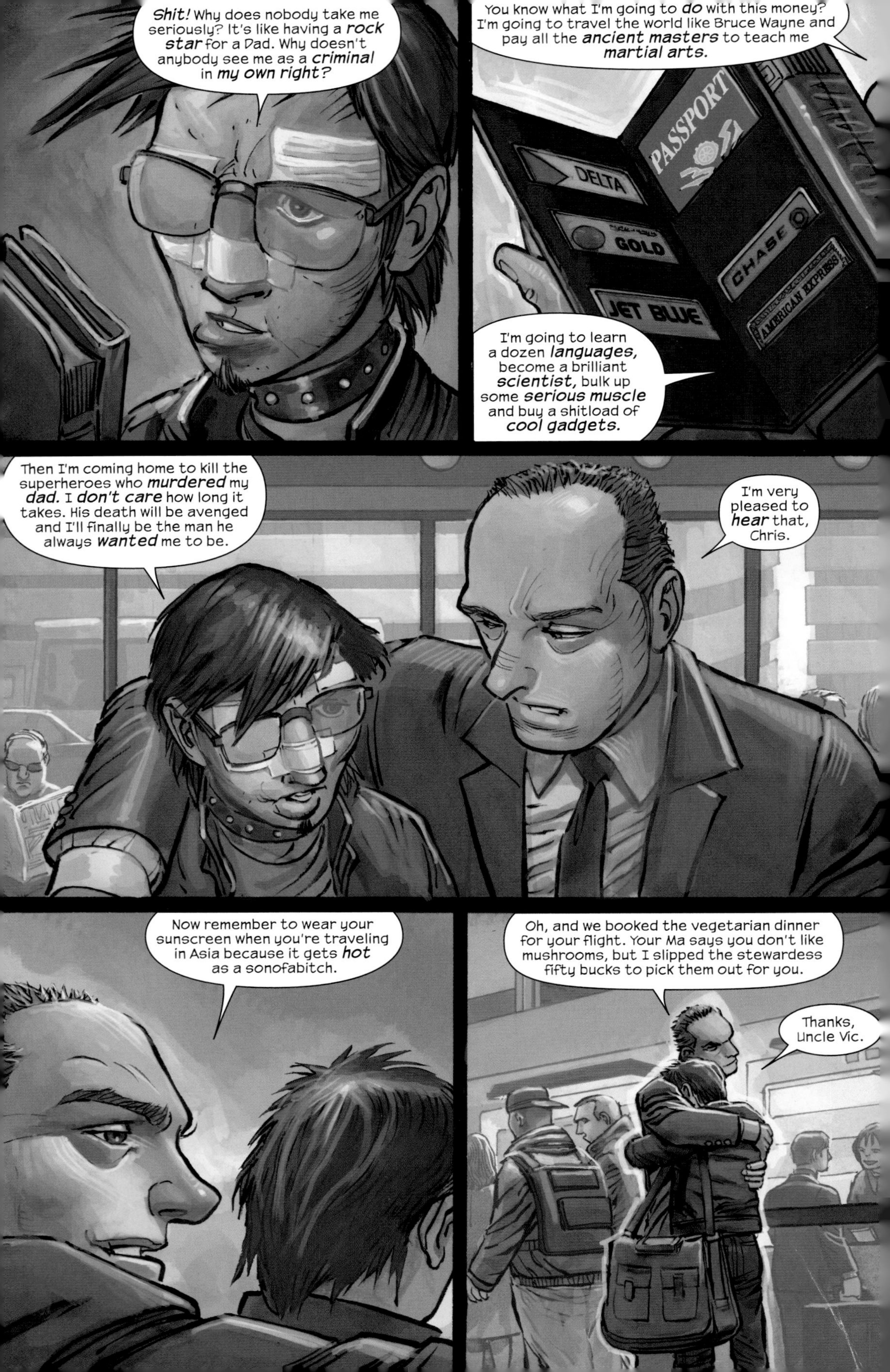
Shit! Why does nobody take me seriously? It's like having a rock star for a Dad. Why doesn't anybody see me as a criminal in my own right?
You know what I'm going to do with this money? I'm going to travel the world like Bruce Wayne and pay all the ancient masters to teach me martial arts.
PASSPORT
DELTA
GOLD
JET BLUE
CHASE
AMERICAN EXPRESS
I'm going to learn a dozen languages, become a brilliant scientist, bulk up some serious muscle and buy a shitload of cool gadgets.
Then I'm coming home to kill the superheroes who murdered my dad. I don't care how long it takes. His death will be avenged and I'll finally be the man he always wanted me to be.
I'm very pleased to hear that, Chris.
Now remember to wear your sunscreen when you're traveling in Asia because it gets hot as a sonofabitch.
Oh, and we booked the vegetarian dinner for your flight. Your Ma says you don't like mushrooms, but I slipped the stewardess fifty bucks to pick them out for you.
Thanks, Uncle Vic.

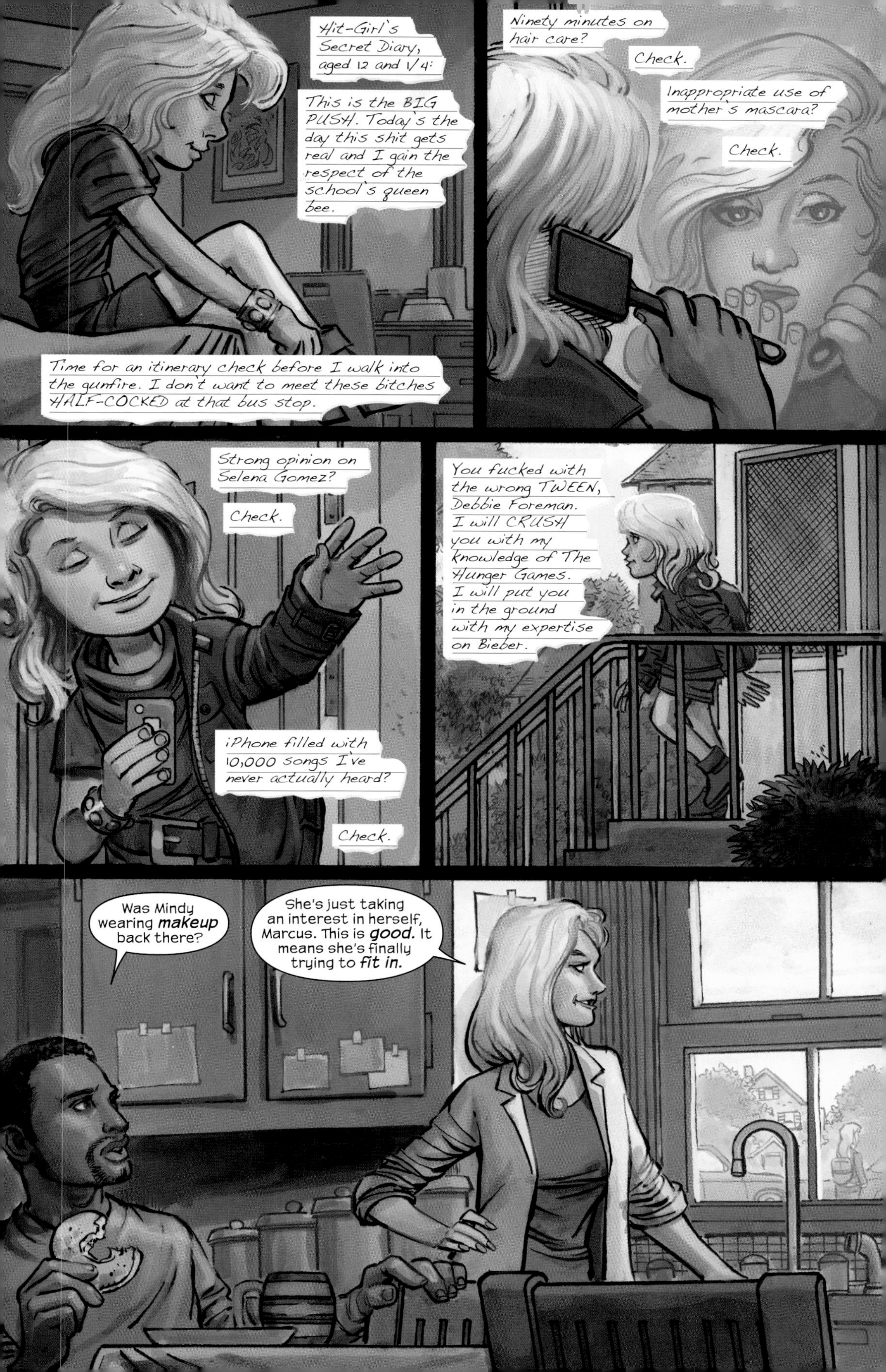
Hit-Girl's Secret Diary, aged 12 and 1/4:
This is the BIG PUSH. Today's the day this shit gets real and I gain the respect of the school's queen bee.
Time for an itinerary check before I walk into the gunfire. I don't want to meet these bitches HALF-COCKED at that bus stop.
Ninety minutes on hair care?
Check.
Inappropriate use of mother's mascara?
Check.
Strong opinion on Selena Gomez?
Check.
iPhone filled with 10,000 songs I've never actually heard?
Check.
You fucked with the wrong TWEEN, Debbie Foreman. I will CRUSH you with my knowledge of The Hunger Games. I will put you in the ground with my expertise on Bieber.
Was Mindy wearing makeup back there?
She's just taking an interest in herself, Marcus. This is good. It means she's finally trying to fit in.

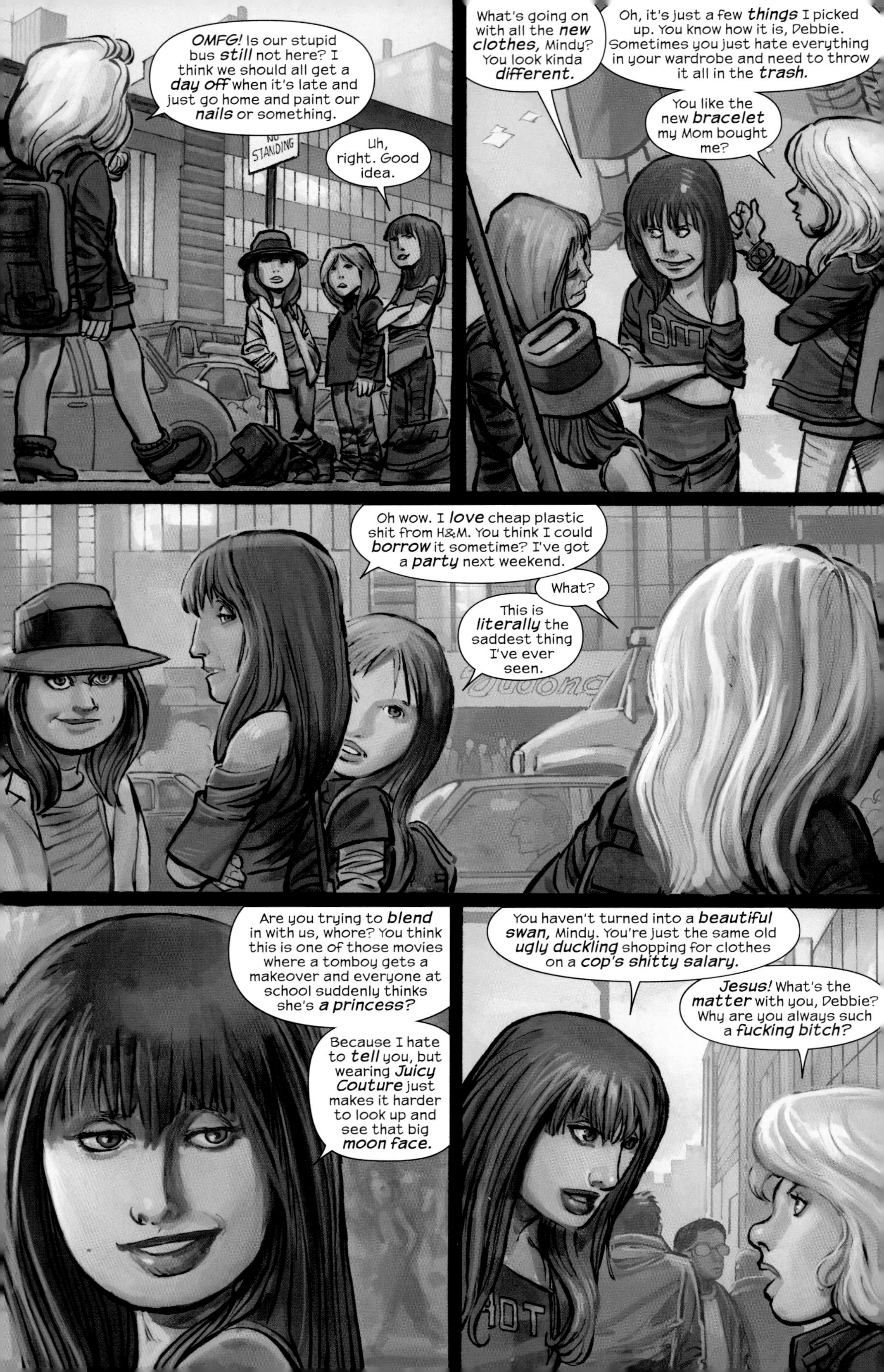
OMFG! Is our stupid bus still not here? I think we should all get a day off when it's late and just go home and paint our nails or something.
NO STANDING
Uh, right. Good idea.
What's going on with all the new clothes, Mindy? You look kinda different.
Oh, it's just a few things I picked up. You know how it is, Debbie. Sometimes you just hate everything in your wardrobe and need to throw it all in the trash.
You like the new bracelet my Mom bought me?
Oh wow. I love cheap plastic shit from H&M. You think I could borrow it sometime? I've got a party next weekend.
What?
This is literally the saddest thing I've ever seen.
Are you trying to blend in with us, whore? You think this is one of those movies where a tomboy gets a makeover and everyone at school suddenly thinks she's a princess?
Because I hate to tell you, but wearing Juicy Couture just makes it harder to look up and see that big moon face.
You haven't turned into a beautiful swan, Mindy. You're just the same old ugly duckling shopping for clothes on a cop's shitty salary.
Jesus! What's the matter with you, Debbie? Why are you always such a fucking bitch?

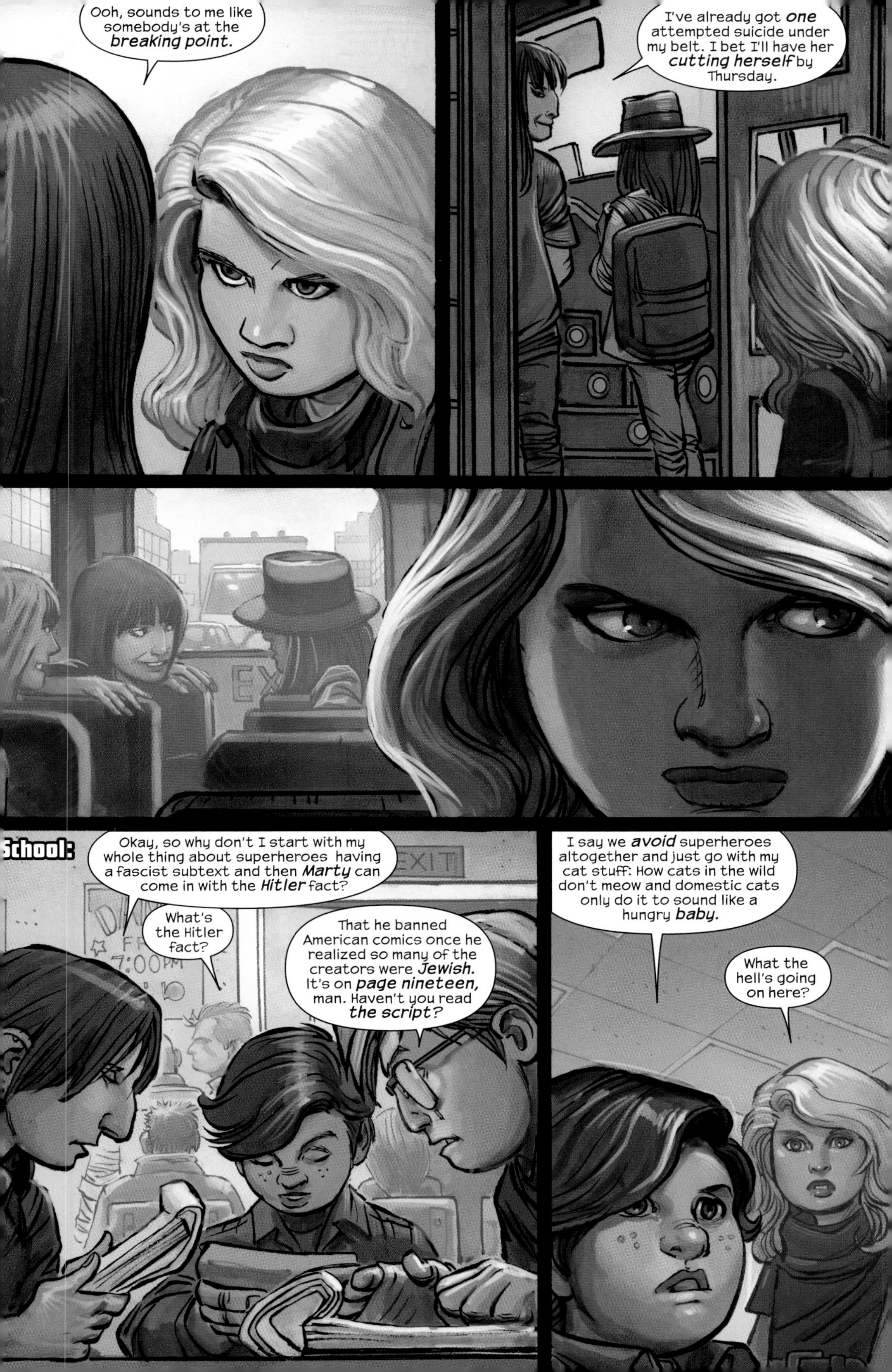

Ooh, sounds to me like somebody's at the *breaking point.*
I've already got *one* attempted suicide under my belt. I bet I'll have her *cutting herself* by Thursday.
EX
School:
Okay, so why don't I start with my whole thing about superheroes having a fascist subtext and then *Marty* can come in with the *Hitler* fact?
EXIT
What's the Hitler fact?
That he banned American comics once he realized so many of the creators were *Jewish.* It's on *page nineteen,* man. Haven't you read *the script?*
7:00PM
I say we *avoid* superheroes altogether and just go with my cat stuff: How cats in the wild don't meow and domestic cats only do it to sound like a hungry *baby.*
What the hell's going on here?

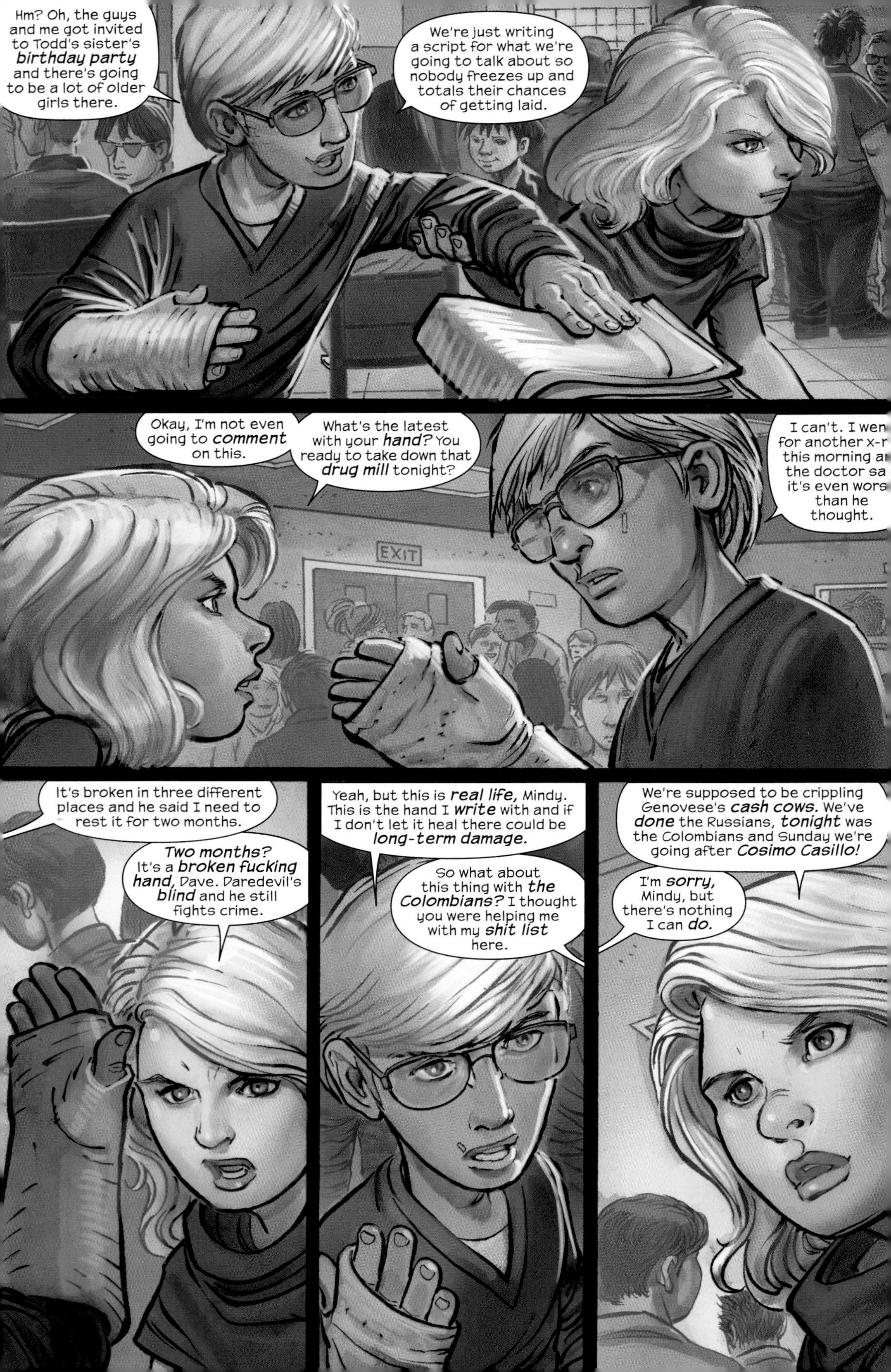
Hm? Oh, the guys and me got invited to Todd's sister's birthday party and there's going to be a lot of older girls there.
We're just writing a script for what we're going to talk about so nobody freezes up and totals their chances of getting laid.
Okay, I'm not even going to comment on this.
What's the latest with your hand? You ready to take down that drug mill tonight?
EXIT
It's broken in three different places and he said I need to rest it for two months.
Two months? It's a broken fucking hand, Dave. Daredevil's blind and he still fights crime.
Yeah, but this is real life, Mindy. This is the hand I write with and if I don't let it heal there could be long-term damage.
So what about this thing with the Colombians? I thought you were helping me with my shit list here.
We're supposed to be crippling Genovese's cash cows. We've done the Russians, tonight was the Colombians and Sunday we're going after Cosimo Casillo!
I'm sorry, Mindy, but there's nothing I can do.

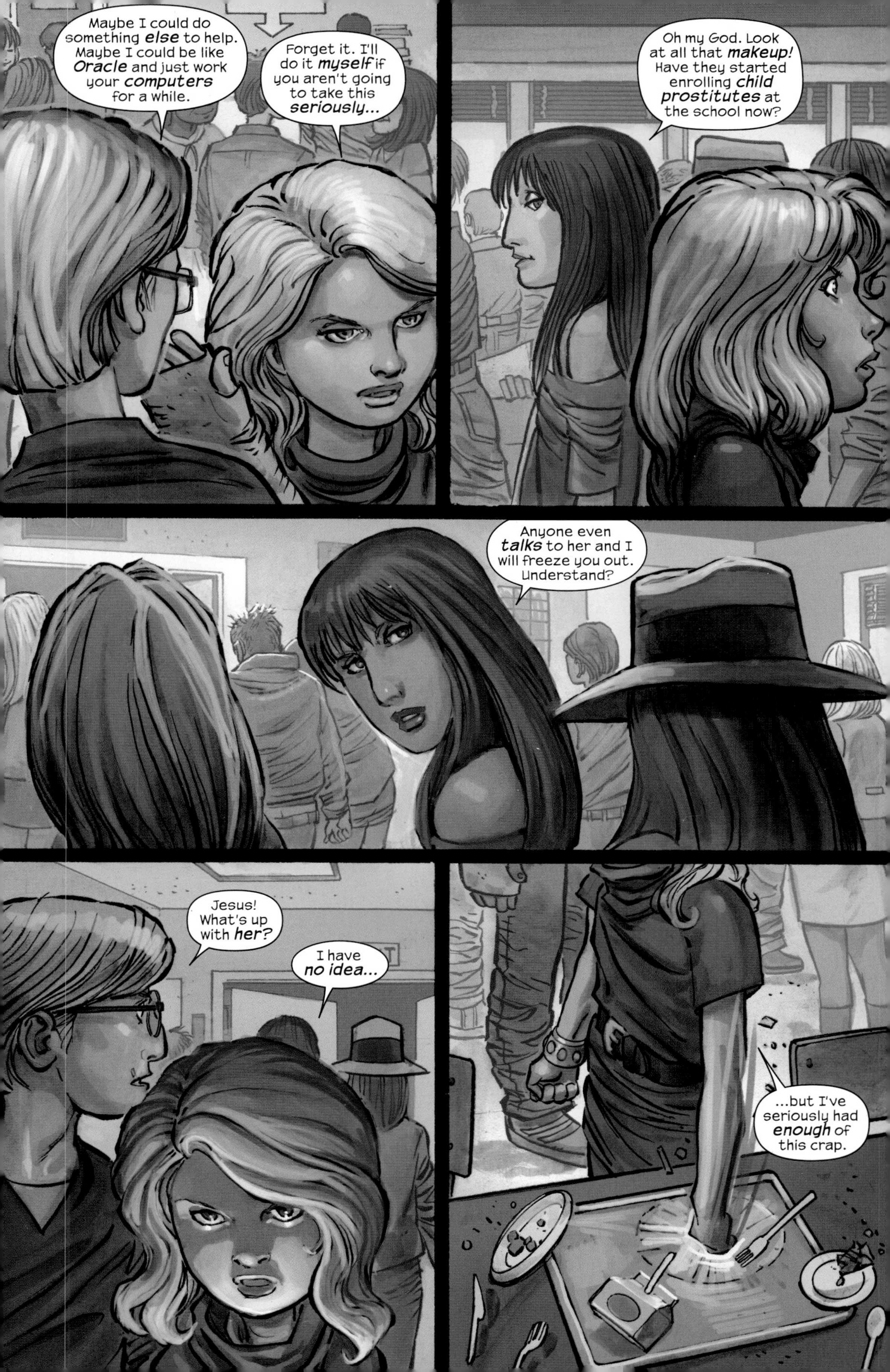
Maybe I could do something else to help. Maybe I could be like Oracle and just work your computers for a while.
Forget it. I'll do it myself if you aren't going to take this seriously...
Oh my God. Look at all that makeup! Have they started enrolling child prostitutes at the school now?
Anyone even talks to her and I will freeze you out. Understand?
Jesus! What's up with her?
I have no idea...
...but I've seriously had enough of this crap.

What the hell? Were you just watching me use the *bathroom,* you lesbian?

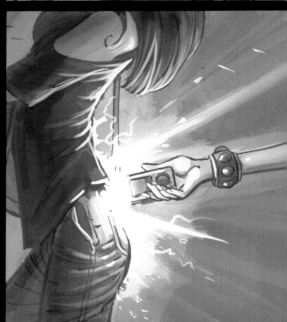

"Wake up, bitch.

"C'mon. I didn't haul your ass up here so you could take a *nap.*"

Wh-What?

Wh-Where am I? I...

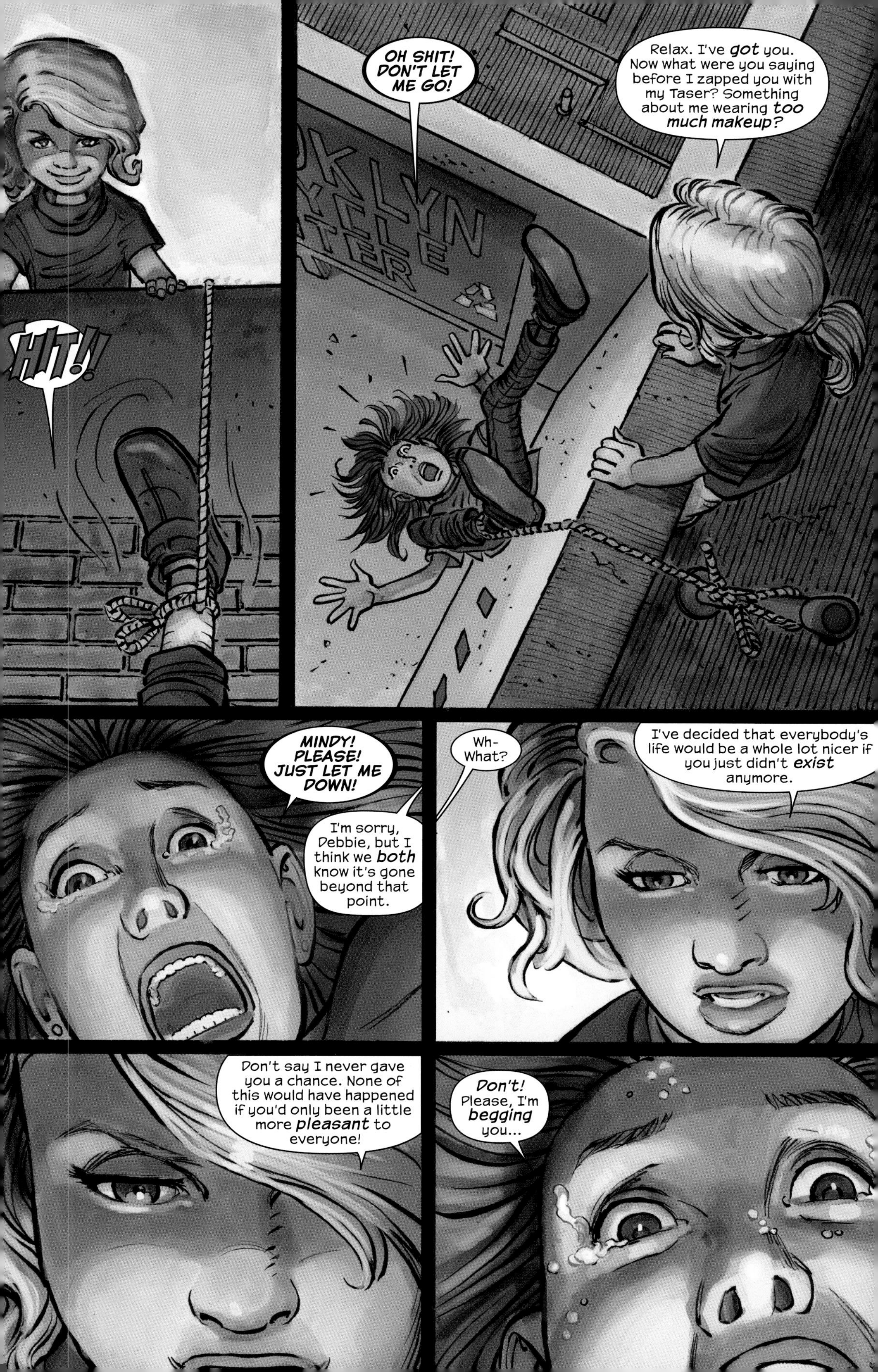
HIT!!
OH SHIT! DON'T LET ME GO!
Relax. I've got you. Now what were you saying before I zapped you with my Taser? Something about me wearing too much makeup?
MINDY! PLEASE! JUST LET ME DOWN!
I'm sorry, Debbie, but I think we both know it's gone beyond that point.
Wh- What?
I've decided that everybody's life would be a whole lot nicer if you just didn't exist anymore.
Don't say I never gave you a chance. None of this would have happened if you'd only been a little more pleasant to everyone!
Don't! Please, I'm begging you...

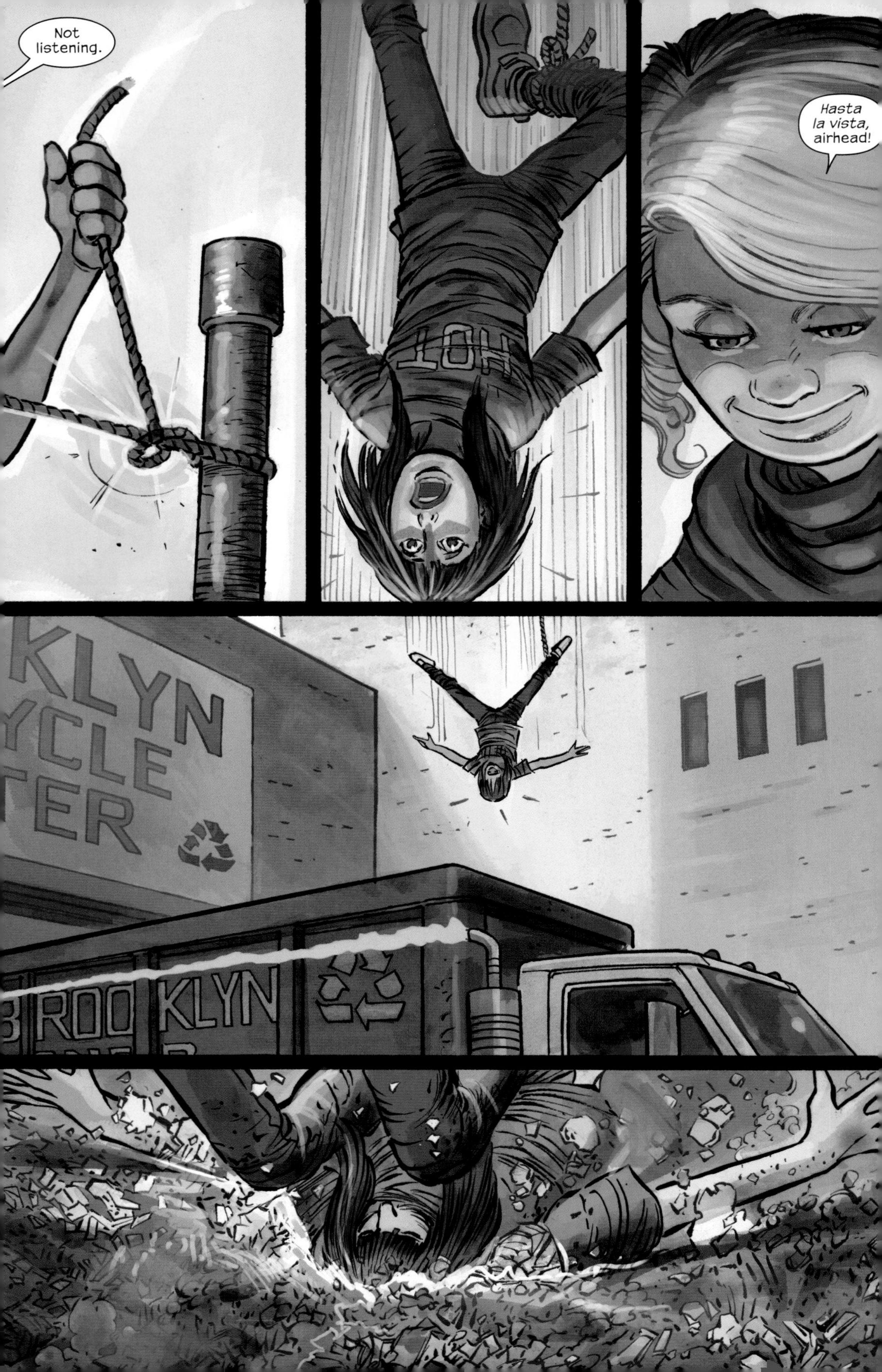

Not listening.
Hasta la vista, airhead!
HOT
KLYN
YCLE
TER
BROOKLYN

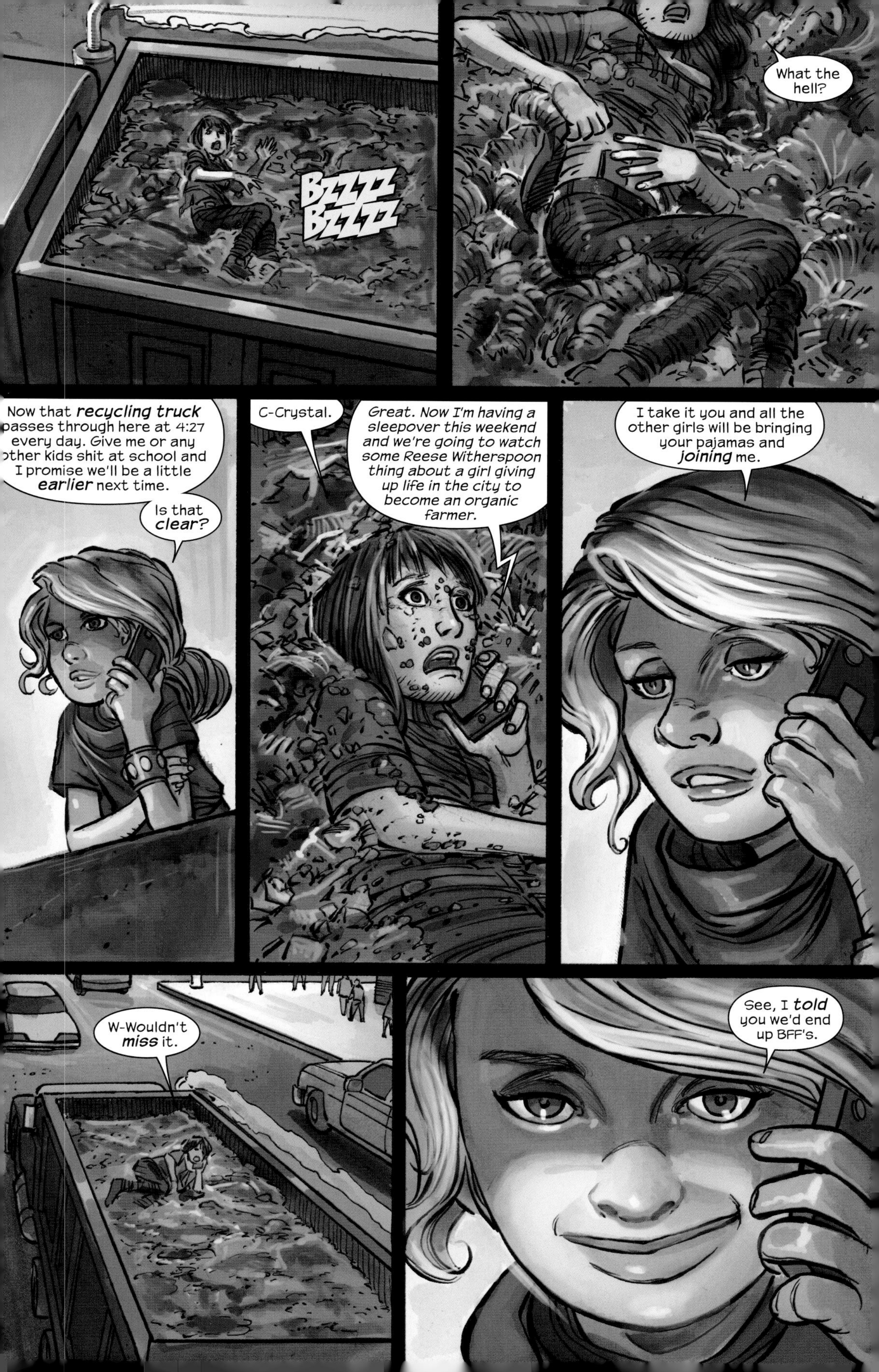
BZZZZ BZZZZ
What the hell?
Now that recycling truck passes through here at 4:27 every day. Give me or any other kids shit at school and I promise we'll be a little earlier next time.
Is that clear?
C-Crystal.
Great. Now I'm having a sleepover this weekend and we're going to watch some Reese Witherspoon thing about a girl giving up life in the city to become an organic farmer.
I take it you and all the other girls will be bringing your pajamas and joining me.
W-Wouldn't miss it.
See, I told you we'd end up BFF's.

Mindy's House:

Hey, honey. What's up?

You *lied* to me, Marcus. You said they weren't *leaning* on you, but look what just got delivered. It says *Mommy Bear, Daddy Bear* and *Baby Bear* on them...

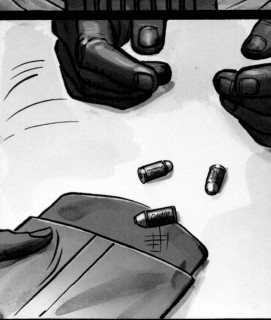

Oh, Jesus.

The Police Department:

Gigante, I need to *talk* to you.

5TH PRECINCT

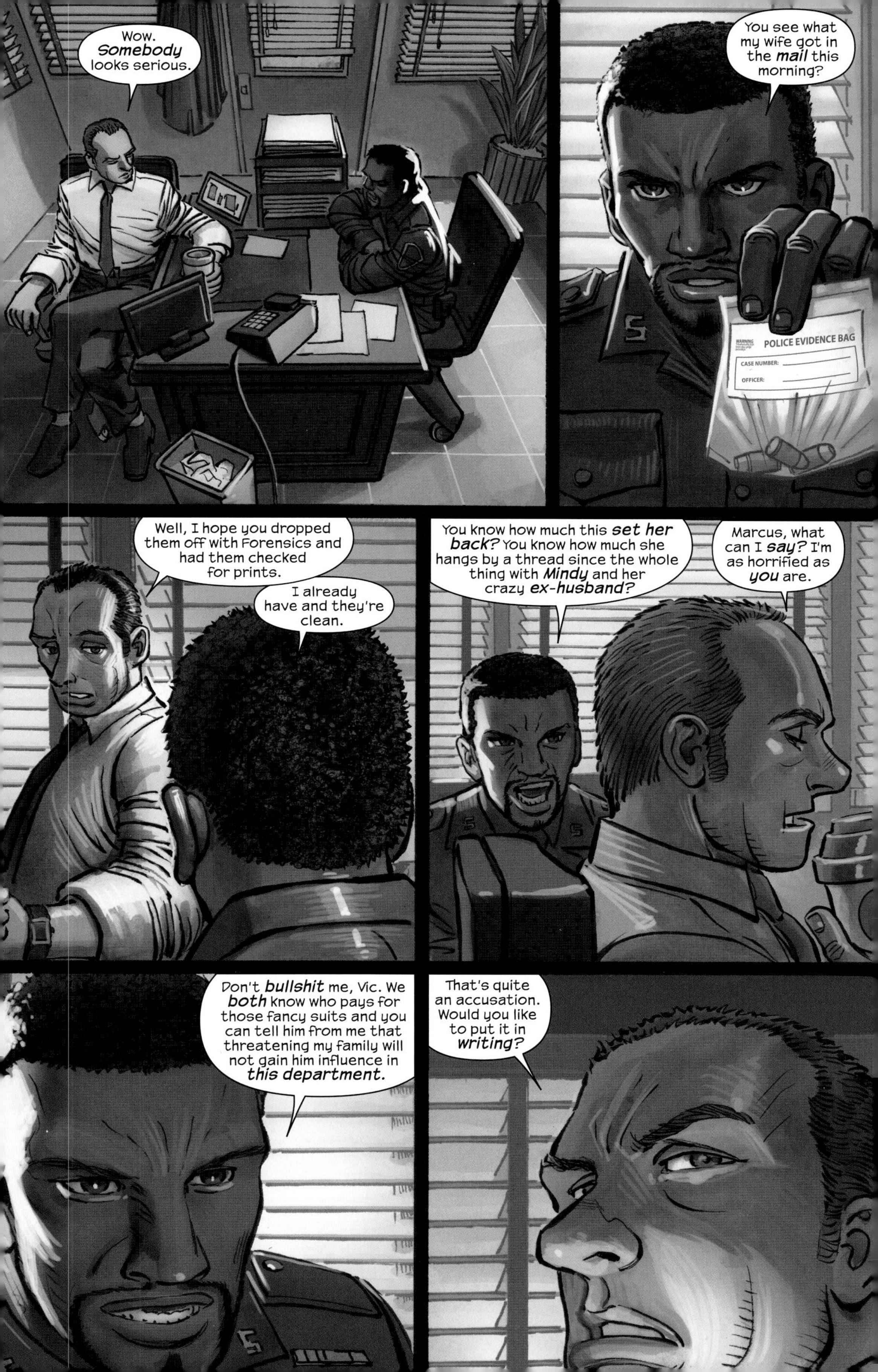
Wow. Somebody looks serious.
You see what my wife got in the mail this morning?
POLICE EVIDENCE BAG
CASE NUMBER:
OFFICER:
Well, I hope you dropped them off with Forensics and had them checked for prints.
I already have and they're clean.
You know how much this set her back? You know how much she hangs by a thread since the whole thing with Mindy and her crazy ex-husband?
Marcus, what can I say? I'm as horrified as you are.
Don't bullshit me, Vic. We both know who pays for those fancy suits and you can tell him from me that threatening my family will not gain him influence in this department.
That's quite an accusation. Would you like to put it in writing?

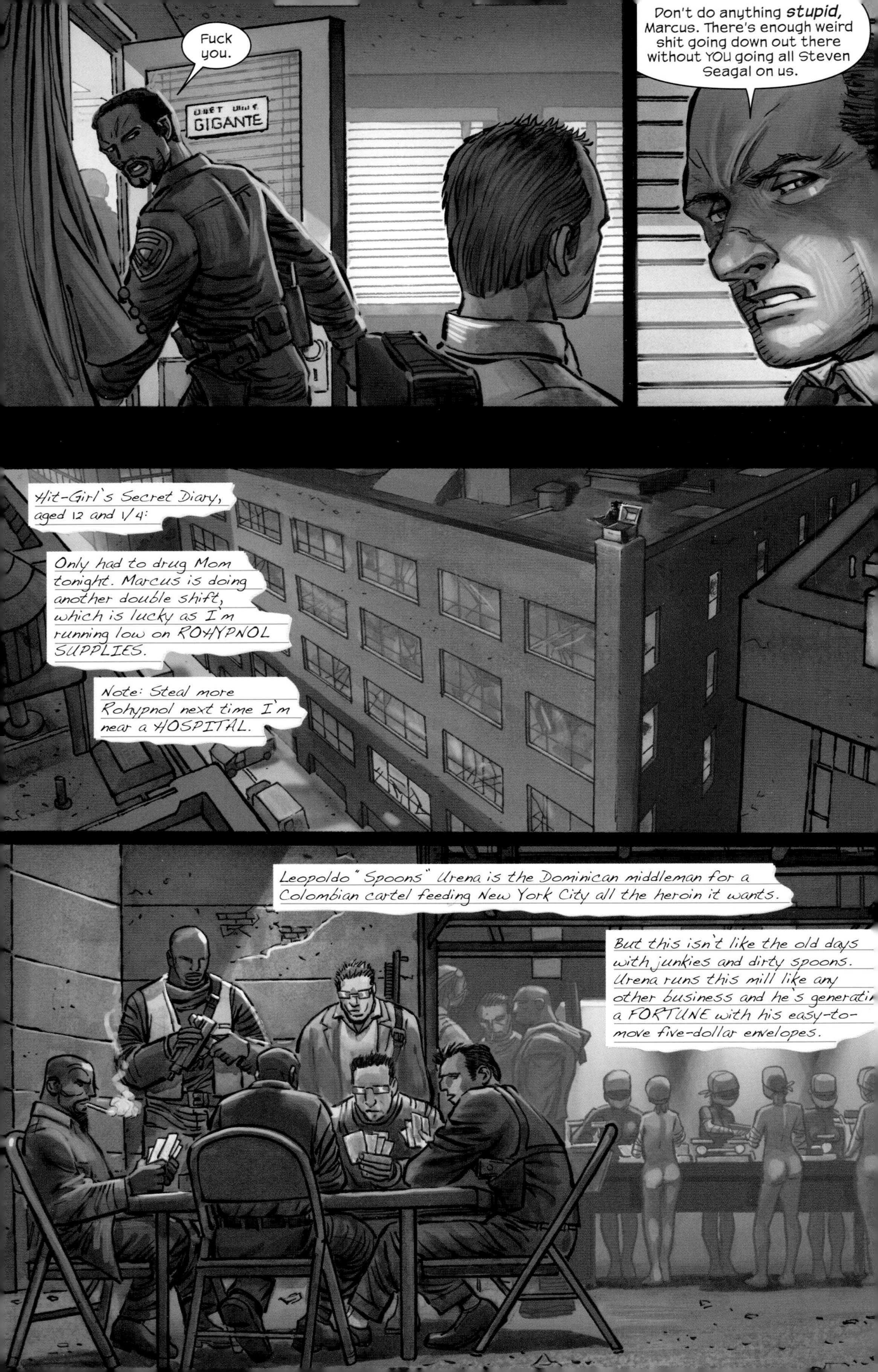
Fuck you.
GIGANTE
Don't do anything stupid, Marcus. There's enough weird shit going down out there without YOU going all Steven Seagal on us.
Hit-Girl's Secret Diary, aged 12 and 1/4:
Only had to drug Mom tonight. Marcus is doing another double shift, which is lucky as I'm running low on ROHYPNOL SUPPLIES.
Note: Steal more Rohypnol next time I'm near a HOSPITAL.
Leopoldo "Spoons" Urena is the Dominican middleman for a Colombian cartel feeding New York City all the heroin it wants.
But this isn't like the old days with junkies and dirty spoons. Urena runs this mill like any other business and he's generati a FORTUNE with his easy-to-move five-dollar envelopes.

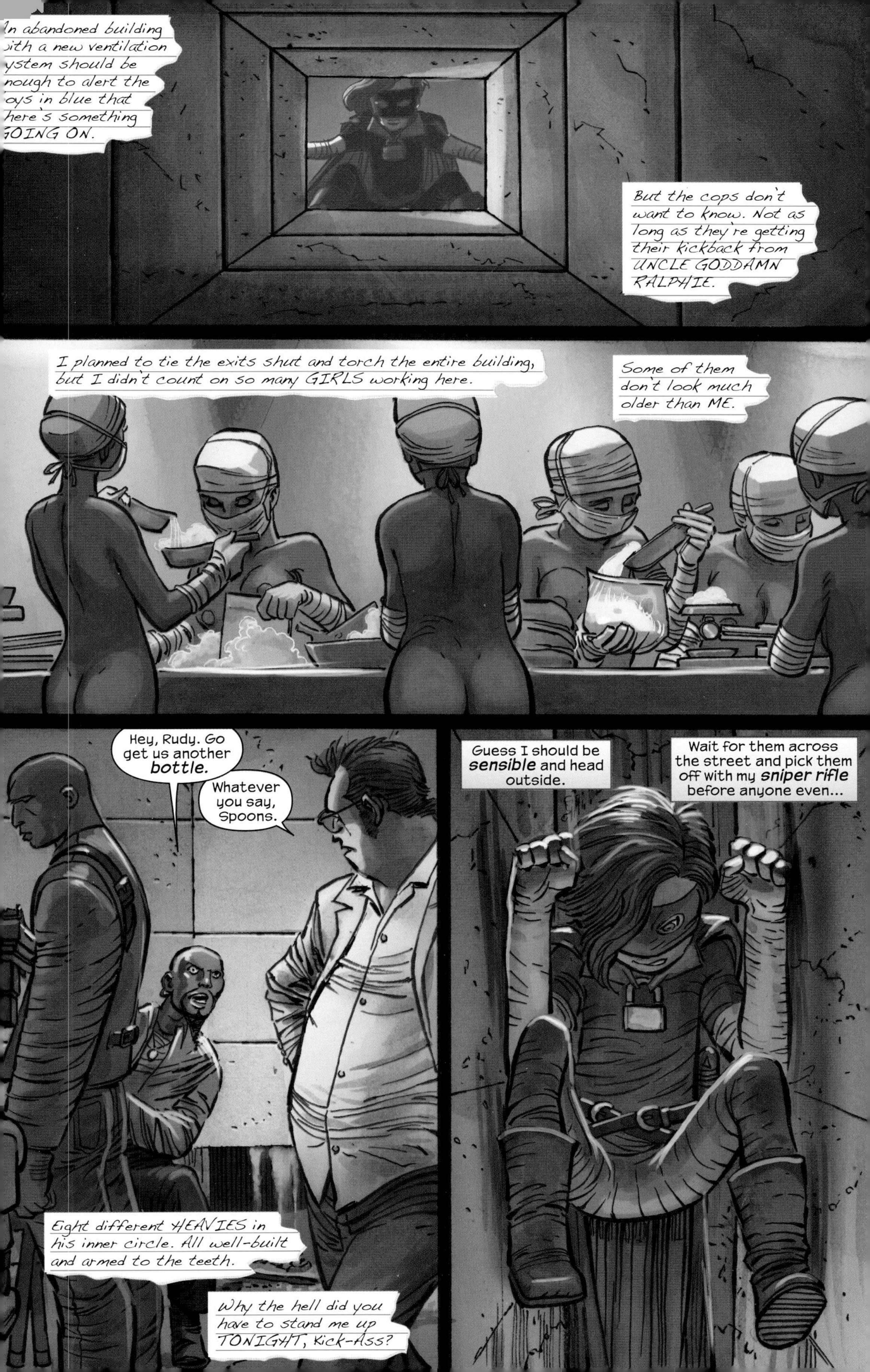

In abandoned building with a new ventilation system should be enough to alert the boys in blue that there's something GOING ON.
But the cops don't want to know. Not as long as they're getting their kickback from UNCLE GODDAMN RALPHIE.
I planned to tie the exits shut and torch the entire building, but I didn't count on so many GIRLS working here.
Some of them don't look much older than ME.
Hey, Rudy. Go get us another bottle.
Whatever you say, Spoons.
Eight different HEAVIES in his inner circle. All well-built and armed to the teeth.
Why the hell did you have to stand me up TONIGHT, Kick-Ass?
Guess I should be sensible and head outside.
Wait for them across the street and pick them off with my sniper rifle before anyone even...

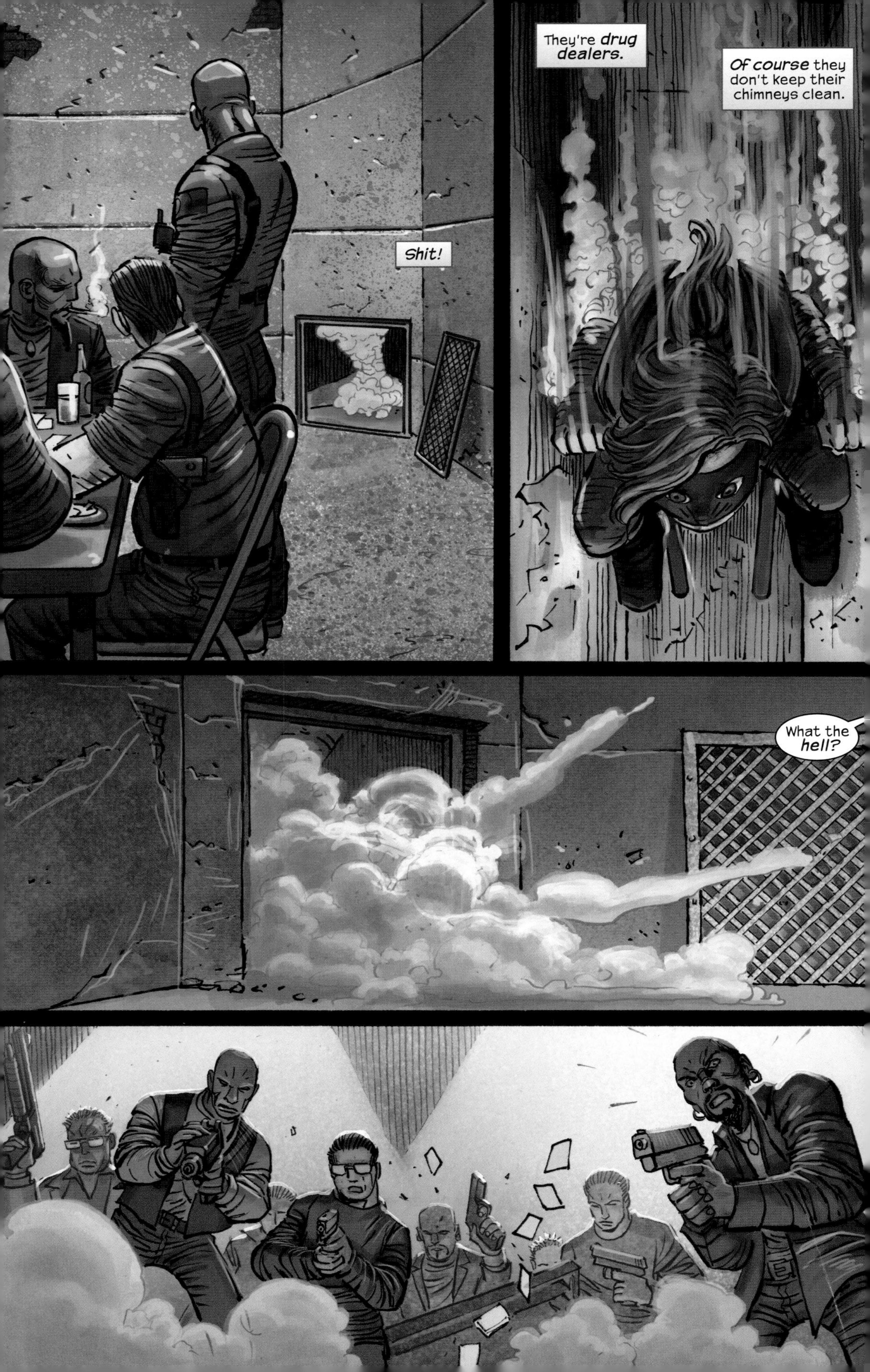
Shit!
They're drug dealers.
Of course they don't keep their chimneys clean.
What the hell?

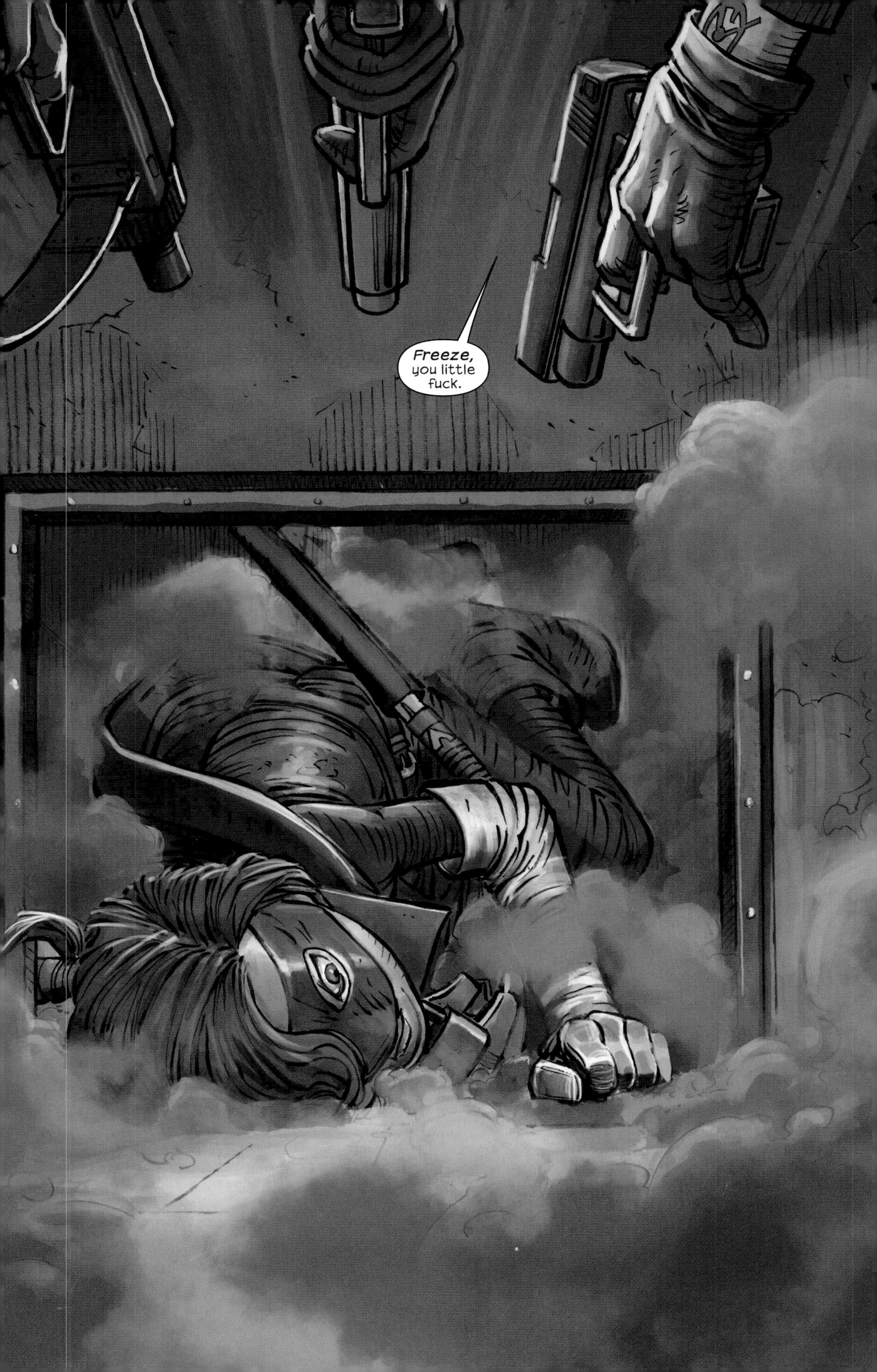
Freeze, you little fuck.

FOUR

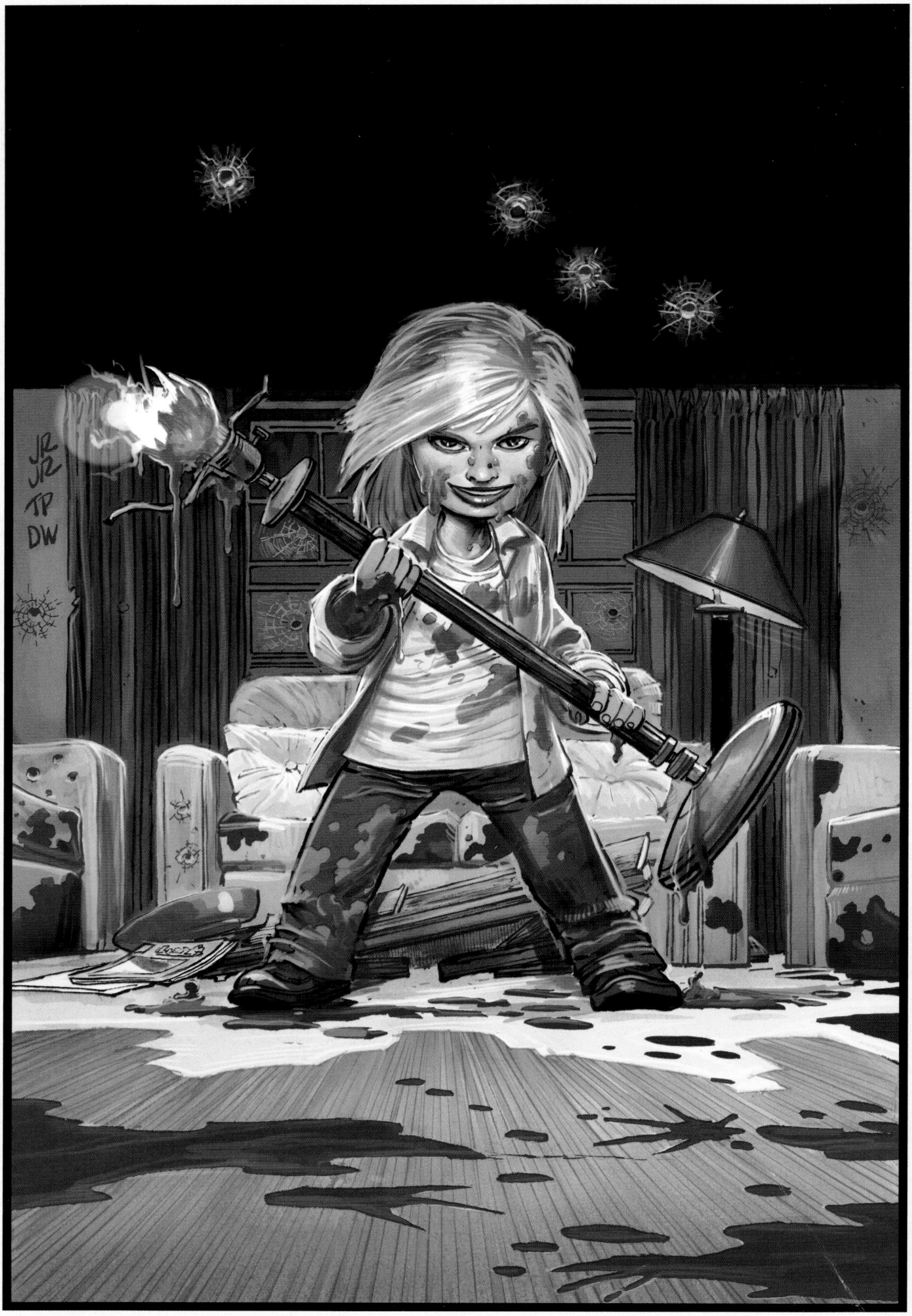
JR JR TP DW

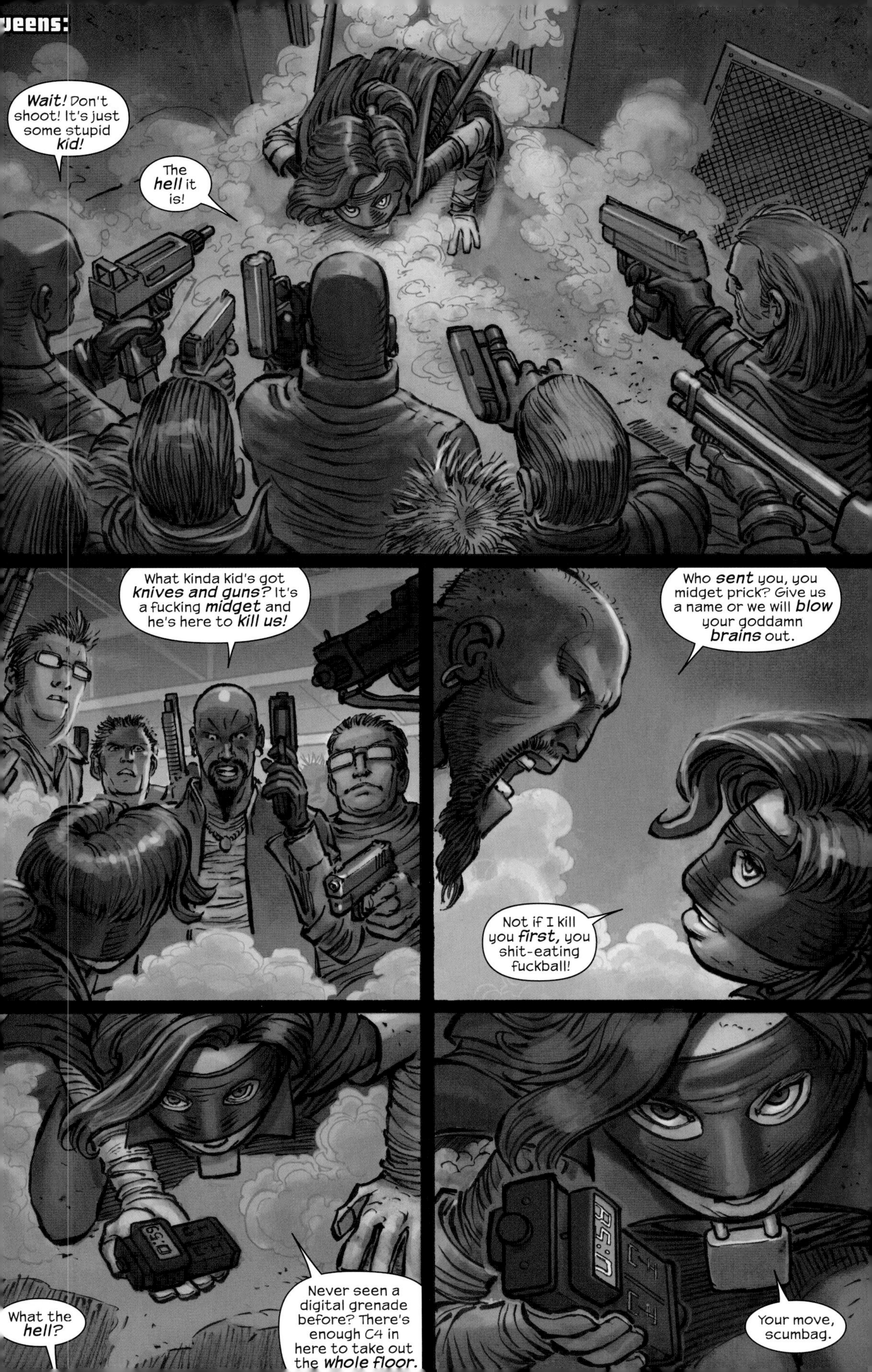

ueens:
Wait! Don't shoot! It's just some stupid kid!
The hell it is!
What kinda kid's got knives and guns? It's a fucking midget and he's here to kill us!
Who sent you, you midget prick? Give us a name or we will blow your goddamn brains out.
Not if I kill you first, you shit-eating fuckball!
What the hell?
Never seen a digital grenade before? There's enough C4 in here to take out the whole floor.
Your move, scumbag.

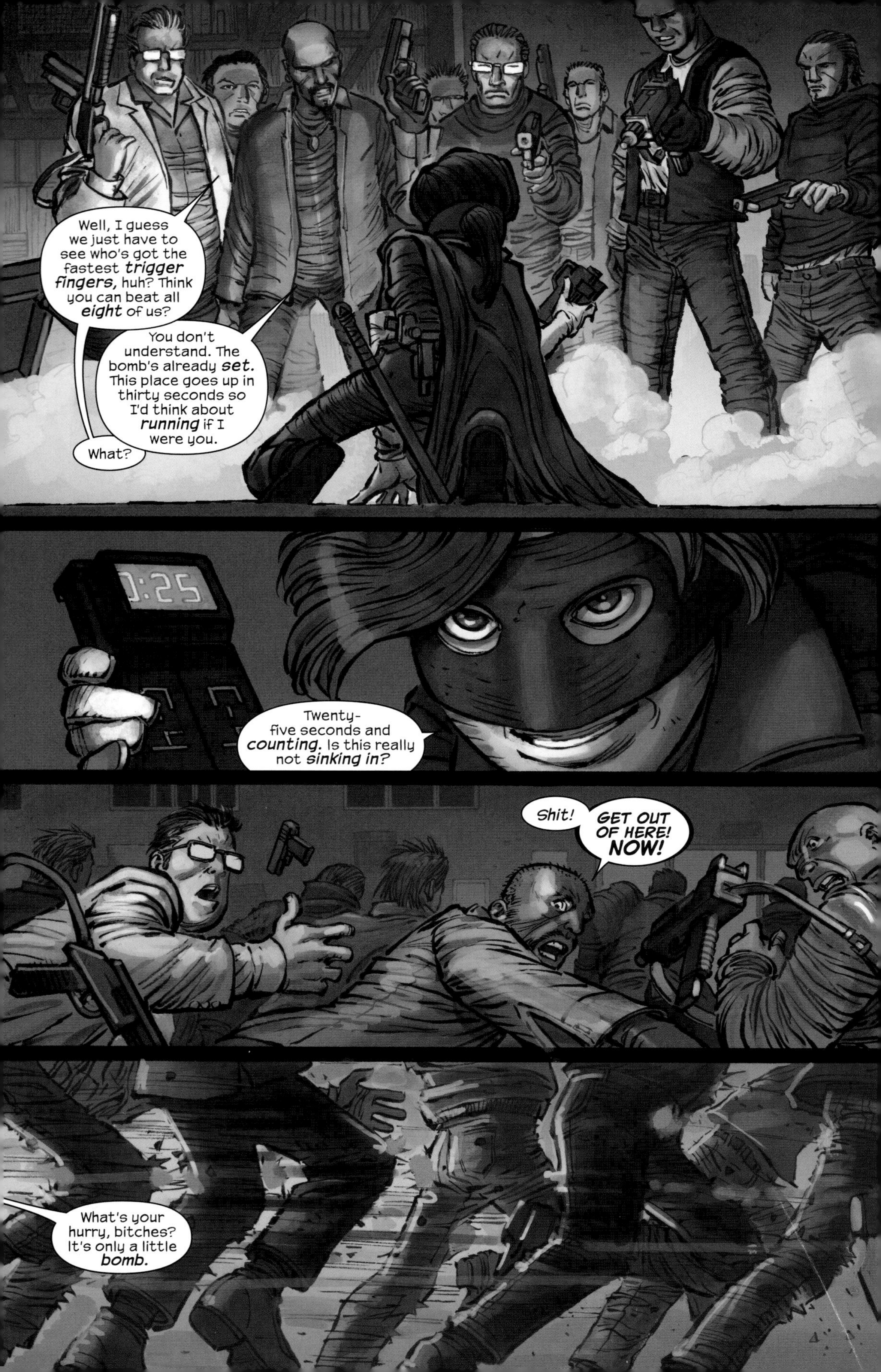
Well, I guess we just have to see who's got the fastest trigger fingers, huh? Think you can beat all eight of us?
You don't understand. The bomb's already set. This place goes up in thirty seconds so I'd think about running if I were you.
What?
0:25
Twenty-five seconds and counting. Is this really not sinking in?
Shit!
GET OUT OF HERE! NOW!
What's your hurry, bitches? It's only a little bomb.

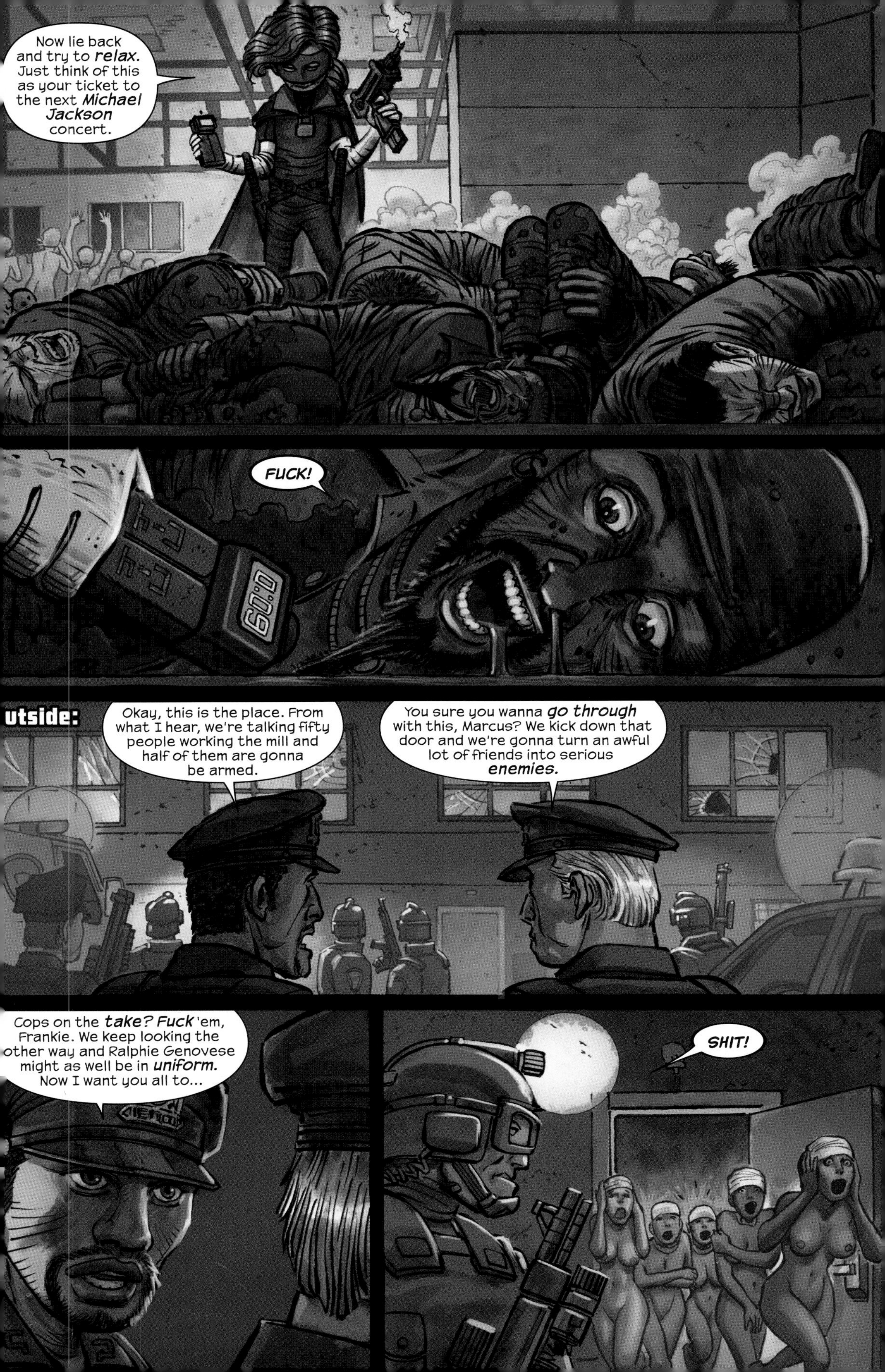
Now lie back and try to *relax.* Just think of this as your ticket to the next *Michael Jackson* concert.
FUCK!
utside:
Okay, this is the place. From what I hear, we're talking fifty people working the mill and half of them are gonna be armed.
You sure you wanna *go through* with this, Marcus? We kick down that door and we're gonna turn an awful lot of friends into serious *enemies.*
Cops on the *take? Fuck* 'em, Frankie. We keep looking the other way and Ralphie Genovese might as well be in *uniform.* Now I want you all to...
SHIT!

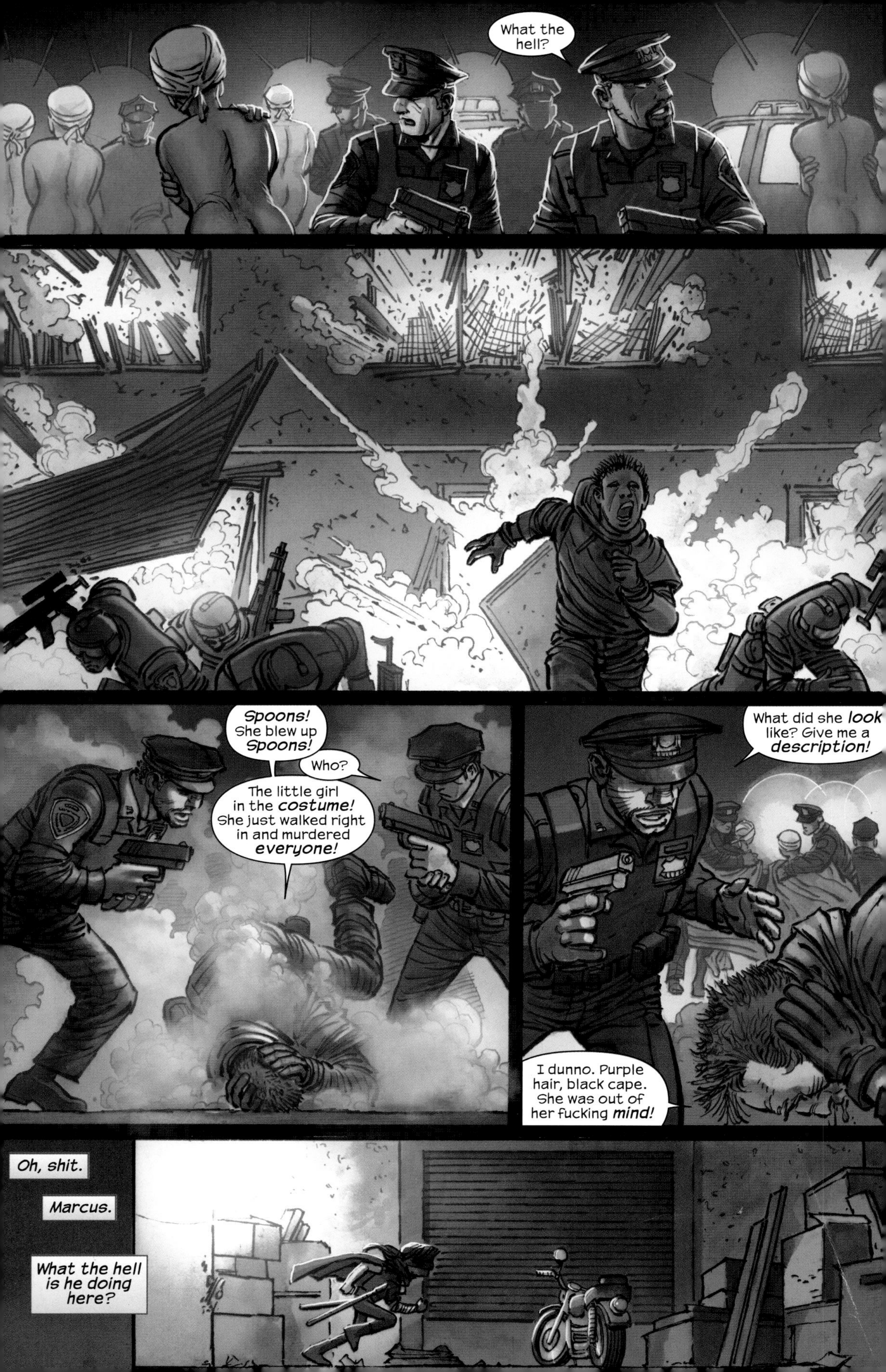

What the hell?
Spoons! She blew up Spoons!
Who?
The little girl in the costume! She just walked right in and murdered everyone!
What did she look like? Give me a description!
I dunno. Purple hair, black cape. She was out of her fucking mind!
Oh, shit.
Marcus.
What the hell is he doing here?

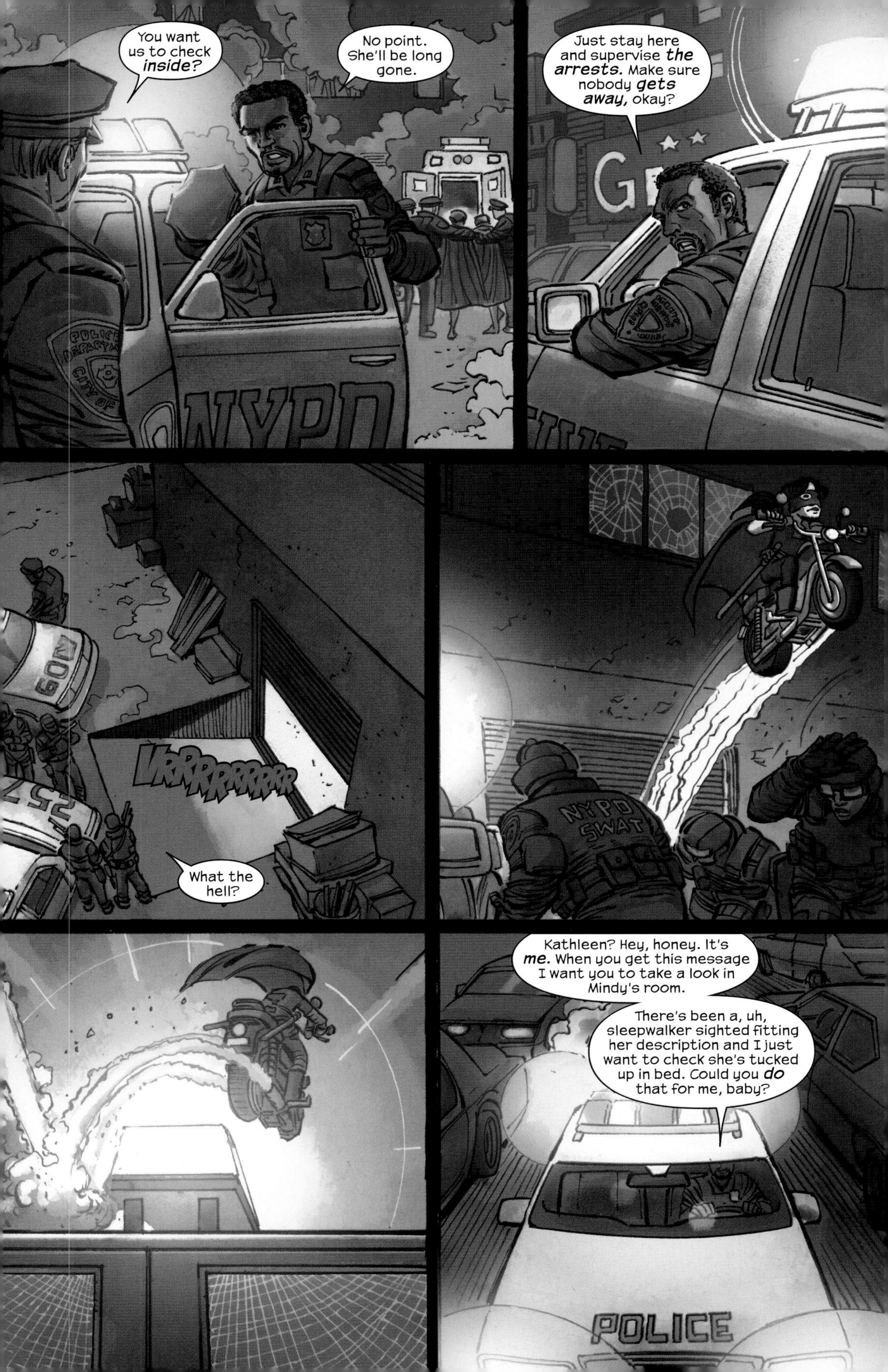
You want us to check inside?
No point. She'll be long gone.
Just stay here and supervise the arrests. Make sure nobody gets away, okay?
NYPD
VRRRRRRRRR
What the hell?
NYPD SWAT
Kathleen? Hey, honey. It's me. When you get this message I want you to take a look in Mindy's room.
There's been a, uh, sleepwalker sighted fitting her description and I just want to check she's tucked up in bed. Could you do that for me, baby?
POLICE

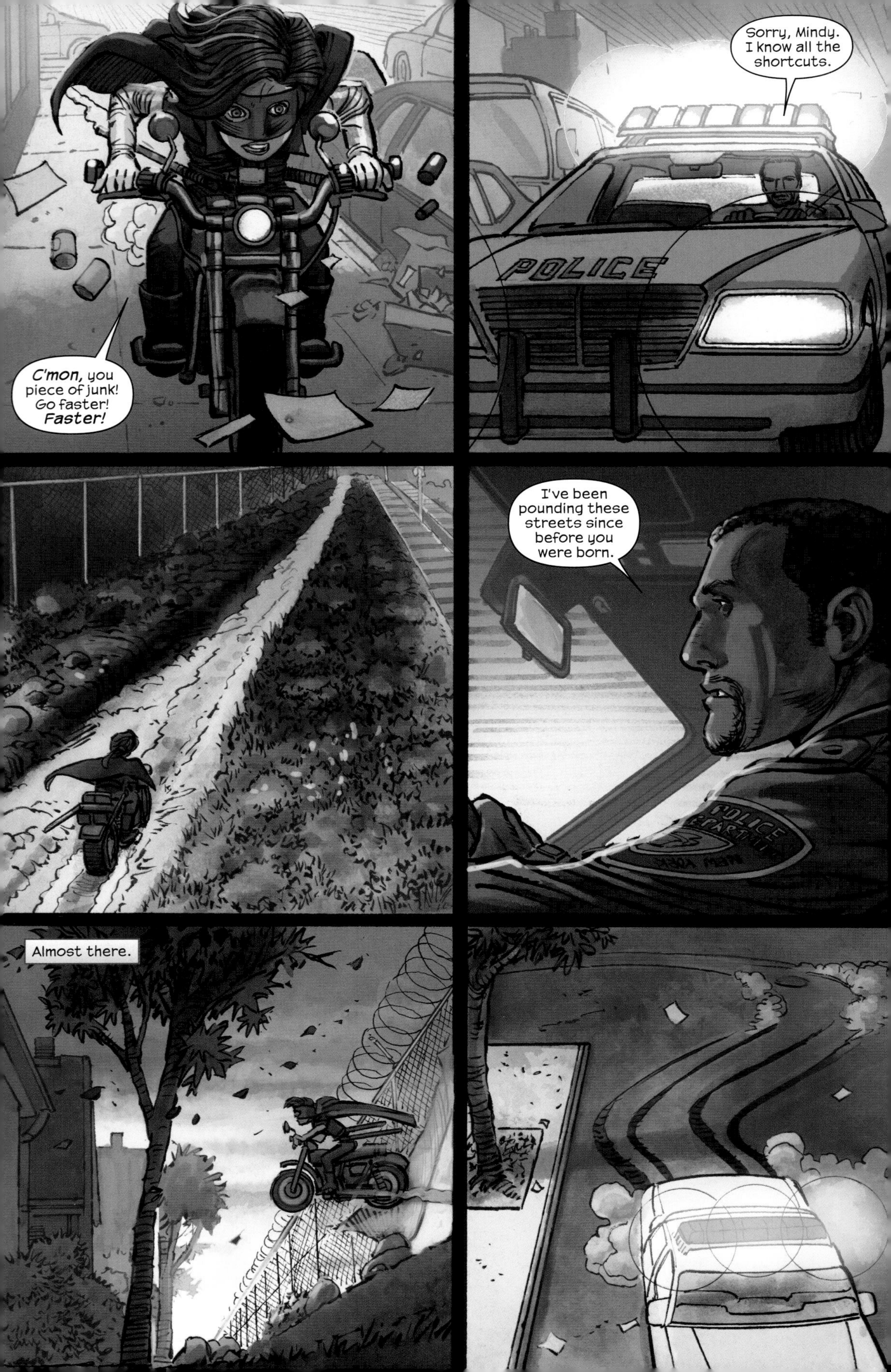
C'mon, you piece of junk! Go faster! ***Faster!***
Sorry, Mindy. I know all the shortcuts.
POLICE
I've been pounding these streets since before you were born.
Almost there.

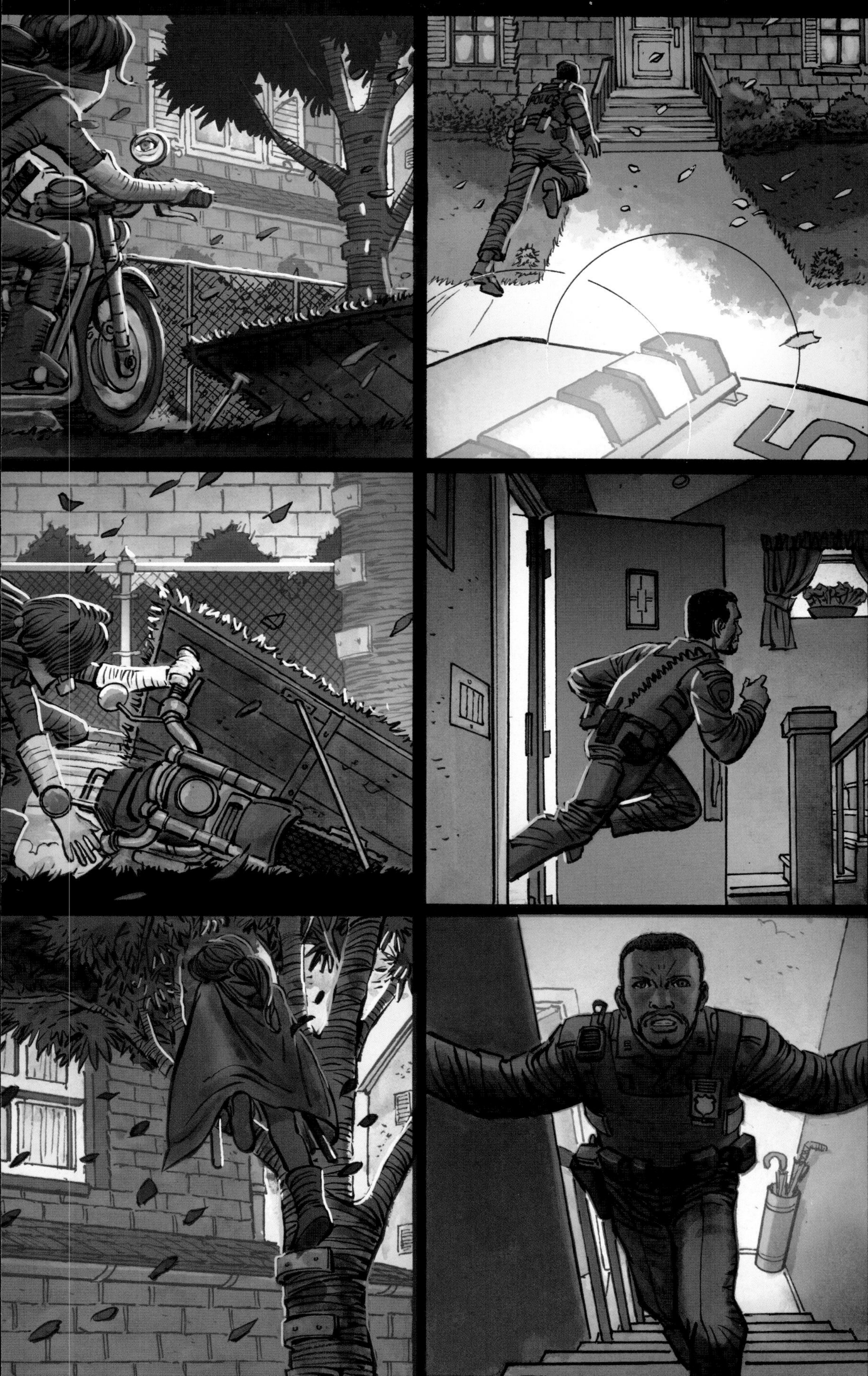
POLICE

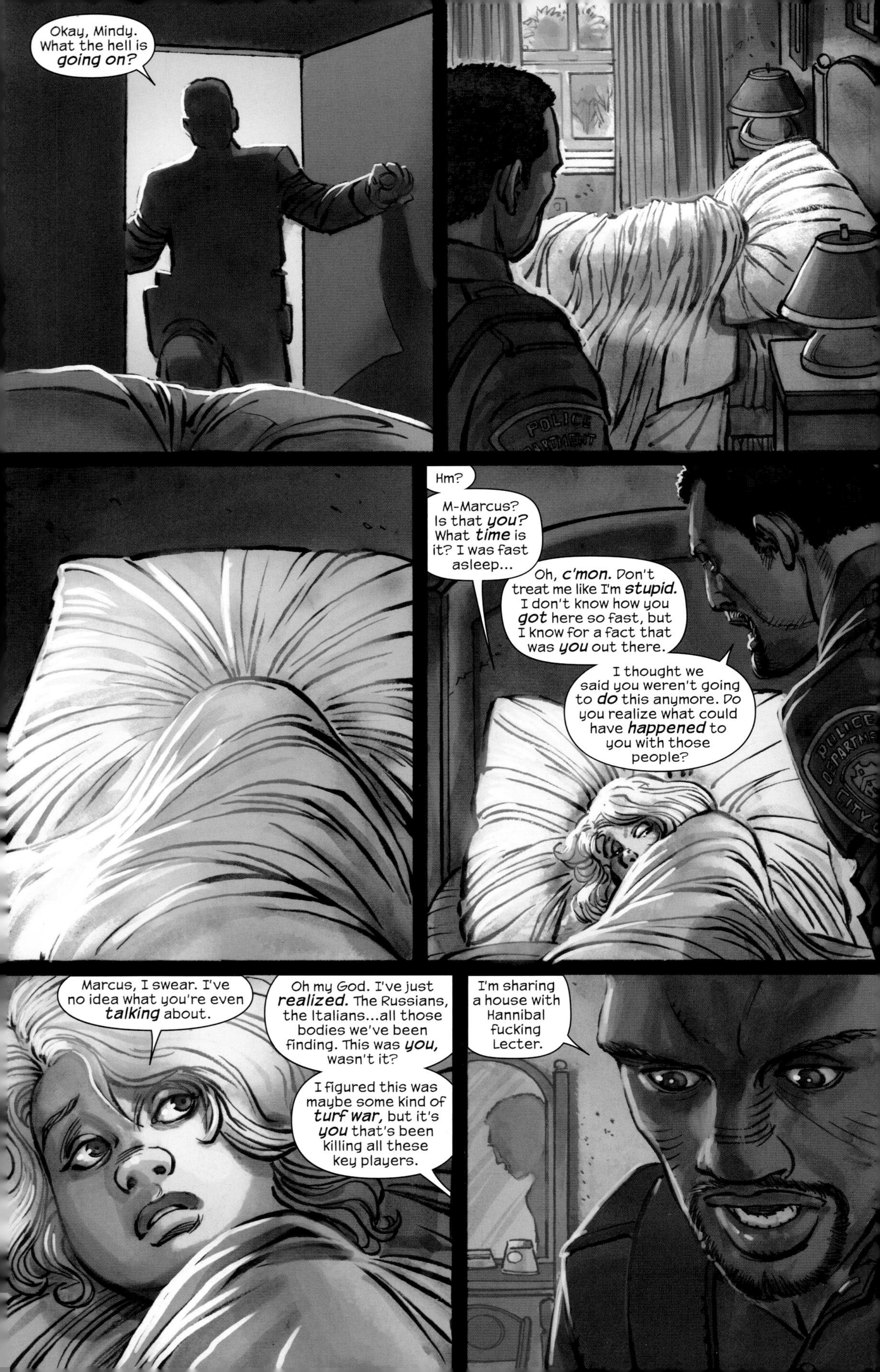

Okay, Mindy. What the hell is going on?
POLICE DEPARTMENT
Hm?
M-Marcus? Is that you? What time is it? I was fast asleep...
Oh, c'mon. Don't treat me like I'm stupid. I don't know how you got here so fast, but I know for a fact that was you out there.
I thought we said you weren't going to do this anymore. Do you realize what could have happened to you with those people?
Marcus, I swear. I've no idea what you're even talking about.
Oh my God. I've just realized. The Russians, the Italians...all those bodies we've been finding. This was you, wasn't it?
I figured this was maybe some kind of turf war, but it's you that's been killing all these key players.
I'm sharing a house with Hannibal fucking Lecter.

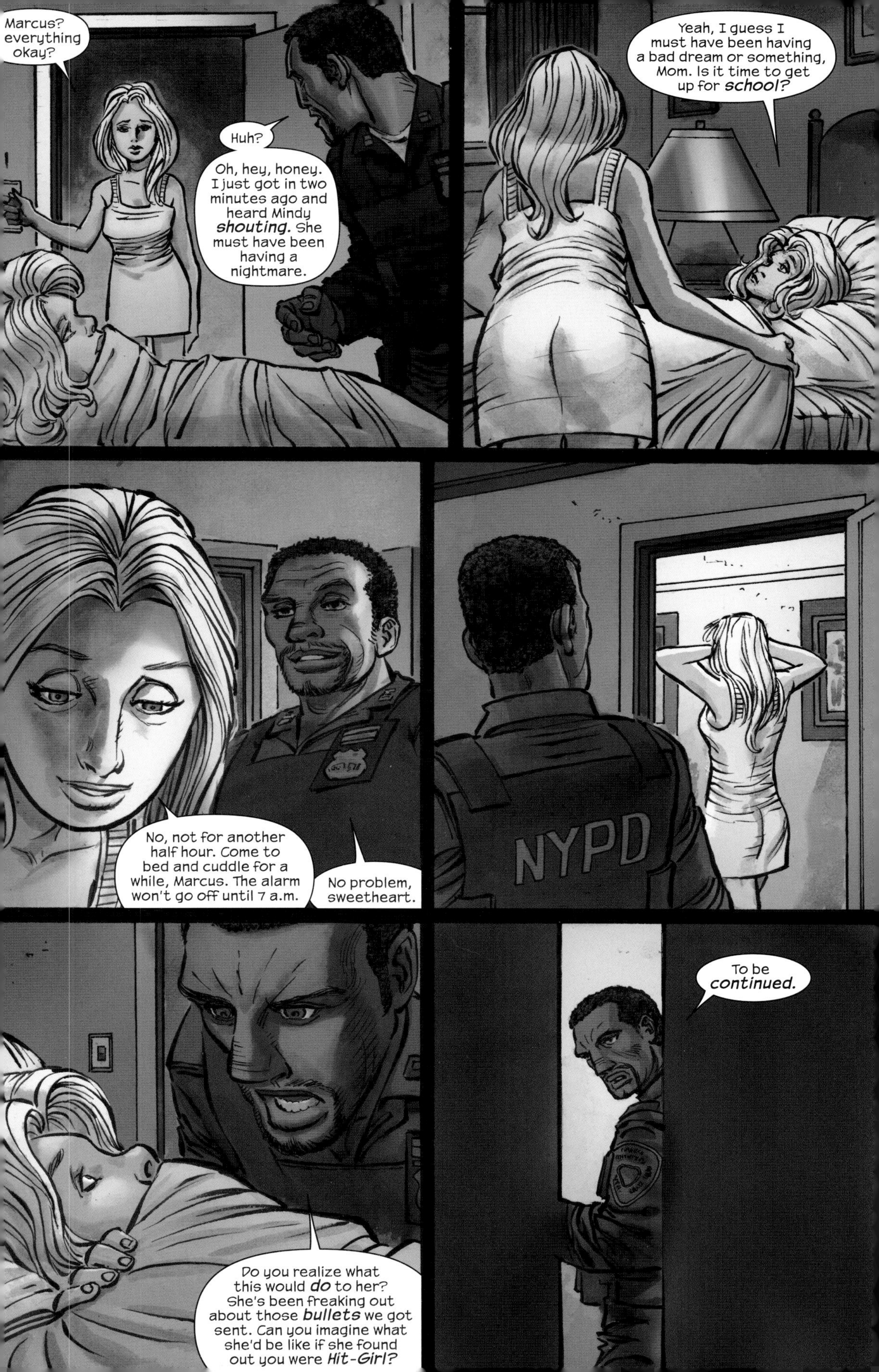
Marcus? everything okay?
Huh?
Oh, hey, honey. I just got in two minutes ago and heard Mindy shouting. She must have been having a nightmare.
Yeah, I guess I must have been having a bad dream or something, Mom. Is it time to get up for school?
No, not for another half hour. Come to bed and cuddle for a while, Marcus. The alarm won't go off until 7 a.m.
No problem, sweetheart.
NYPD
Do you realize what this would do to her? She's been freaking out about those bullets we got sent. Can you imagine what she'd be like if she found out you were Hit-Girl?
To be continued.

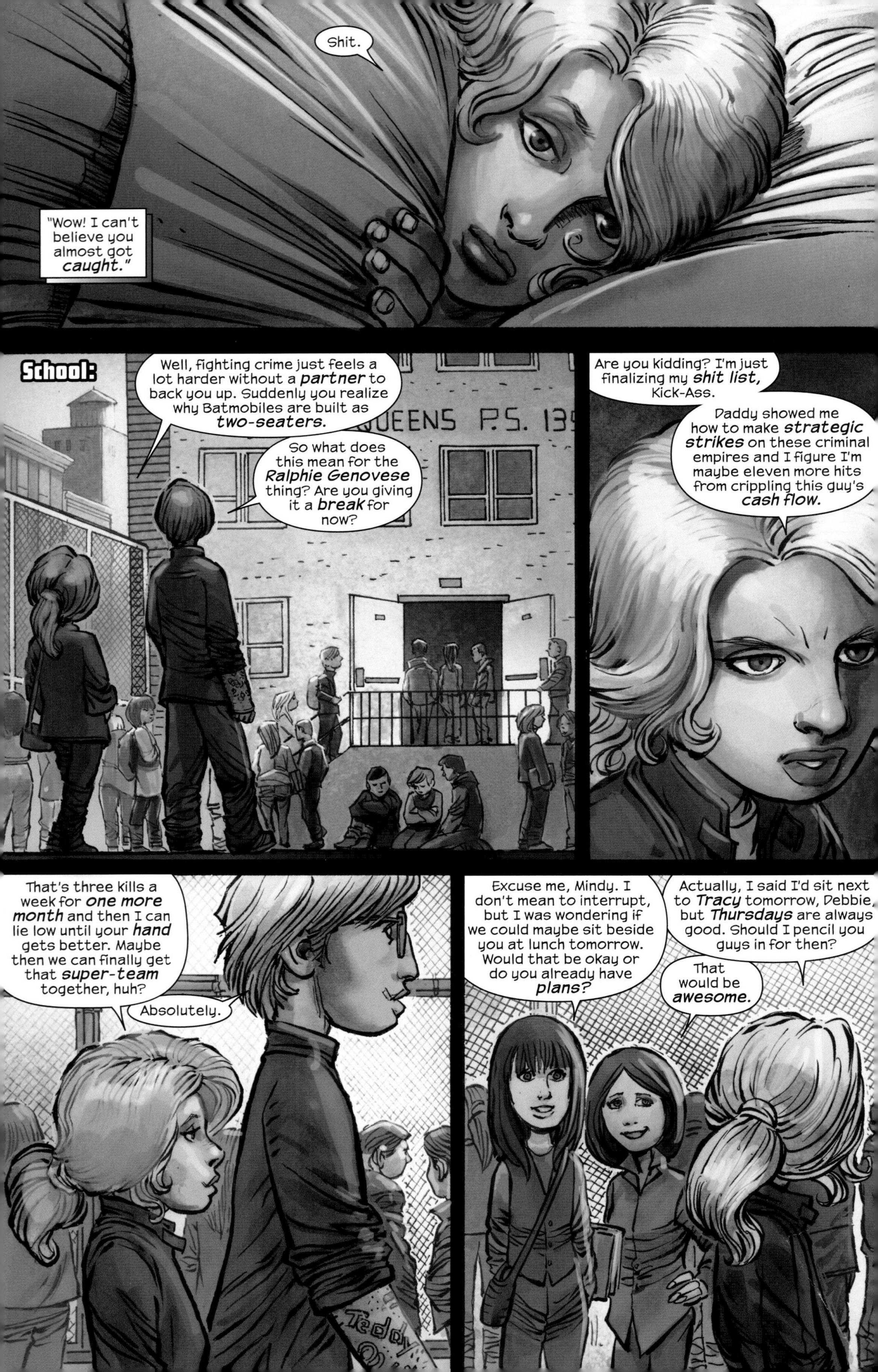

Shit.
"Wow! I can't believe you almost got caught."
School:
Well, fighting crime just feels a lot harder without a partner to back you up. Suddenly you realize why Batmobiles are built as two-seaters.
QUEENS P.S. 13
So what does this mean for the Ralphie Genovese thing? Are you giving it a break for now?
Are you kidding? I'm just finalizing my shit list, Kick-Ass.
Daddy showed me how to make strategic strikes on these criminal empires and I figure I'm maybe eleven more hits from crippling this guy's cash flow.
That's three kills a week for one more month and then I can lie low until your hand gets better. Maybe then we can finally get that super-team together, huh?
Absolutely.
Teddy
Excuse me, Mindy. I don't mean to interrupt, but I was wondering if we could maybe sit beside you at lunch tomorrow. Would that be okay or do you already have plans?
Actually, I said I'd sit next to Tracy tomorrow, Debbie, but Thursdays are always good. Should I pencil you guys in for then?
That would be awesome.

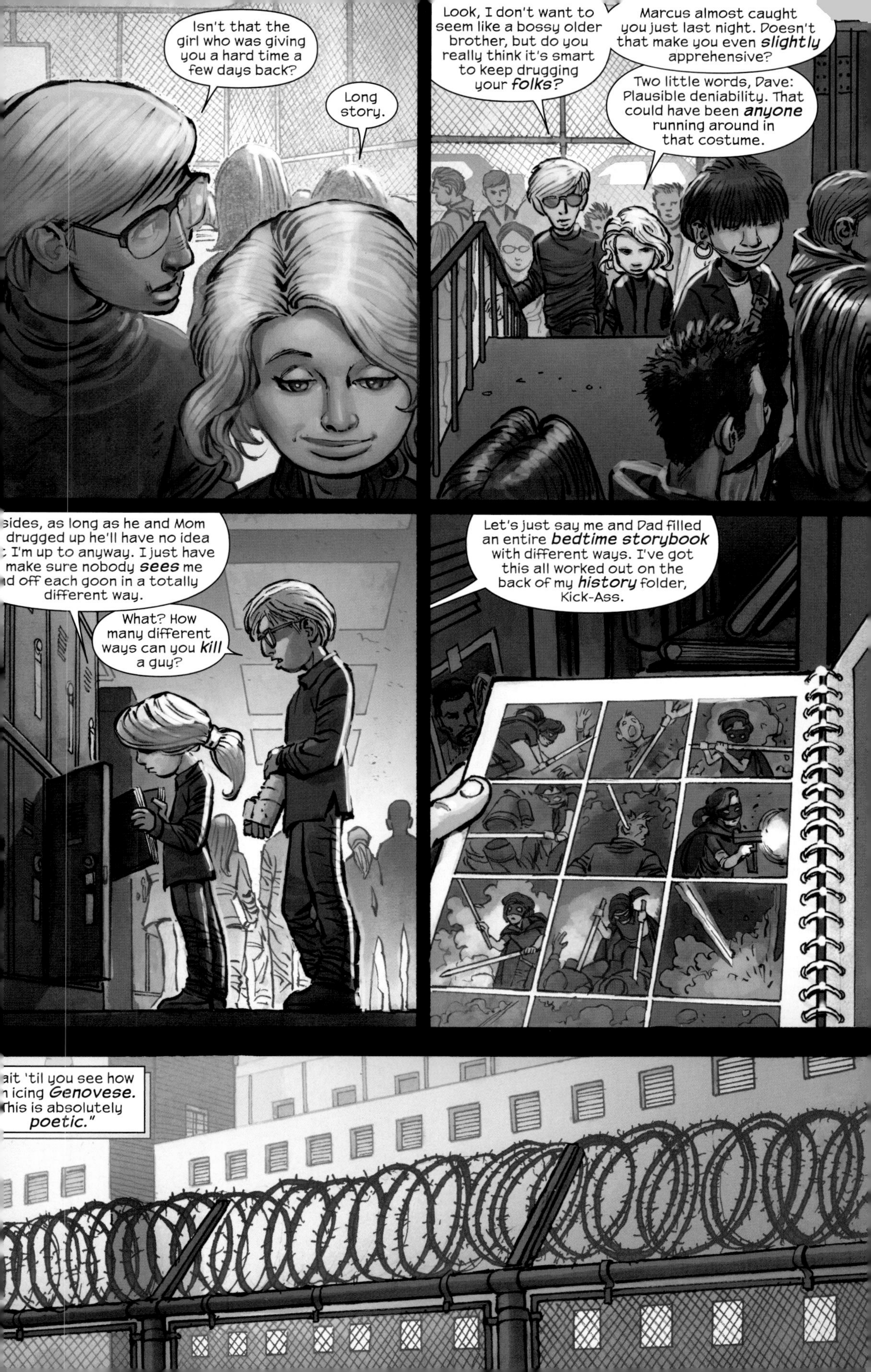

Isn't that the girl who was giving you a hard time a few days back?
Long story.
Look, I don't want to seem like a bossy older brother, but do you really think it's smart to keep drugging your *folks?*
Marcus almost caught you just last night. Doesn't that make you even *slightly* apprehensive?
Two little words, Dave: Plausible deniability. That could have been *anyone* running around in that costume.
sides, as long as he and Mom drugged up he'll have no idea I'm up to anyway. I just have make sure nobody *sees* me d off each goon in a totally different way.
What? How many different ways can you *kill* a guy?
Let's just say me and Dad filled an entire *bedtime storybook* with different ways. I've got this all worked out on the back of my *history* folder, Kick-Ass.
ait 'til you see how n icing *Genovese.* This is absolutely *poetic."*

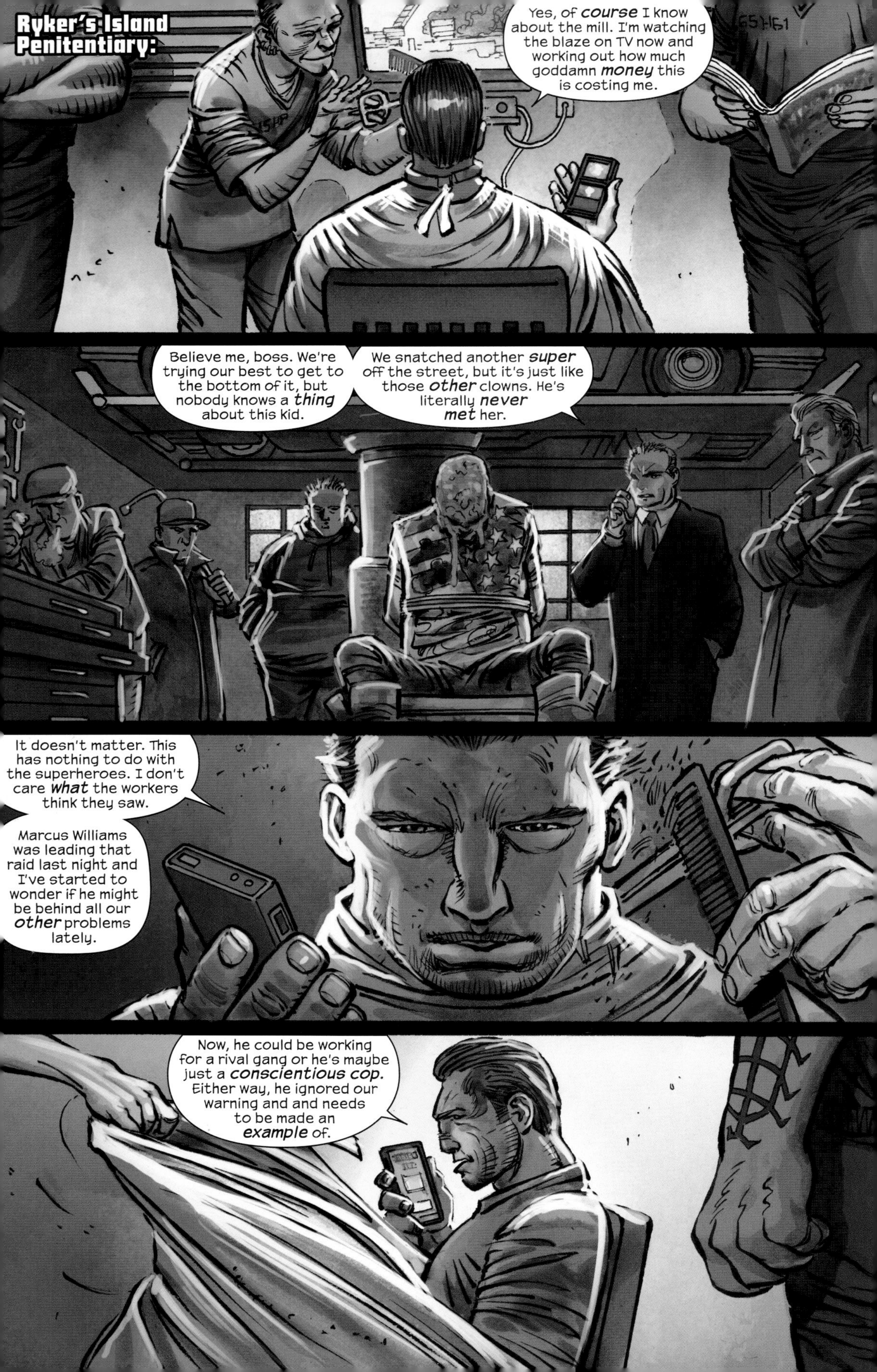
Ryker's Island Penitentiary:
Yes, of course I know about the mill. I'm watching the blaze on TV now and working out how much goddamn money this is costing me.
Believe me, boss. We're trying our best to get to the bottom of it, but nobody knows a thing about this kid.
We snatched another super off the street, but it's just like those other clowns. He's literally never met her.
It doesn't matter. This has nothing to do with the superheroes. I don't care what the workers think they saw.
Marcus Williams was leading that raid last night and I've started to wonder if he might be behind all our other problems lately.
Now, he could be working for a rival gang or he's maybe just a conscientious cop. Either way, he ignored our warning and and needs to be made an example of.

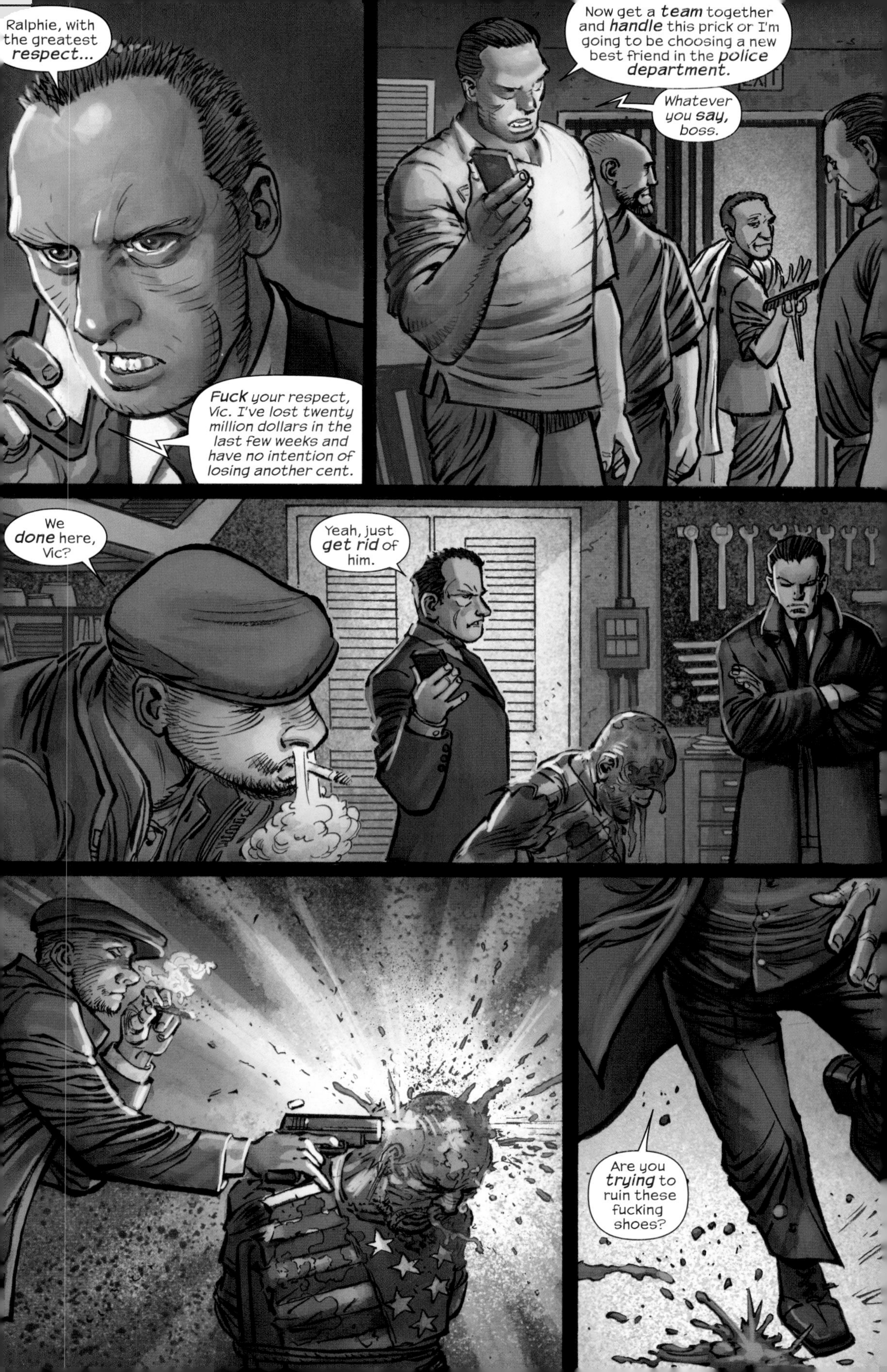
Ralphie, with the greatest respect...
Fuck your respect, Vic. I've lost twenty million dollars in the last few weeks and have no intention of losing another cent.
Now get a team together and handle this prick or I'm going to be choosing a new best friend in the police department.
Whatever you say, boss.
We done here, Vic?
Yeah, just get rid of him.
Are you trying to ruin these fucking shoes?

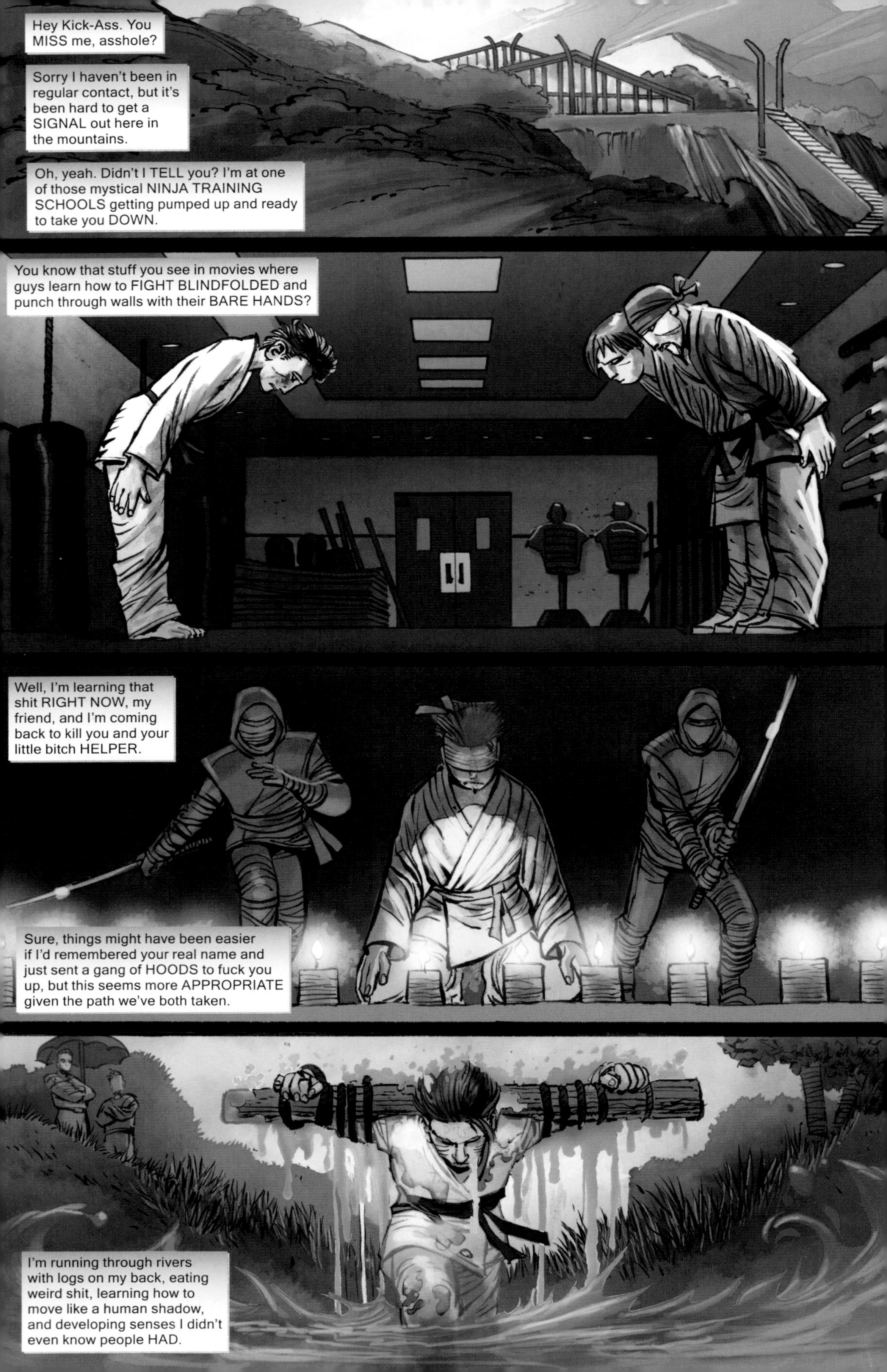
Hey Kick-Ass. You MISS me, asshole?
Sorry I haven't been in regular contact, but it's been hard to get a SIGNAL out here in the mountains.
Oh, yeah. Didn't I TELL you? I'm at one of those mystical NINJA TRAINING SCHOOLS getting pumped up and ready to take you DOWN.
You know that stuff you see in movies where guys learn how to FIGHT BLINDFOLDED and punch through walls with their BARE HANDS?
Well, I'm learning that shit RIGHT NOW, my friend, and I'm coming back to kill you and your little bitch HELPER.
Sure, things might have been easier if I'd remembered your real name and just sent a gang of HOODS to fuck you up, but this seems more APPROPRIATE given the path we've both taken.
I'm running through rivers with logs on my back, eating weird shit, learning how to move like a human shadow, and developing senses I didn't even know people HAD.

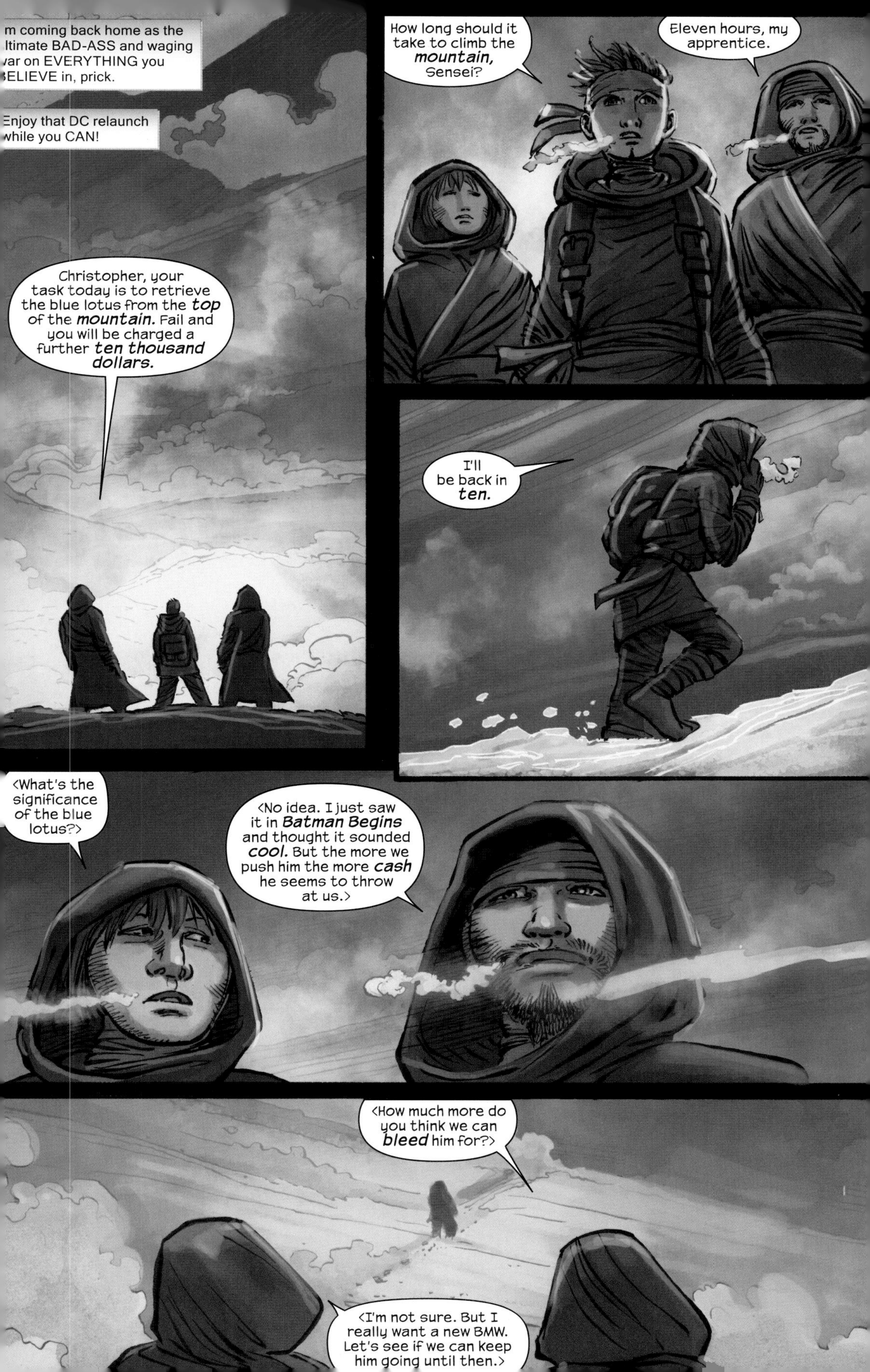
m coming back home as the ltimate BAD-ASS and waging var on EVERYTHING you 3ELIEVE in, prick.
Enjoy that DC relaunch while you CAN!
Christopher, your task today is to retrieve the blue lotus from the *top* of the *mountain.* Fail and you will be charged a further *ten thousand dollars.*
How long should it take to climb the *mountain,* Sensei?
Eleven hours, my apprentice.
I'll be back in *ten.*
<What's the significance of the blue lotus?>
<No idea. I just saw it in *Batman Begins* and thought it sounded *cool.* But the more we push him the more *cash* he seems to throw at us.>
<How much more do you think we can *bleed* him for?>
<I'm not sure. But I really want a new BMW. Let's see if we can keep him going until then.>

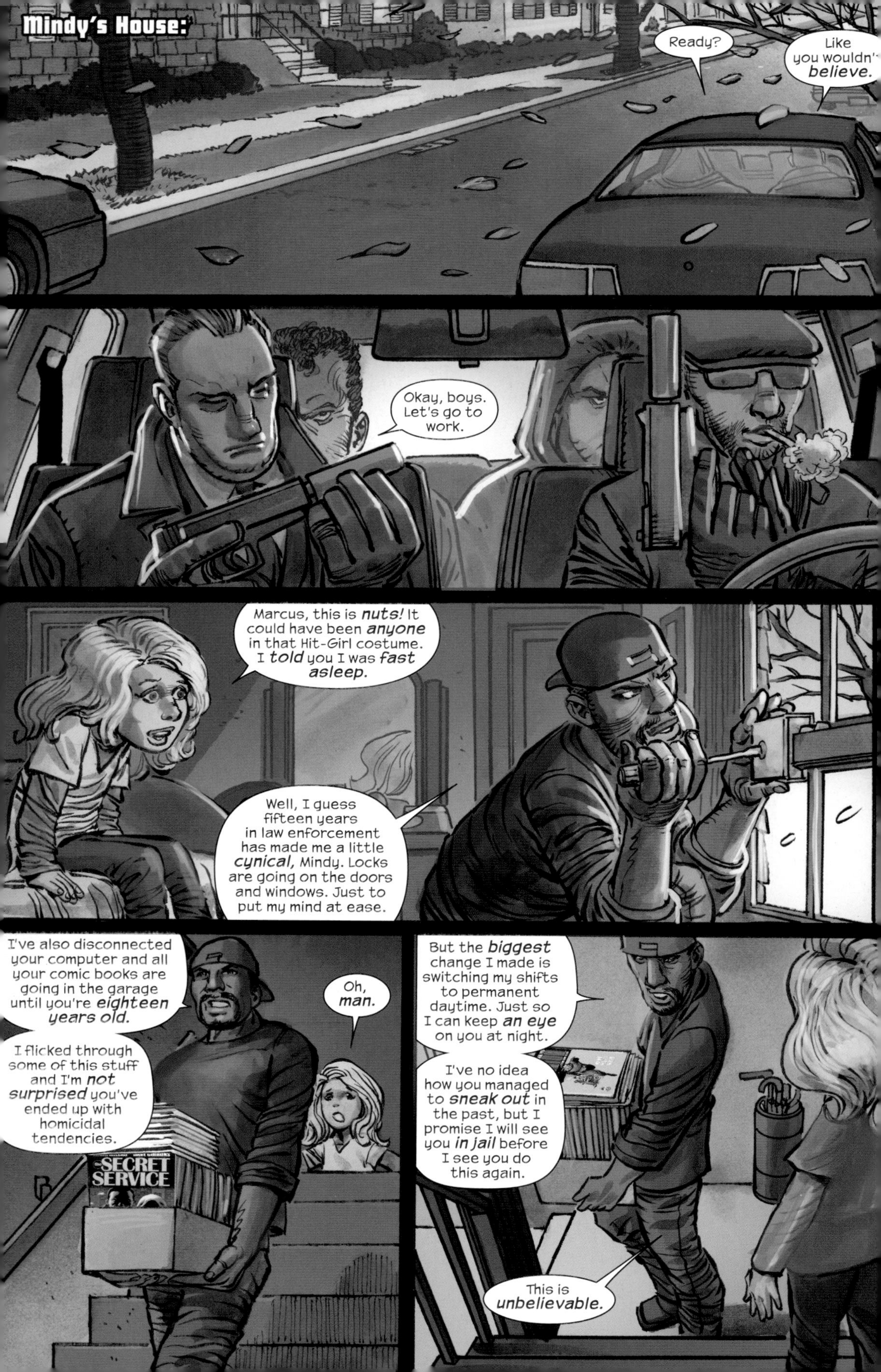
Mindy's House:
Ready?
Like you wouldn't believe.
Okay, boys. Let's go to work.
Marcus, this is nuts! It could have been anyone in that Hit-Girl costume. I told you I was fast asleep.
Well, I guess fifteen years in law enforcement has made me a little cynical, Mindy. Locks are going on the doors and windows. Just to put my mind at ease.
I've also disconnected your computer and all your comic books are going in the garage until you're eighteen years old.
I flicked through some of this stuff and I'm not surprised you've ended up with homicidal tendencies.
Oh, man.
SECRET SERVICE
But the biggest change I made is switching my shifts to permanent daytime. Just so I can keep an eye on you at night.
I've no idea how you managed to sneak out in the past, but I promise I will see you in jail before I see you do this again.
This is unbelievable.

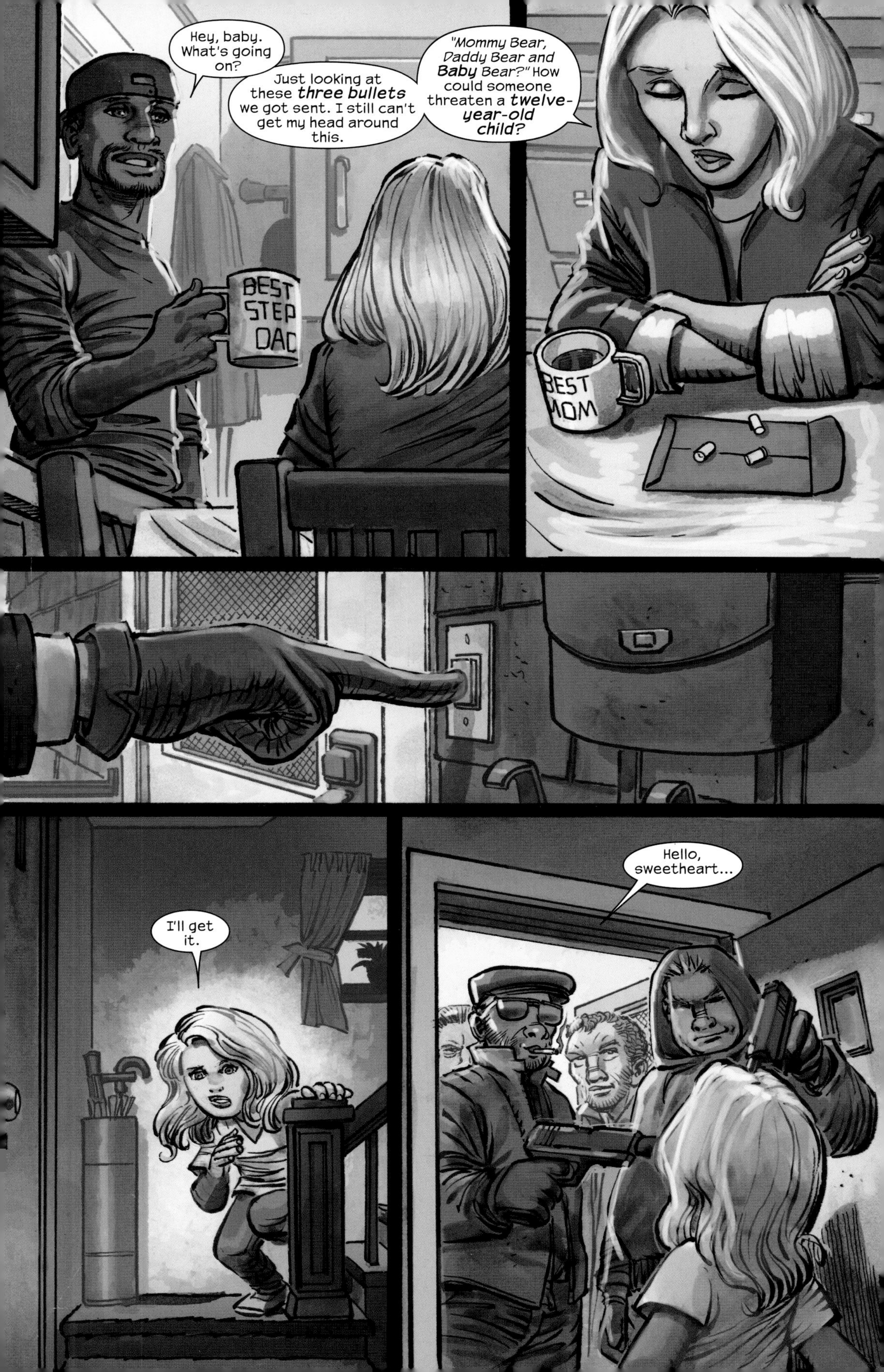

Hey, baby. What's going on?
Just looking at these *three bullets* we got sent. I still can't get my head around this.
"Mommy Bear, Daddy Bear and Baby Bear?" How could someone threaten a *twelve-year-old child?*
BEST STEP DAD
BEST MOM
I'll get it.
Hello, sweetheart...

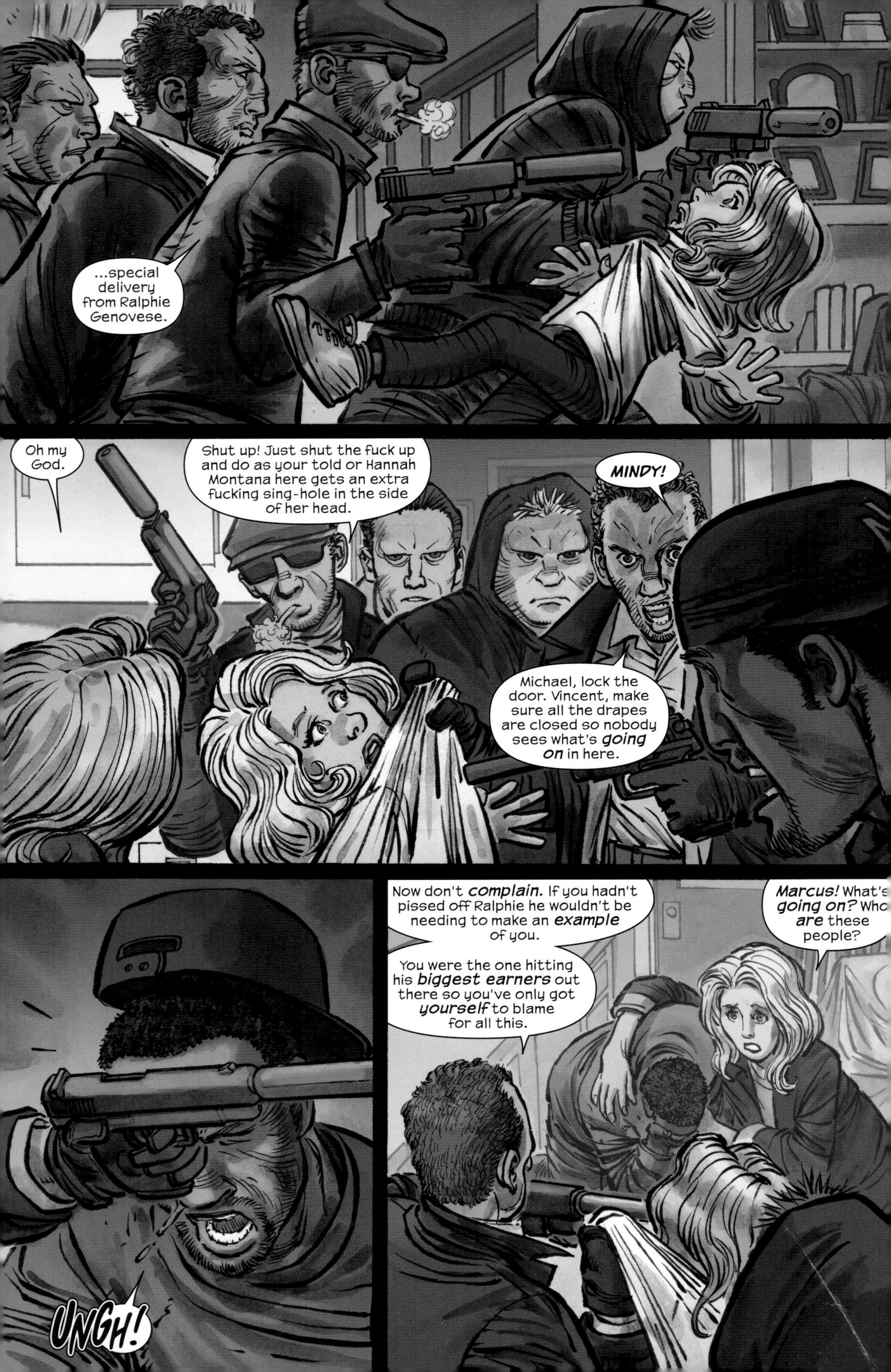
...special delivery from Ralphie Genovese.
Oh my God.
Shut up! Just shut the fuck up and do as your told or Hannah Montana here gets an extra fucking sing-hole in the side of her head.
MINDY!
Michael, lock the door. Vincent, make sure all the drapes are closed so nobody sees what's going on in here.
UNGH!
Now don't complain. If you hadn't pissed off Ralphie he wouldn't be needing to make an example of you.
You were the one hitting his biggest earners out there so you've only got yourself to blame for all this.
Marcus! What's going on? Who are these people?

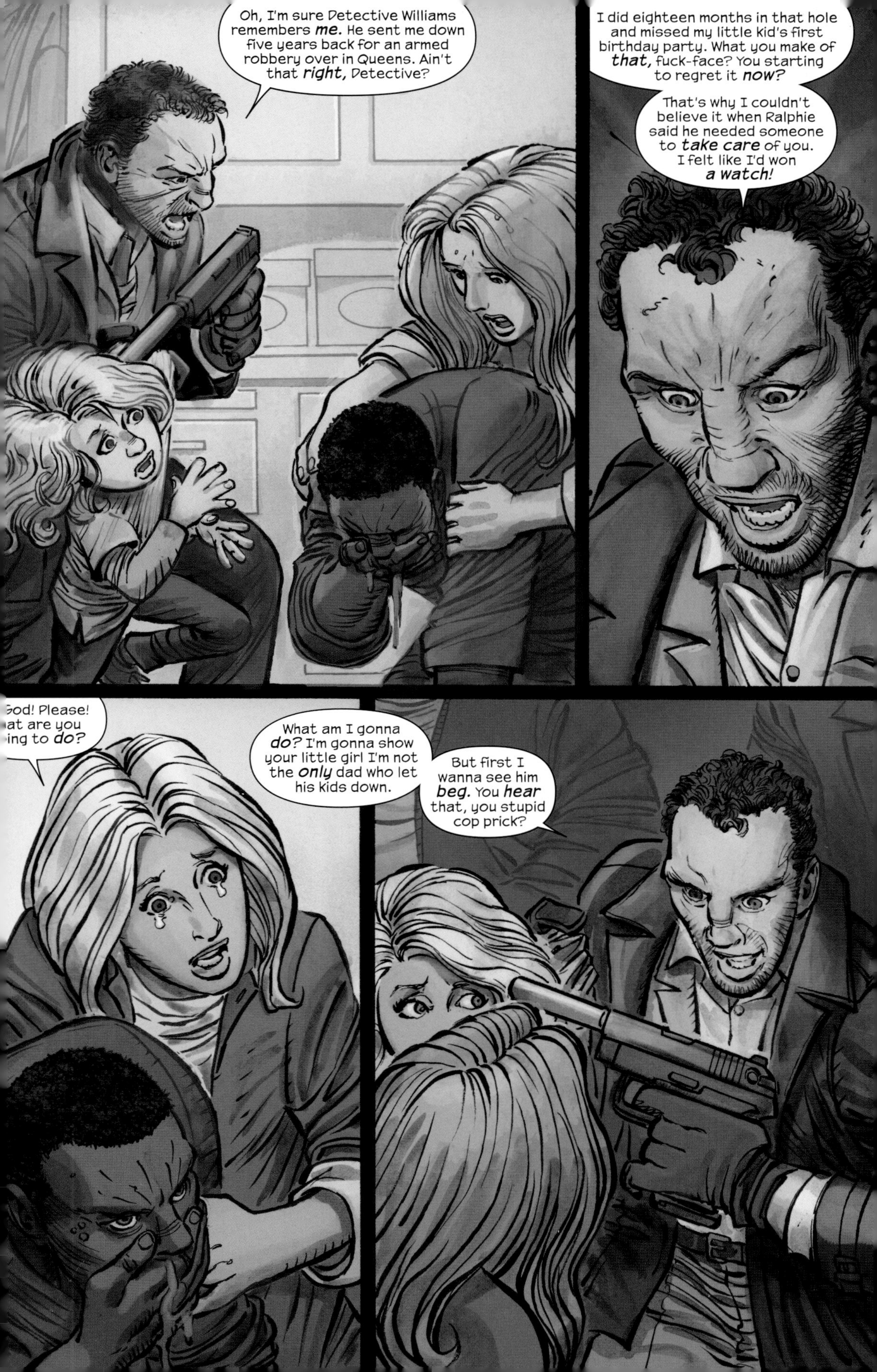

Oh, I'm sure Detective Williams remembers *me.* He sent me down five years back for an armed robbery over in Queens. Ain't that *right,* Detective?
I did eighteen months in that hole and missed my little kid's first birthday party. What you make of *that,* fuck-face? You starting to regret it *now?*
That's why I couldn't believe it when Ralphie said he needed someone to *take care* of you. I felt like I'd won *a watch!*
God! Please! ...at are you ...ing to *do?*
What am I gonna *do?* I'm gonna show your little girl I'm not the *only* dad who let his kids down.
But first I wanna see him *beg.* You *hear* that, you stupid cop prick?

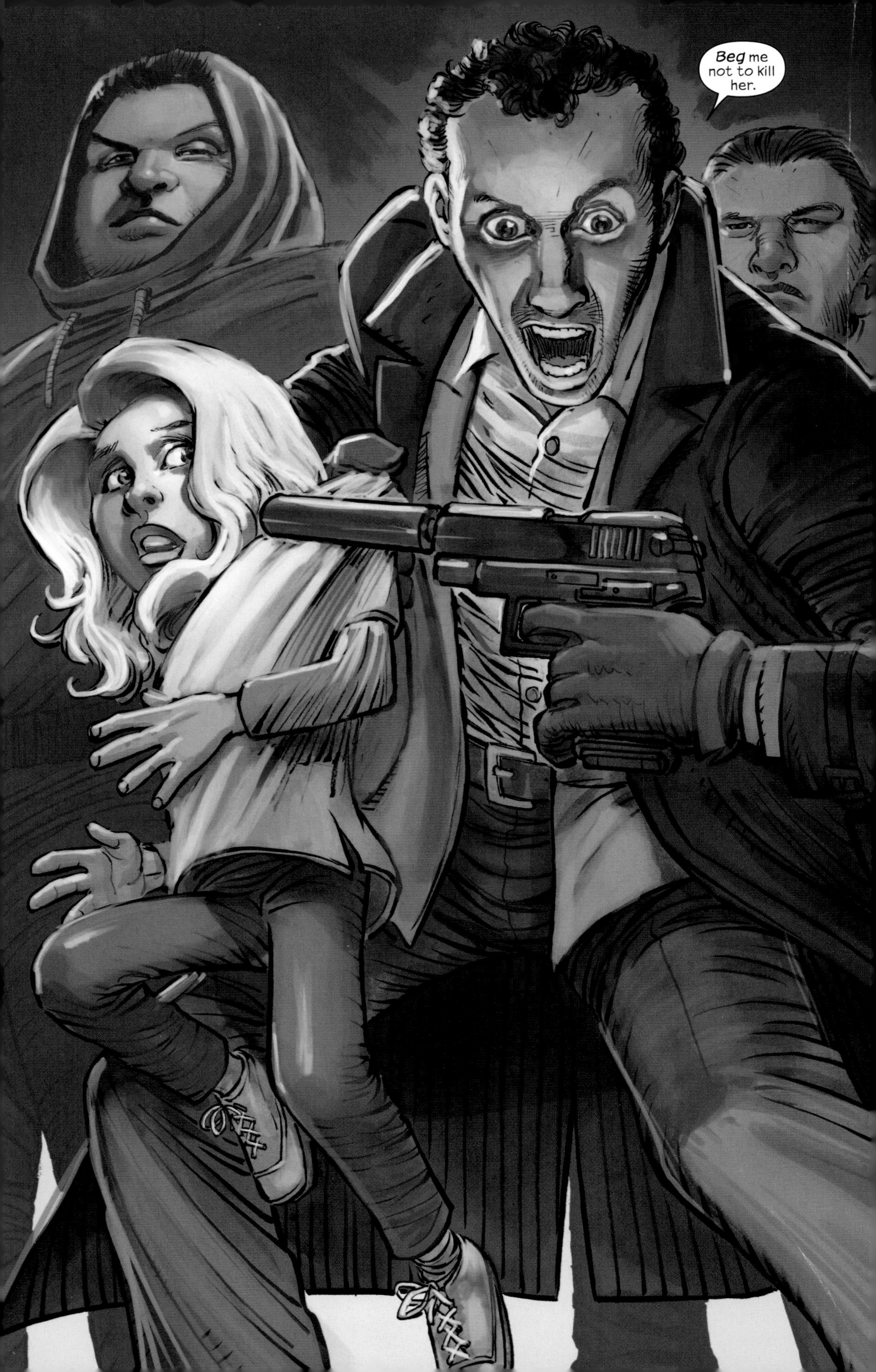
Beg me not to kill her.

FIVE

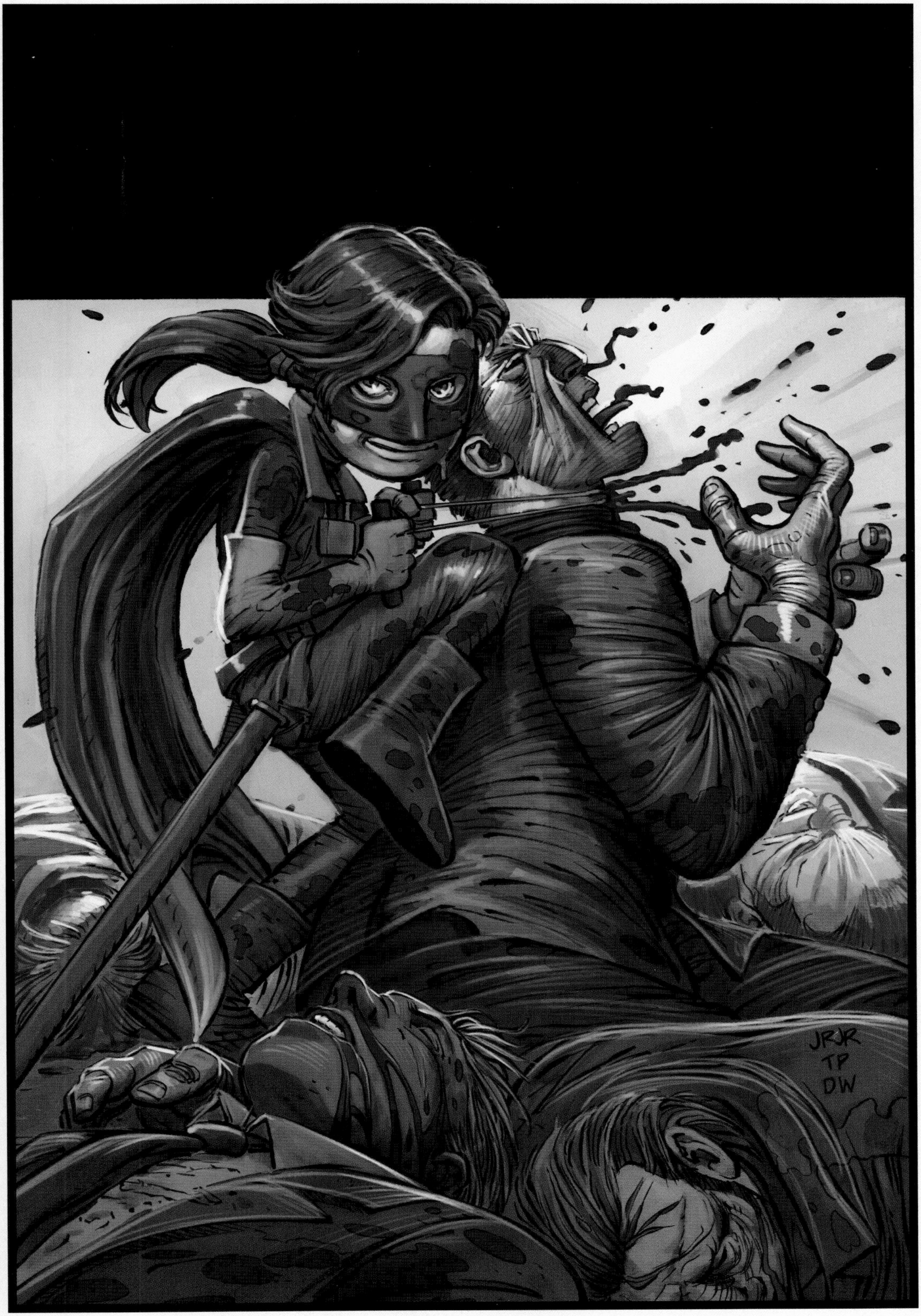
JRJR
TP
DW

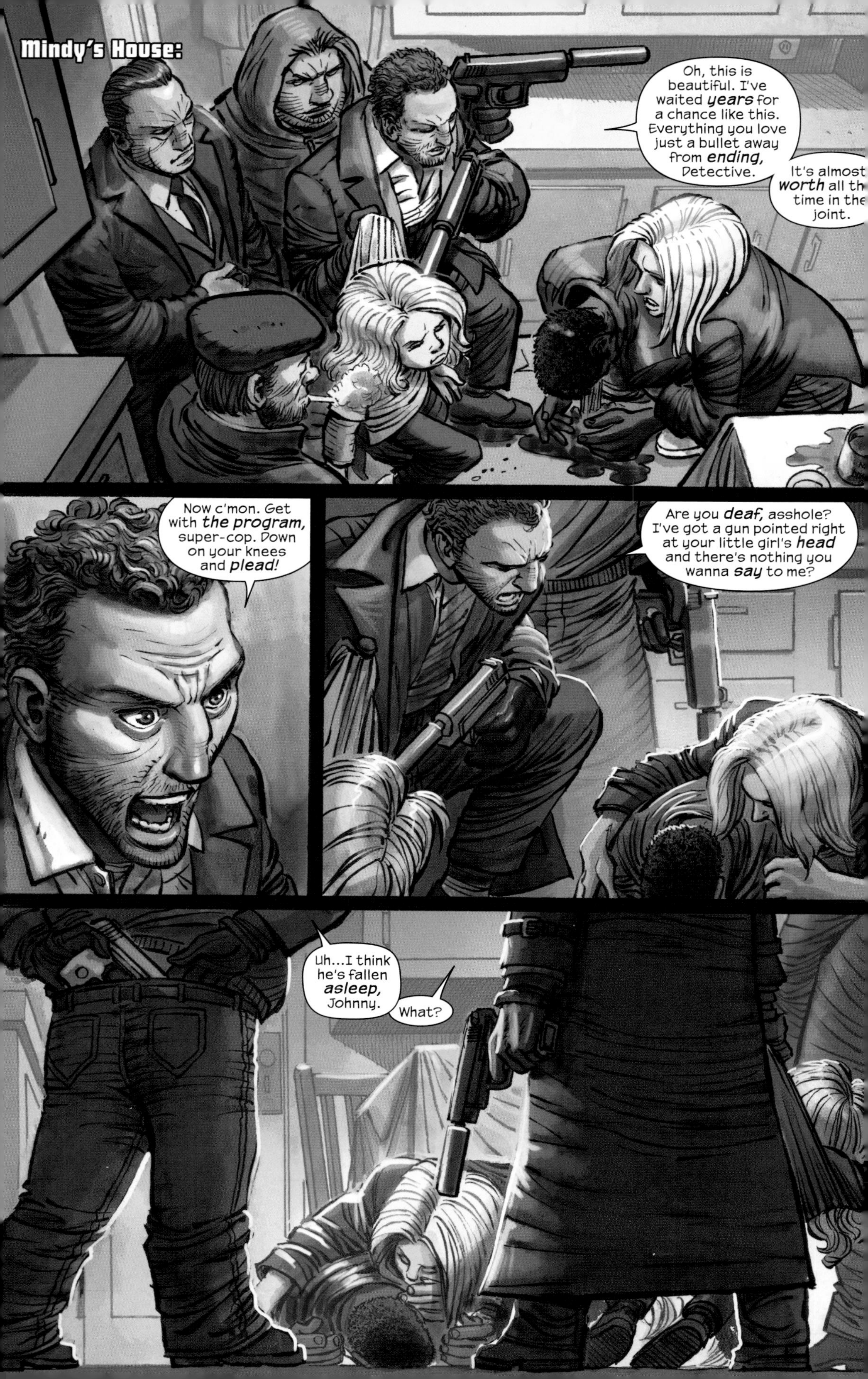
Mindy's House:
Oh, this is beautiful. I've waited *years* for a chance like this. Everything you love just a bullet away from *ending,* Detective.
It's almost *worth* all th time in the joint.
Now c'mon. Get with *the program,* super-cop. Down on your knees and *plead!*
Are you *deaf,* asshole? I've got a gun pointed right at your little girl's *head* and there's nothing you wanna *say* to me?
Uh...I think he's fallen *asleep,* Johnny.
What?

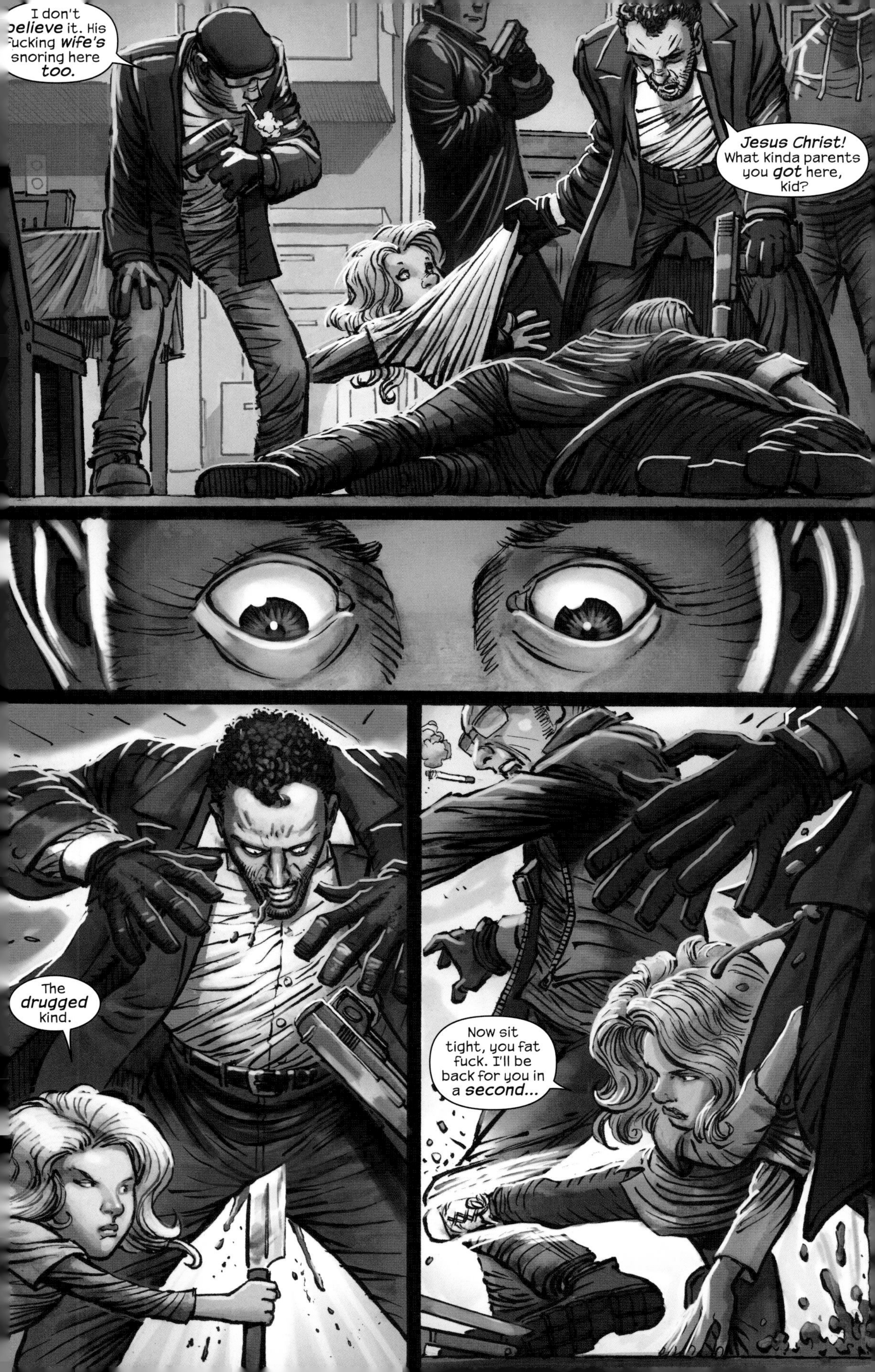
I don't believe it. His fucking wife's snoring here too.
Jesus Christ! What kinda parents you got here, kid?
The drugged kind.
Now sit tight, you fat fuck. I'll be back for you in a second...

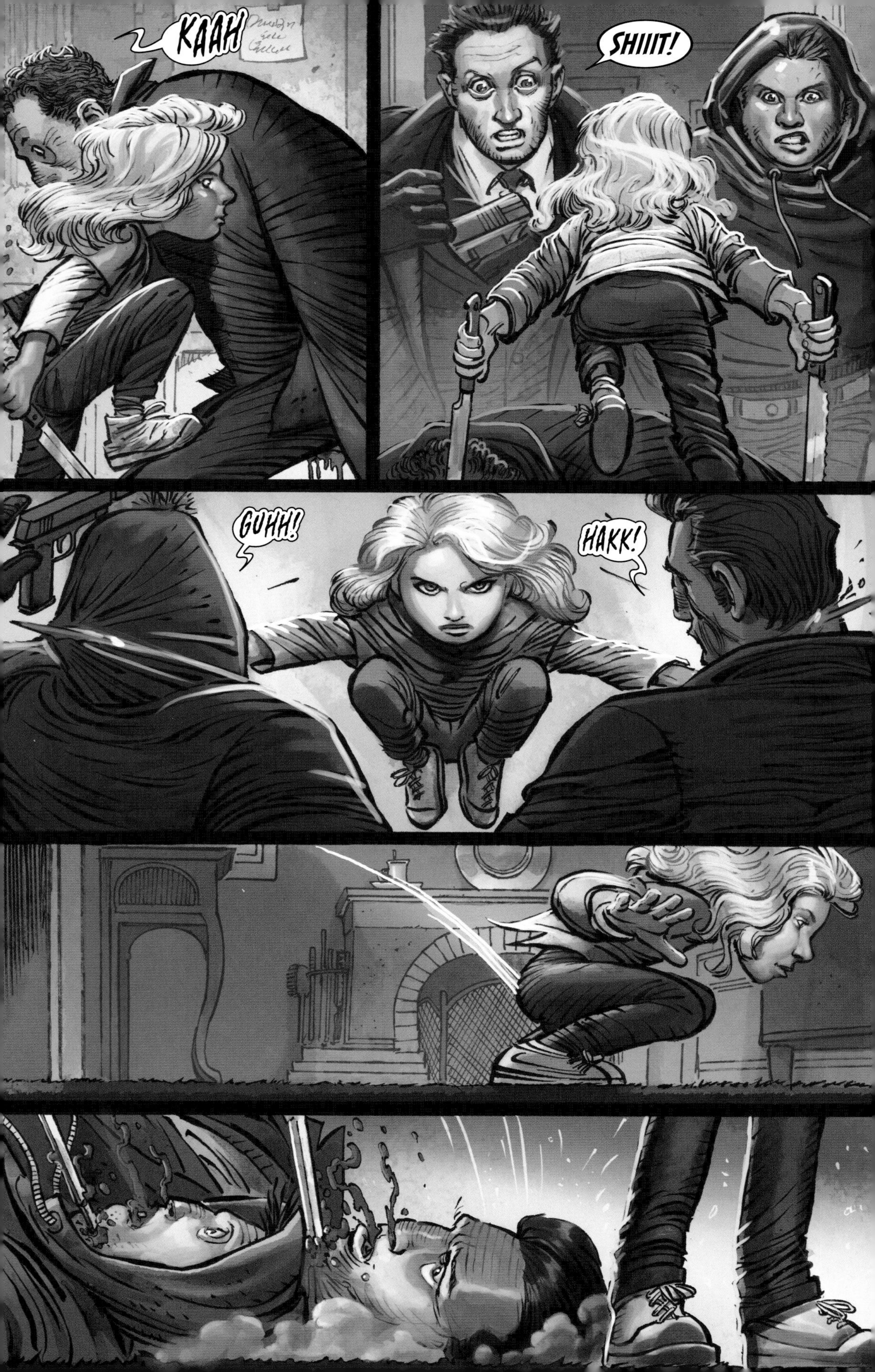
KAAH
SHIIIT!
GUHH!
HAKK!

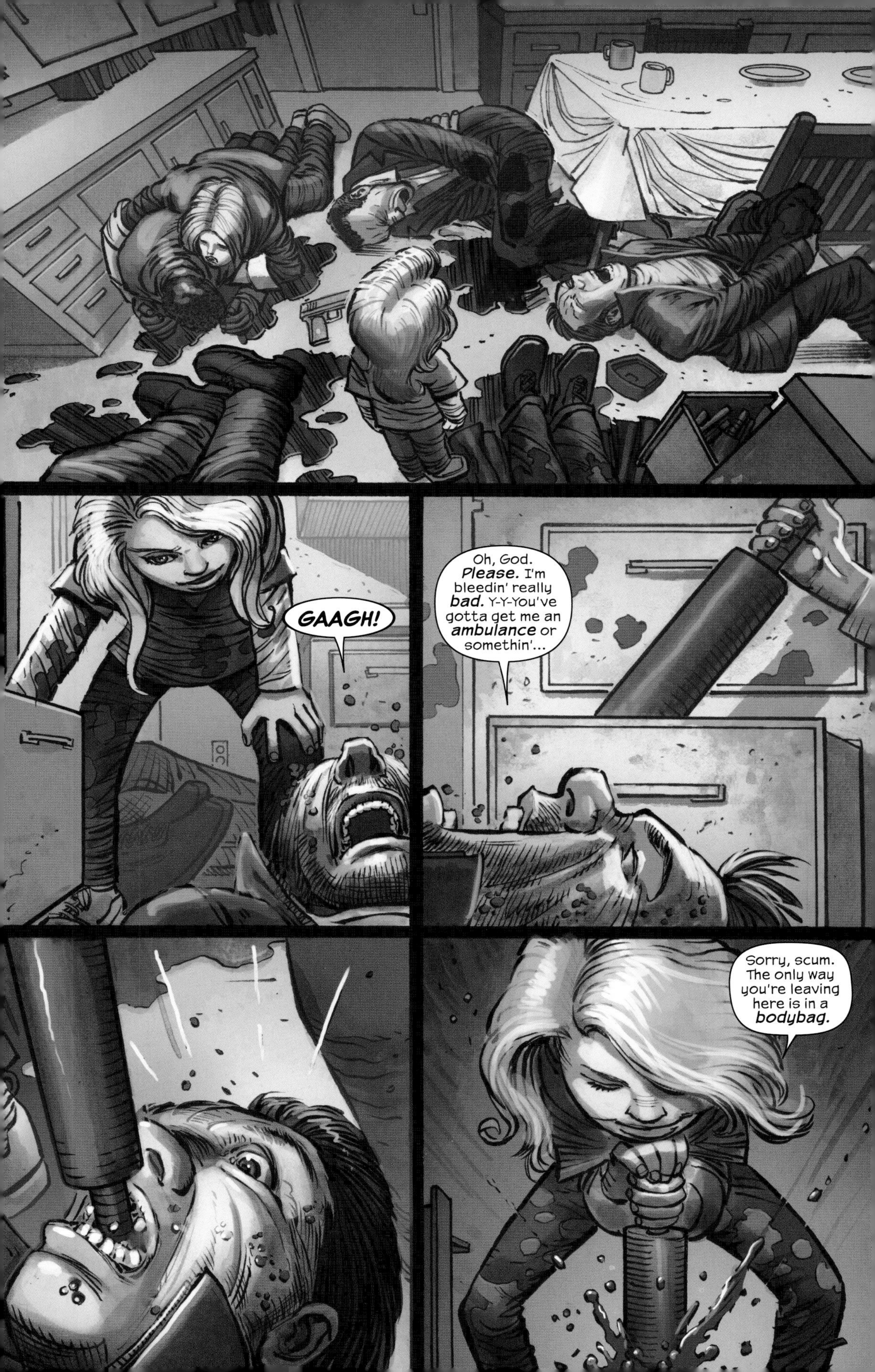
GAAGH!
Oh, God. Please. I'm bleedin' really bad. Y-Y-You've gotta get me an ambulance or somethin'...
Sorry, scum. The only way you're leaving here is in a bodybag.

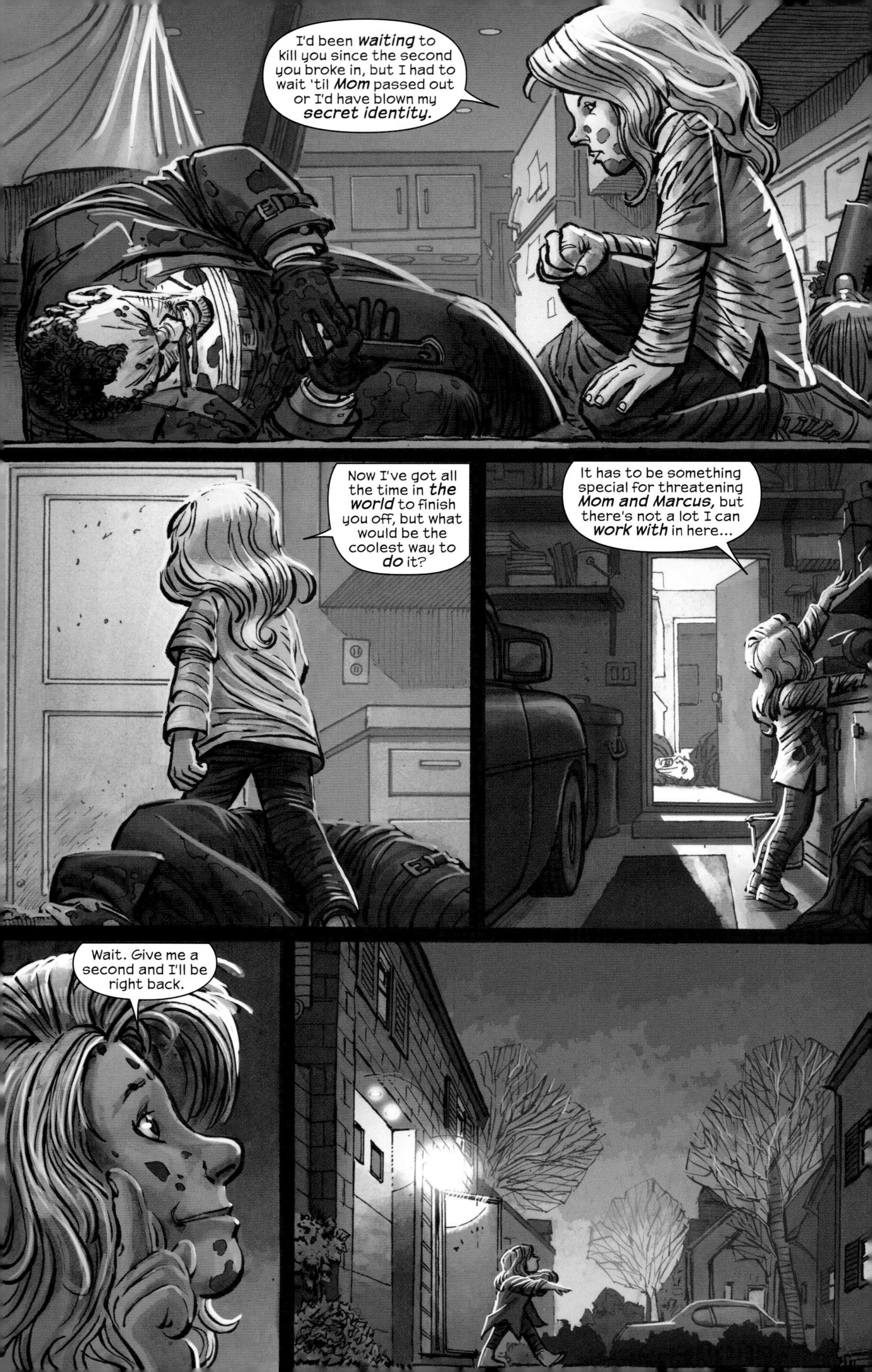

I'd been waiting to kill you since the second you broke in, but I had to wait 'til Mom passed out or I'd have blown my secret identity.
Now I've got all the time in the world to finish you off, but what would be the coolest way to do it?
It has to be something special for threatening Mom and Marcus, but there's not a lot I can work with in here...
Wait. Give me a second and I'll be right back.

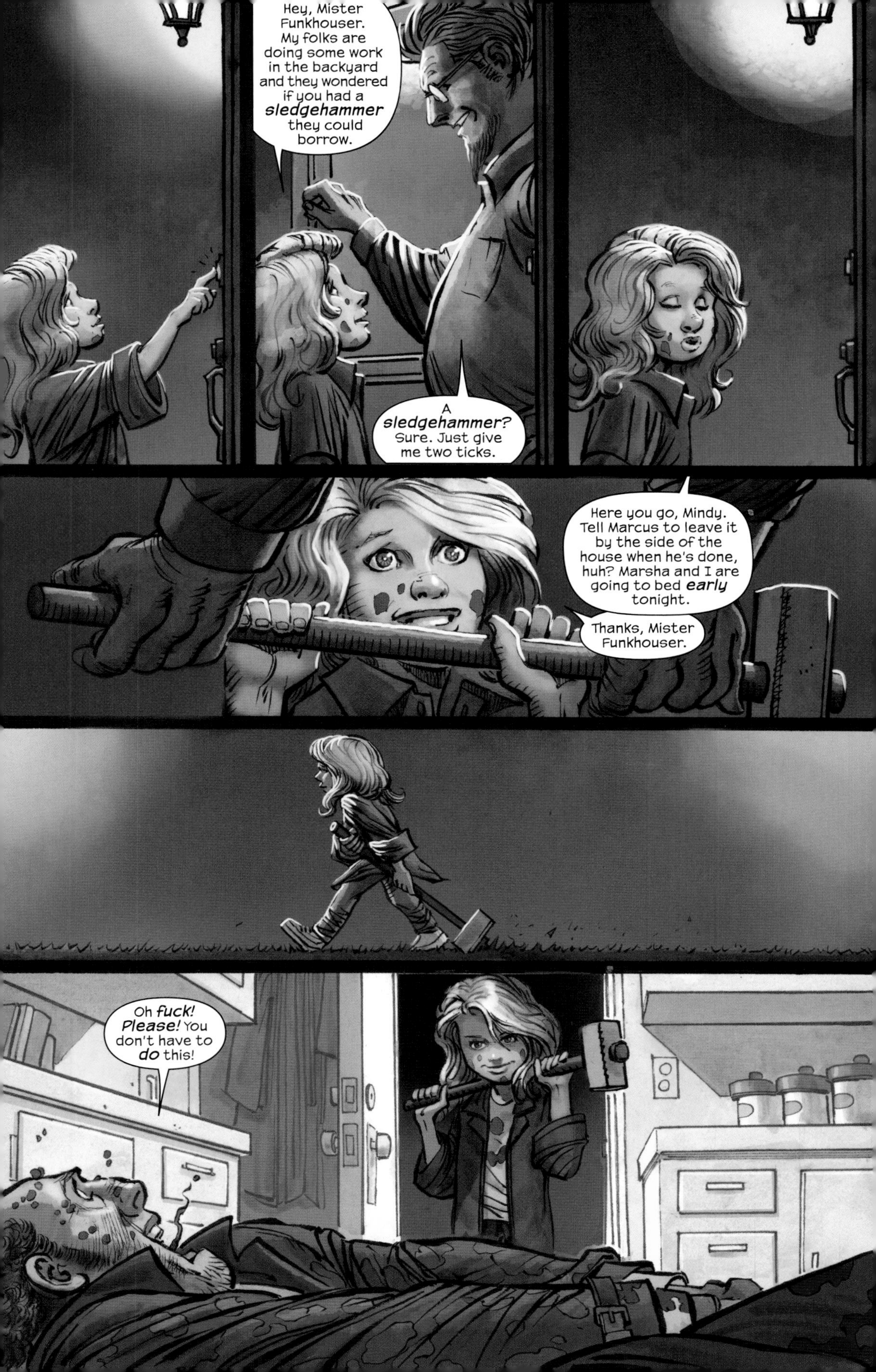

Hey, Mister Funkhouser. My folks are doing some work in the backyard and they wondered if you had a *sledgehammer* they could borrow.
A *sledgehammer?* Sure. Just give me two ticks.
Here you go, Mindy. Tell Marcus to leave it by the side of the house when he's done, huh? Marsha and I are going to bed *early* tonight.
Thanks, Mister Funkhouser.
Oh *fuck! Please!* You don't have to *do* this!

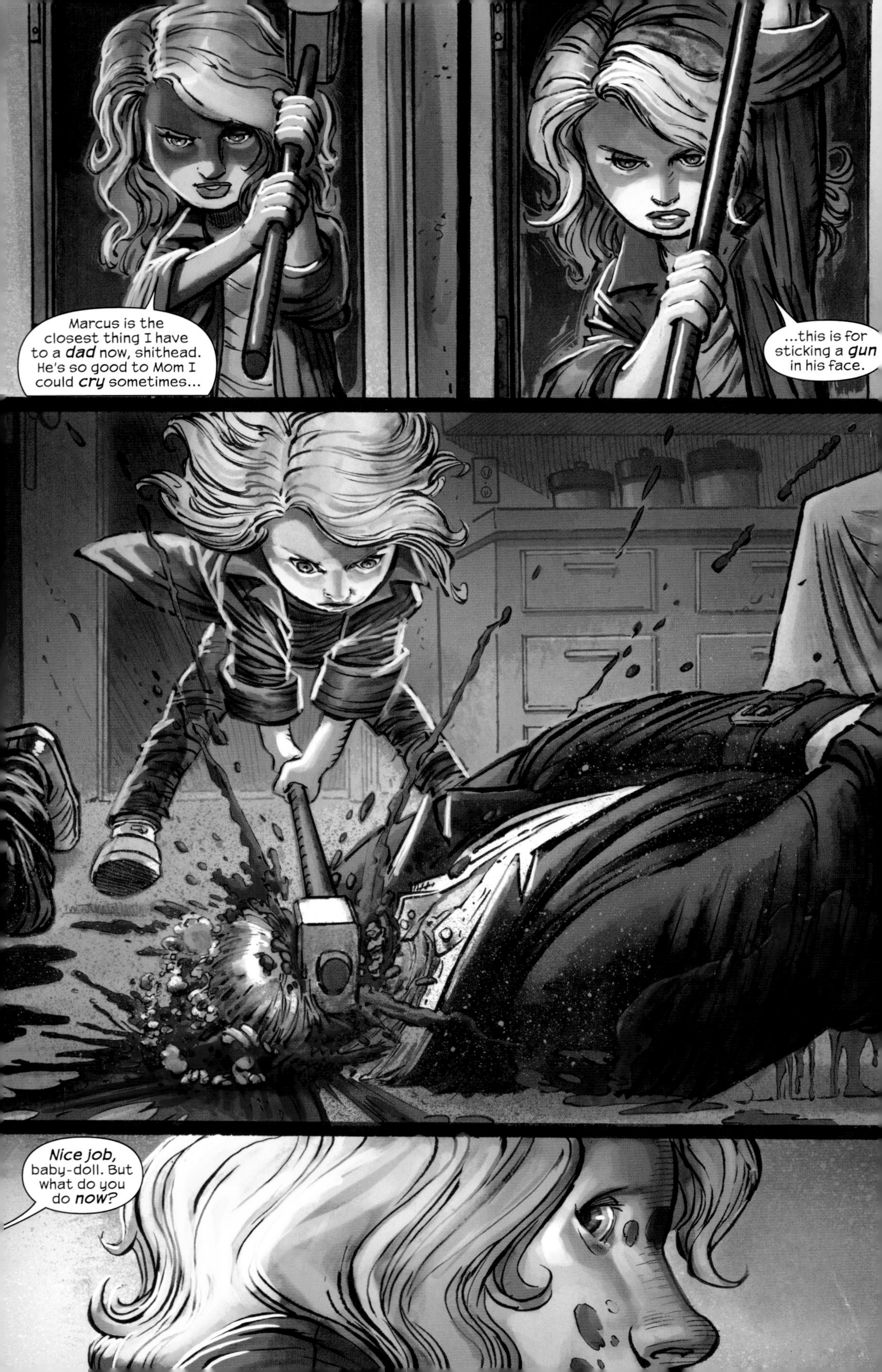
Marcus is the closest thing I have to a *dad* now, shithead. He's so good to Mom I could *cry* sometimes...
...this is for sticking a *gun* in his face.
Nice job, baby-doll. But what do you do *now?*

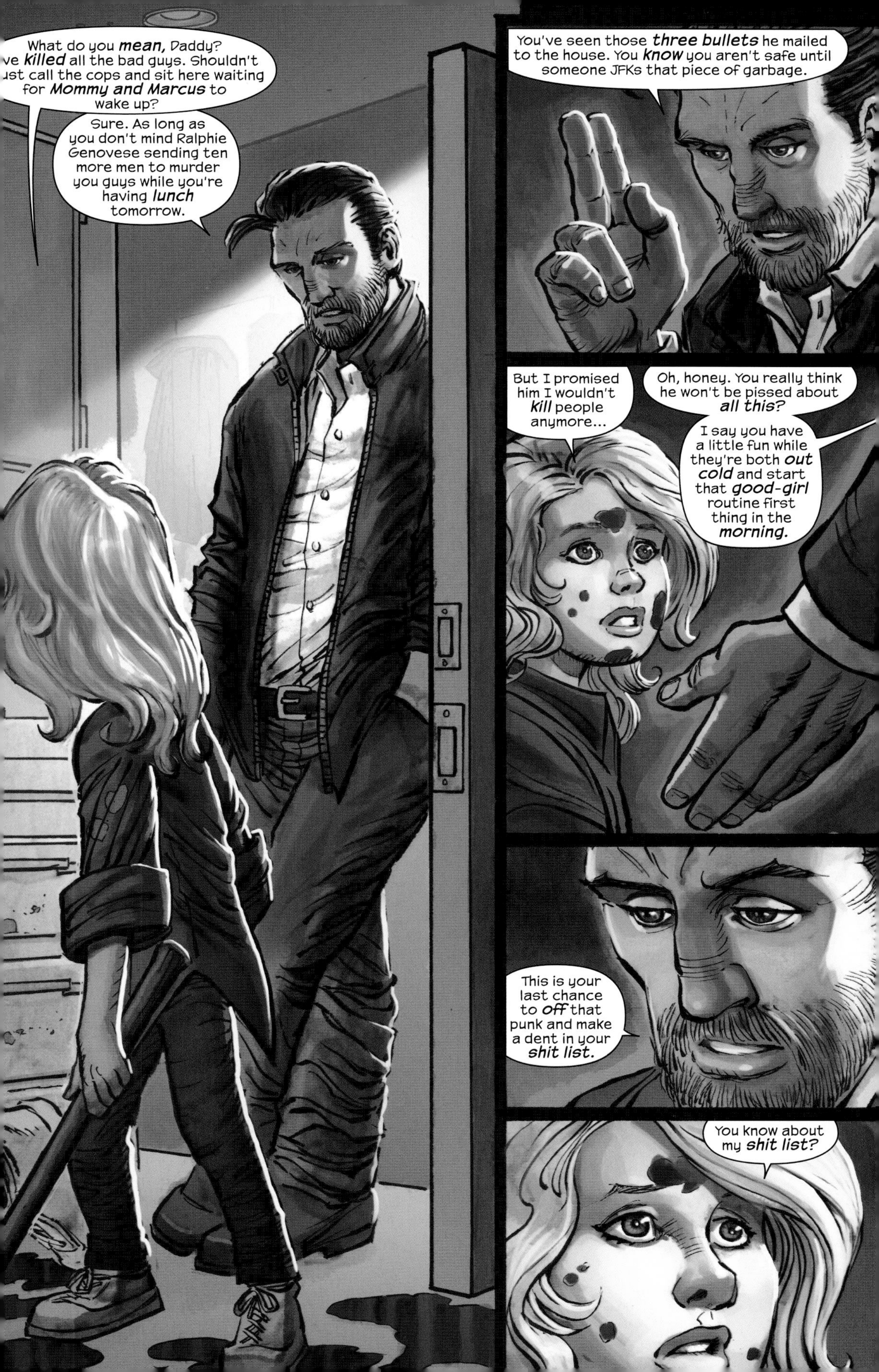

What do you mean, Daddy? ve killed all the bad guys. Shouldn't ust call the cops and sit here waiting for Mommy and Marcus to wake up?
Sure. As long as you don't mind Ralphie Genovese sending ten more men to murder you guys while you're having lunch tomorrow.
You've seen those three bullets he mailed to the house. You know you aren't safe until someone JFKs that piece of garbage.
But I promised him I wouldn't kill people anymore...
Oh, honey. You really think he won't be pissed about all this?
I say you have a little fun while they're both out cold and start that good-girl routine first thing in the morning.
This is your last chance to off that punk and make a dent in your shit list.
You know about my shit list?

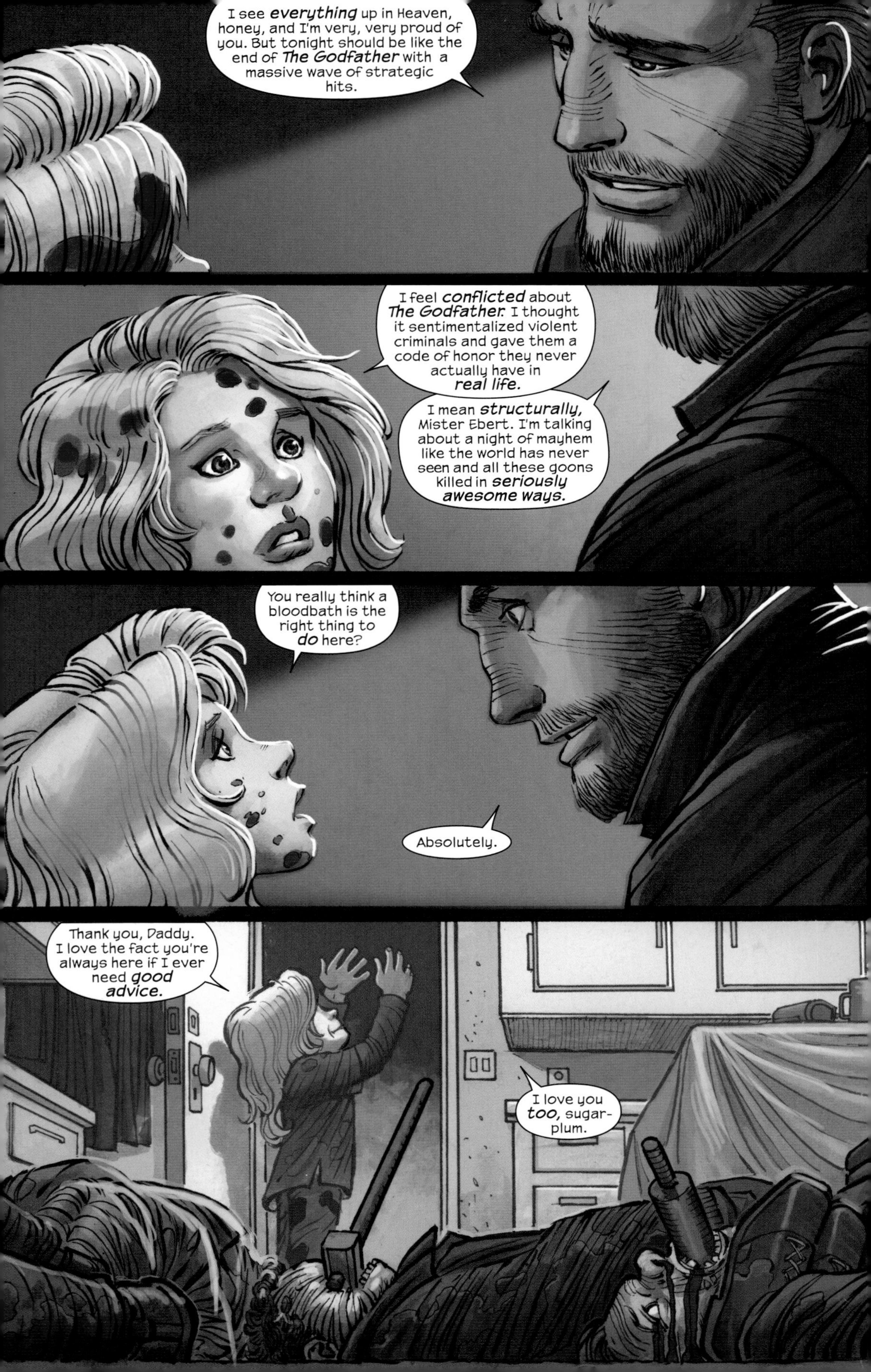
I see everything up in Heaven, honey, and I'm very, very proud of you. But tonight should be like the end of The Godfather with a massive wave of strategic hits.
I feel conflicted about The Godfather. I thought it sentimentalized violent criminals and gave them a code of honor they never actually have in real life.
I mean structurally, Mister Ebert. I'm talking about a night of mayhem like the world has never seen and all these goons killed in seriously awesome ways.
You really think a bloodbath is the right thing to do here?
Absolutely.
Thank you, Daddy. I love the fact you're always here if I ever need good advice.
I love you too, sugar-plum.

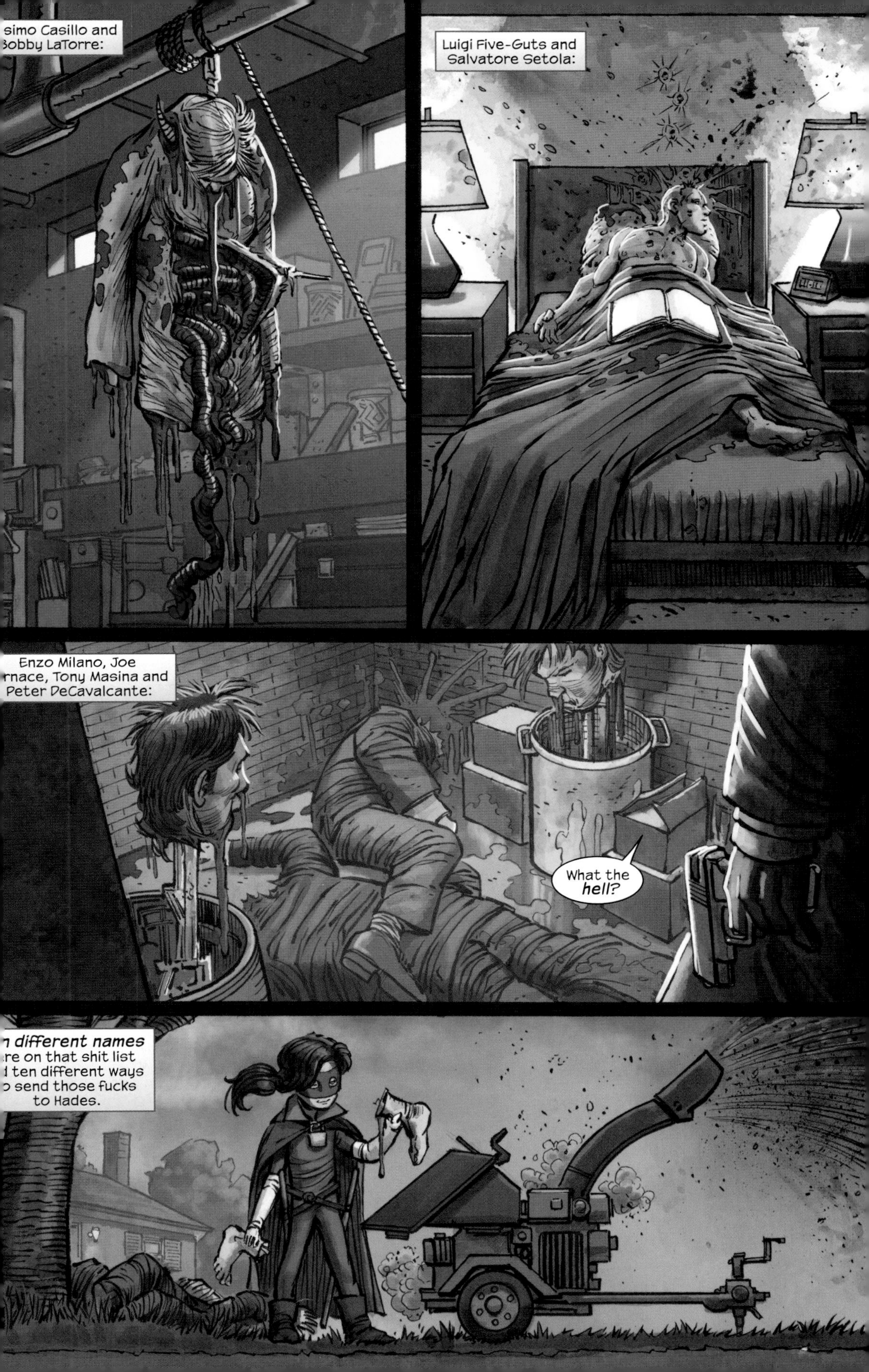
simo Casillo and
Bobby LaTorre:
Luigi Five-Guts and
Salvatore Setola:
Enzo Milano, Joe
rnace, Tony Masina and
Peter DeCavalcante:
What the *hell?*
n different names
re on that shit list
d ten different ways
o send those fucks
to Hades.

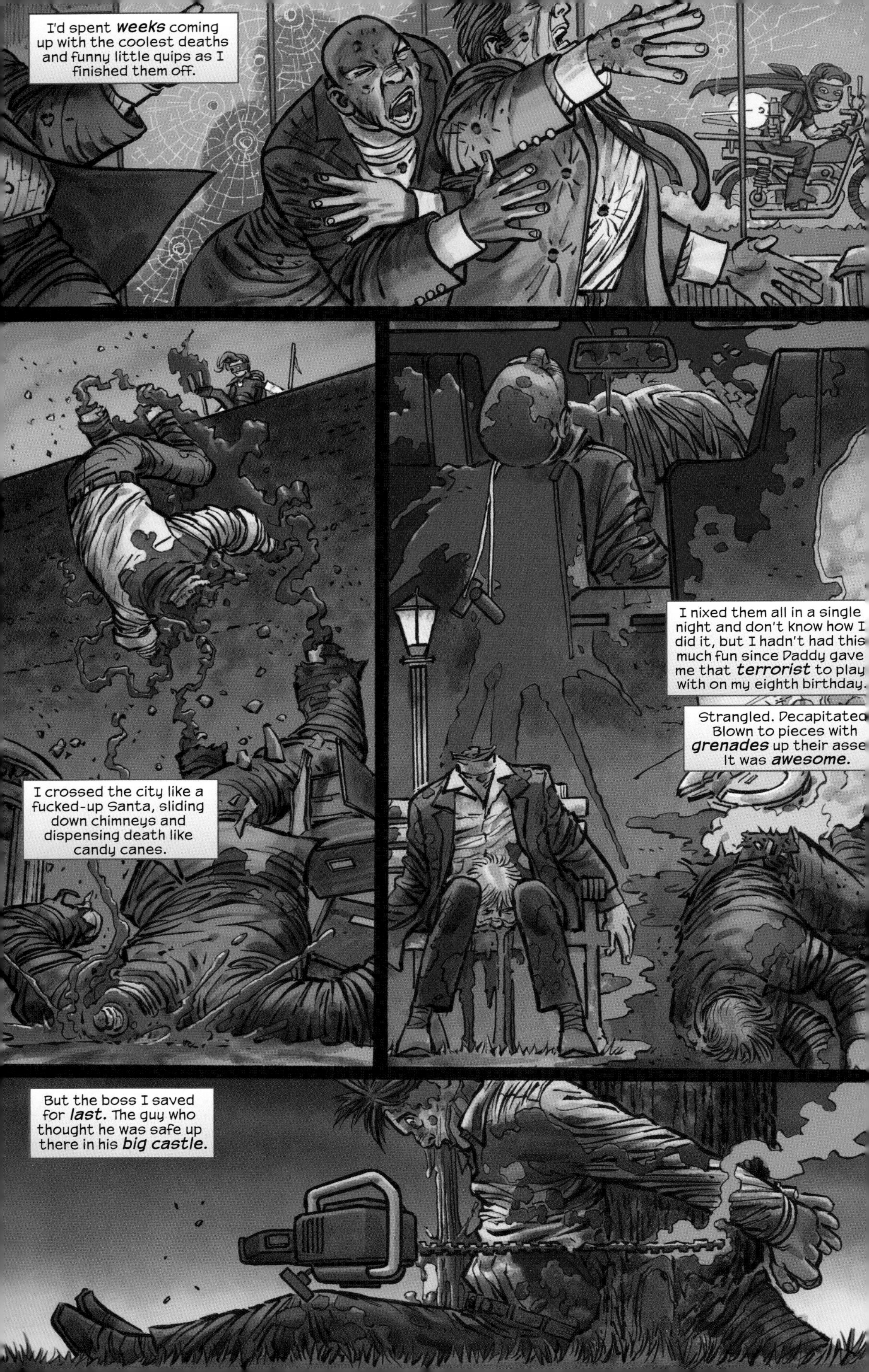
I'd spent *weeks* coming up with the coolest deaths and funny little quips as I finished them off.
I crossed the city like a fucked-up Santa, sliding down chimneys and dispensing death like candy canes.
I nixed them all in a single night and don't know how I did it, but I hadn't had this much fun since Daddy gave me that *terrorist* to play with on my eighth birthday.
Strangled. Decapitated. Blown to pieces with *grenades* up their asse It was *awesome.*
But the boss I saved for *last.* The guy who thought he was safe up there in his *big castle.*

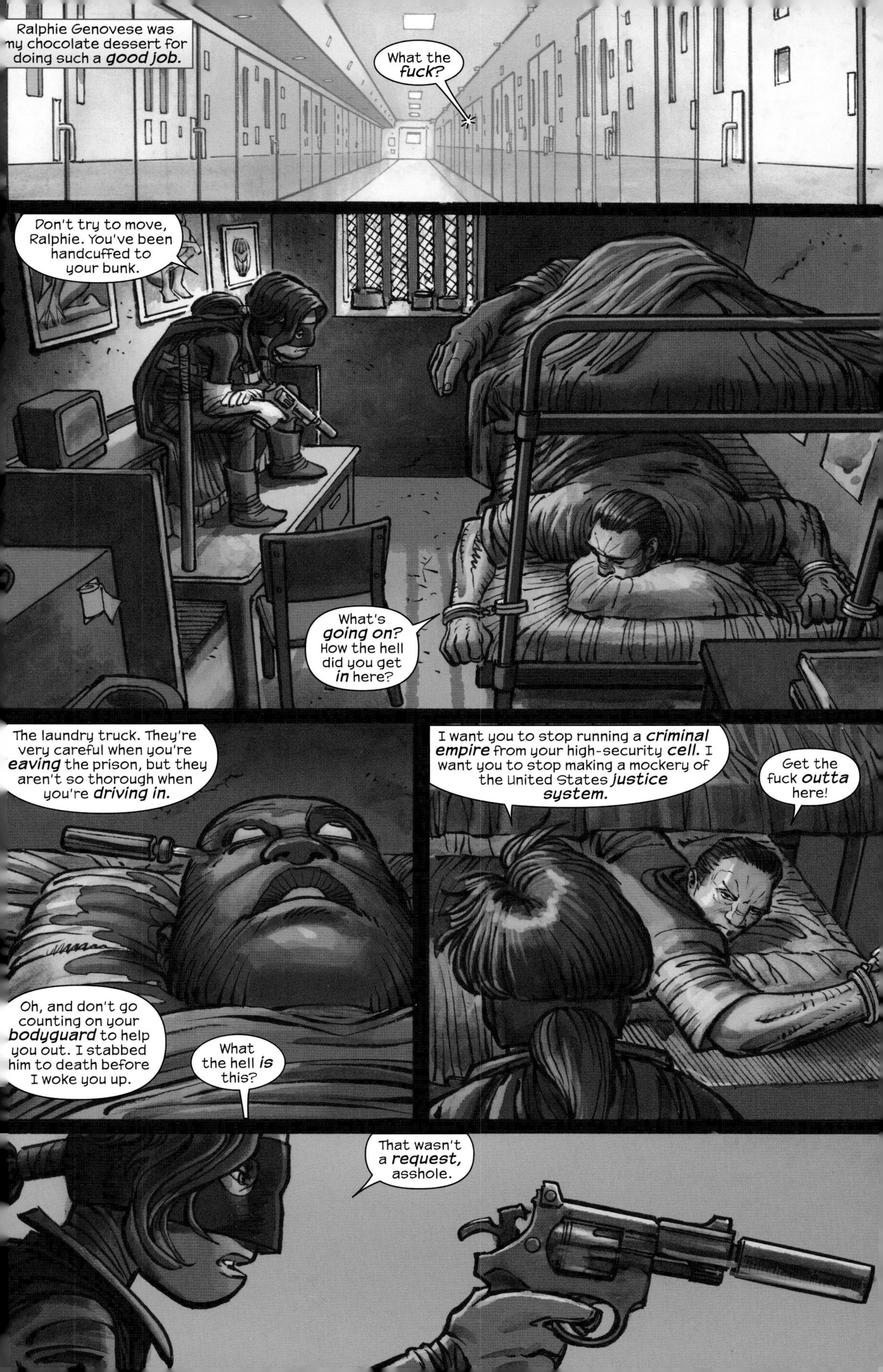
Ralphie Genovese was my chocolate dessert for doing such a good job.
What the fuck?
Don't try to move, Ralphie. You've been handcuffed to your bunk.
What's going on? How the hell did you get in here?
The laundry truck. They're very careful when you're eaving the prison, but they aren't so thorough when you're driving in.
Oh, and don't go counting on your bodyguard to help you out. I stabbed him to death before I woke you up.
What the hell is this?
I want you to stop running a criminal empire from your high-security cell. I want you to stop making a mockery of the United States justice system.
Get the fuck outta here!
That wasn't a request, asshole.

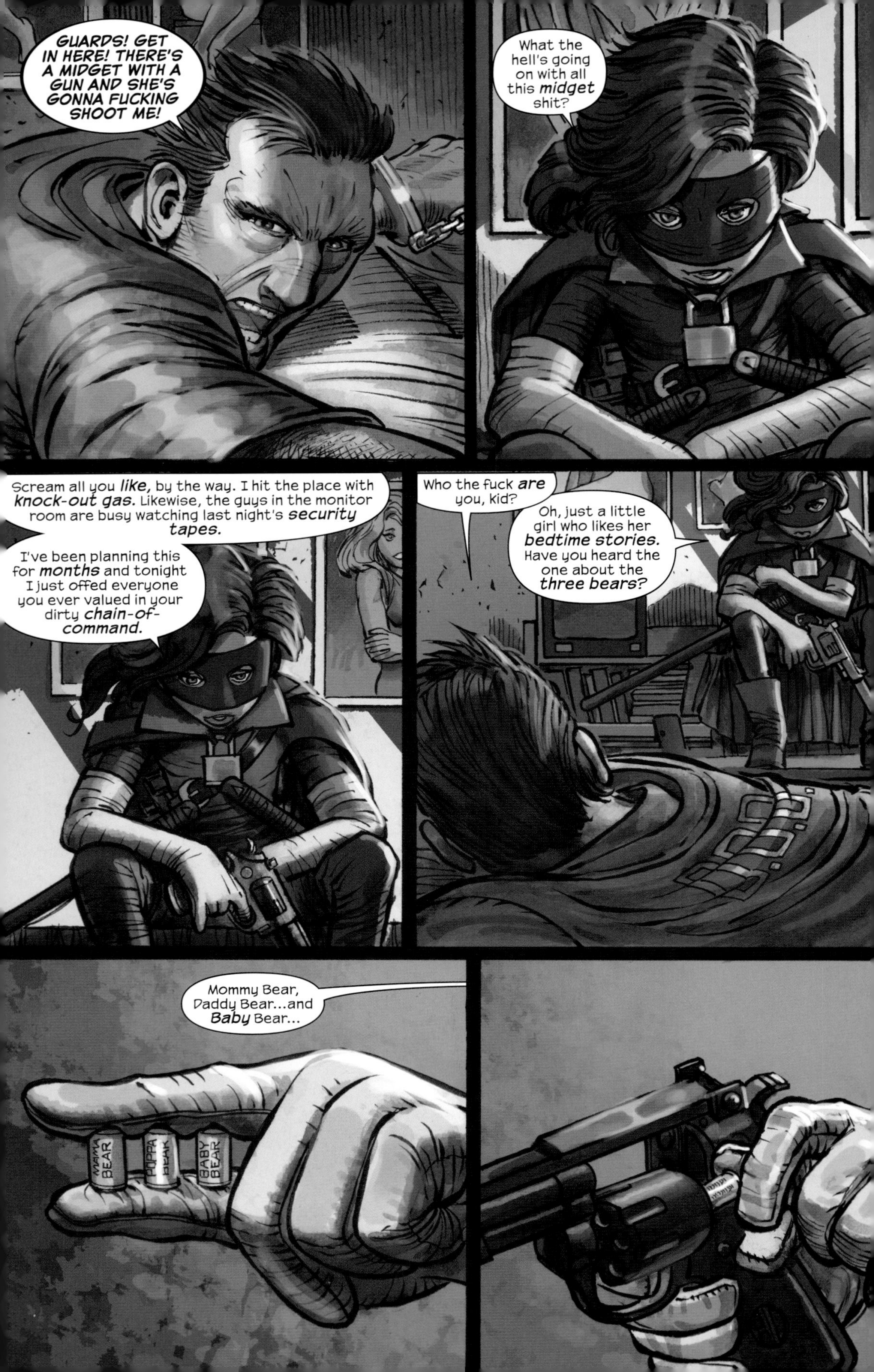
GUARDS! GET IN HERE! THERE'S A MIDGET WITH A GUN AND SHE'S GONNA FUCKING SHOOT ME!
What the hell's going on with all this *midget* shit?
Scream all you *like,* by the way. I hit the place with *knock-out gas.* Likewise, the guys in the monitor room are busy watching last night's *security tapes.*
I've been planning this for *months* and tonight I just offed everyone you ever valued in your dirty *chain-of-command.*
Who the fuck *are* you, kid?
Oh, just a little girl who likes her *bedtime stories.* Have you heard the one about the *three bears?*
Mommy Bear, Daddy Bear...and *Baby* Bear...
MAMA BEAR
POPPA BEAR
BABY BEAR

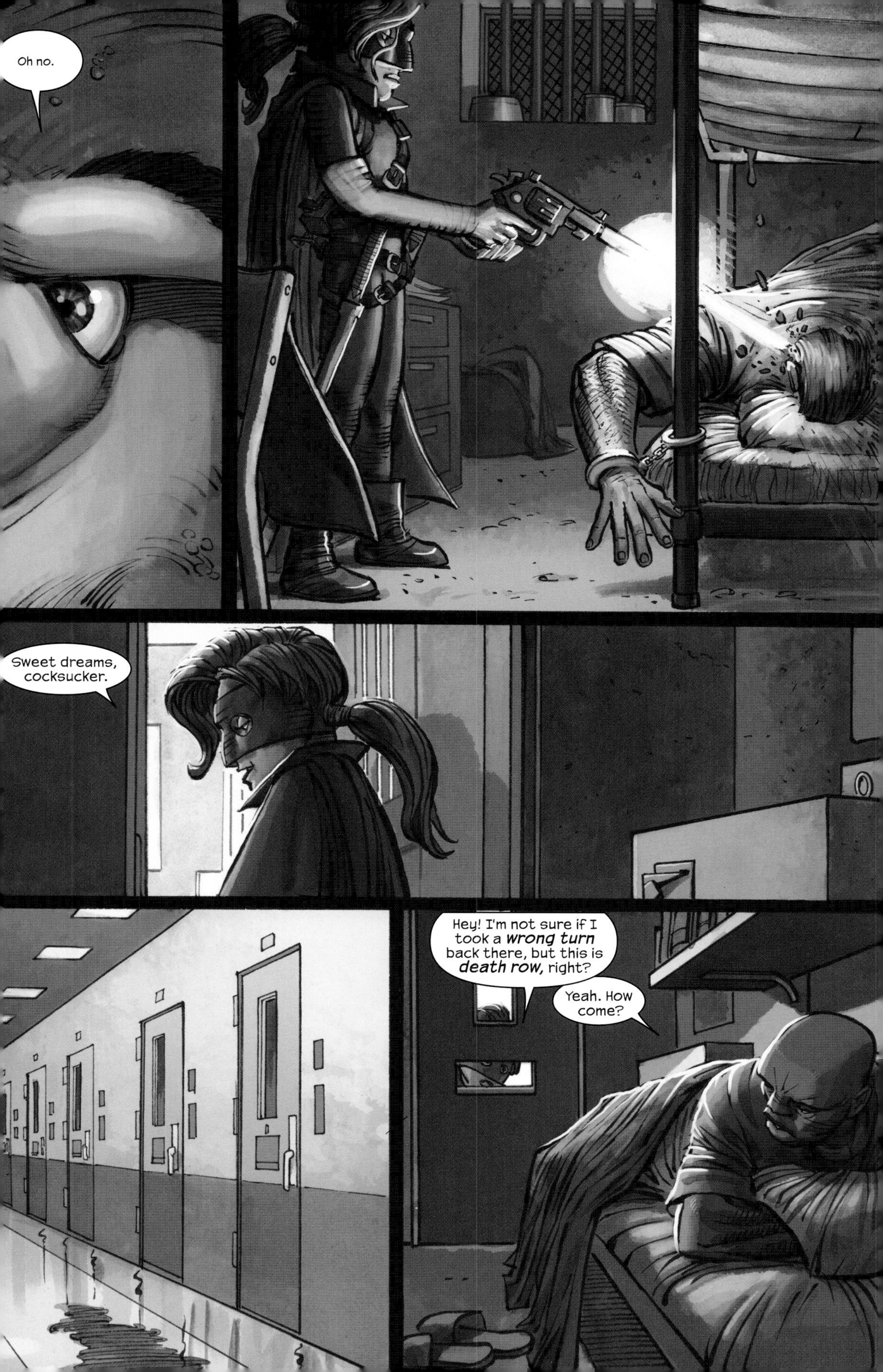
Oh no.
Sweet dreams, cocksucker.
Hey! I'm not sure if I took a *wrong turn* back there, but this is *death row,* right?
Yeah. How come?

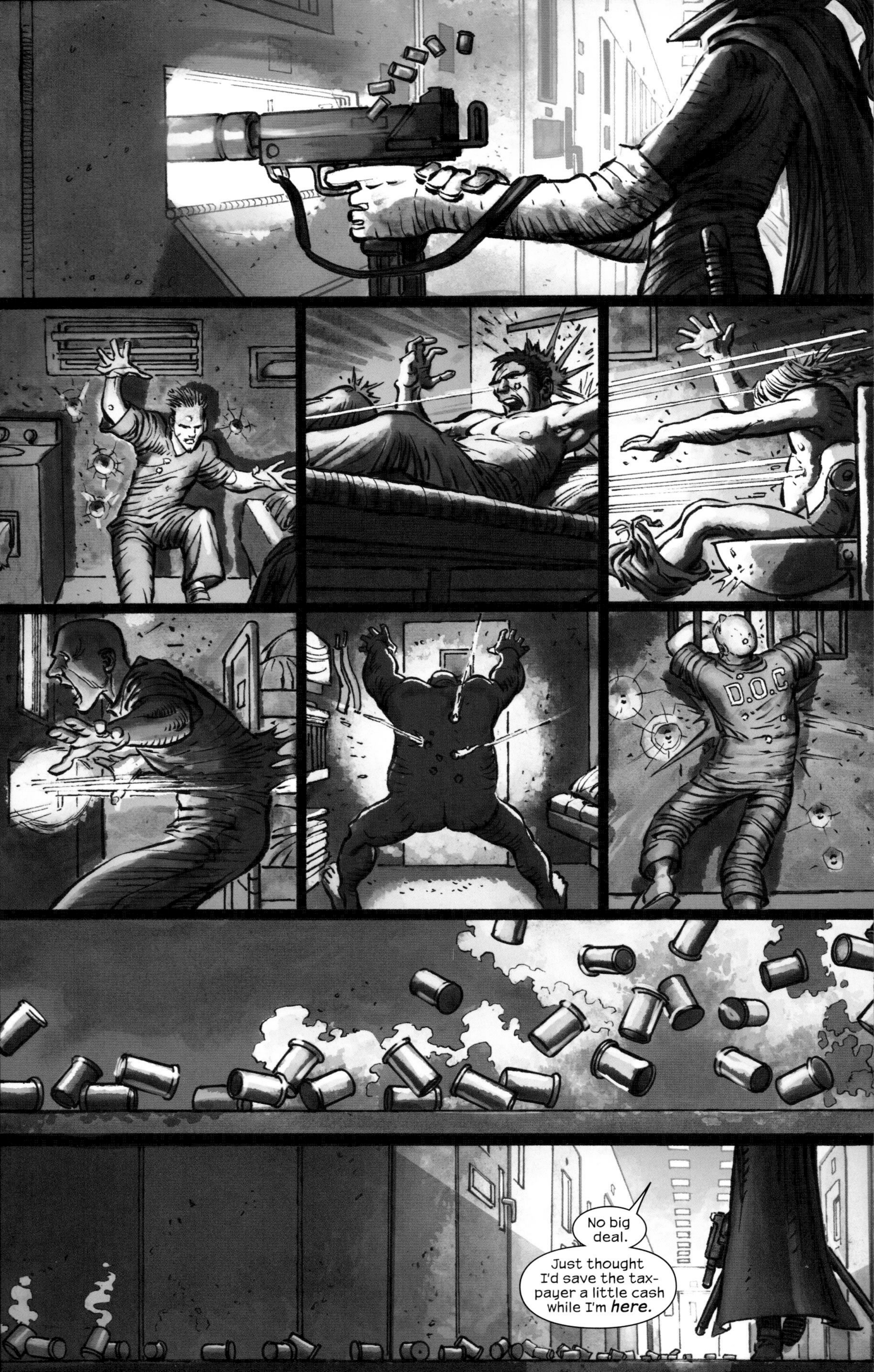
D.O.C
No big deal.
Just thought I'd save the tax-payer a little cash while I'm *here.*

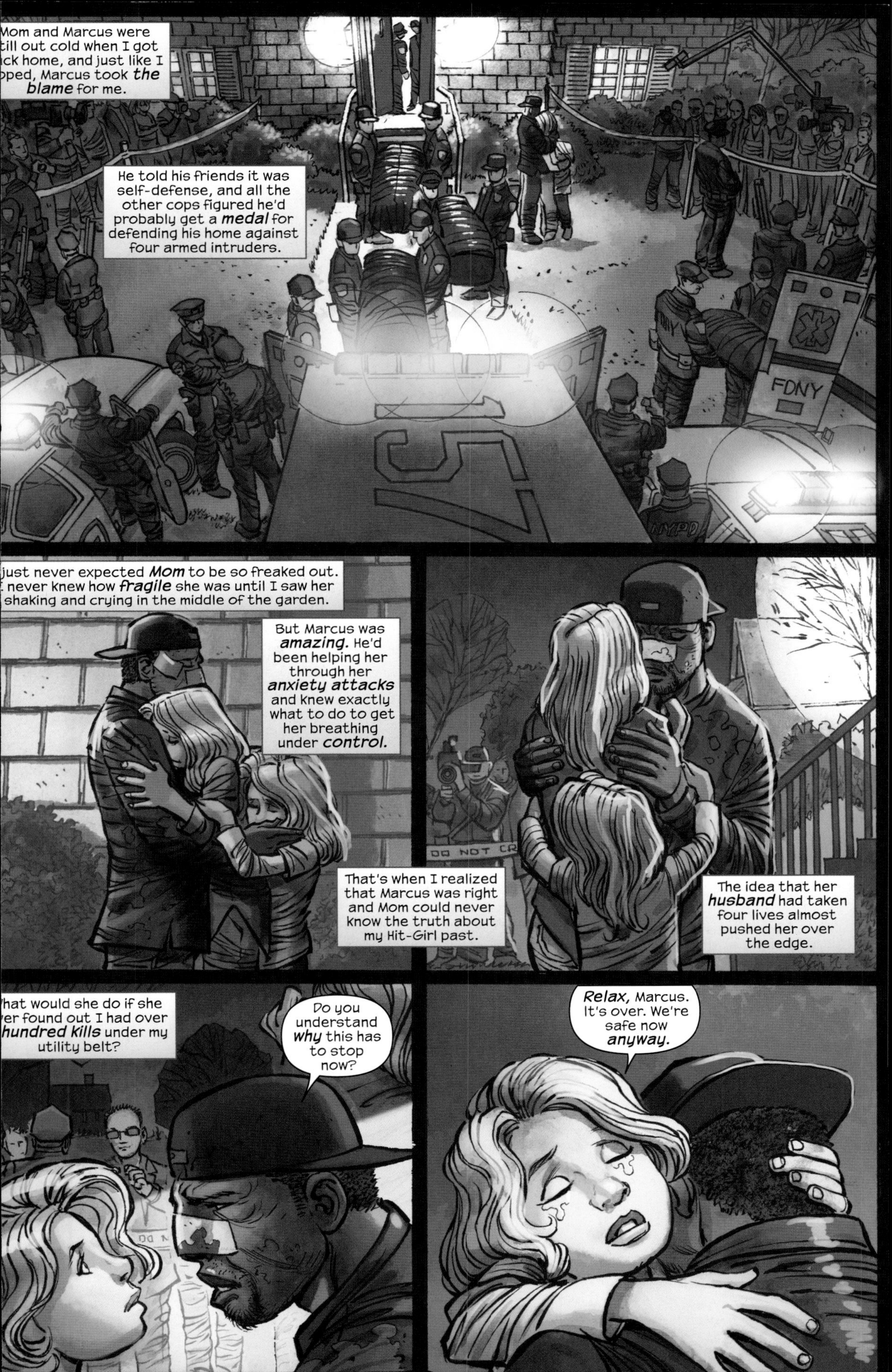

Mom and Marcus were
till out cold when I got
ck home, and just like I
oped, Marcus took *the blame* for me.
He told his friends it was self-defense, and all the other cops figured he'd probably get a *medal* for defending his home against four armed intruders.
FDNY
NYPD
just never expected *Mom* to be so freaked out.
never knew how *fragile* she was until I saw her
shaking and crying in the middle of the garden.
But Marcus was *amazing.* He'd been helping her through her *anxiety attacks* and knew exactly what to do to get her breathing under *control.*
That's when I realized that Marcus was right and Mom could never know the truth about my Hit-Girl past.
DO NOT CR
The idea that her *husband* had taken four lives almost pushed her over the edge.
hat would she do if she
er found out I had over
hundred kills under my
utility belt?
Do you understand *why* this has to stop now?
Relax, Marcus. It's over. We're safe now *anyway.*

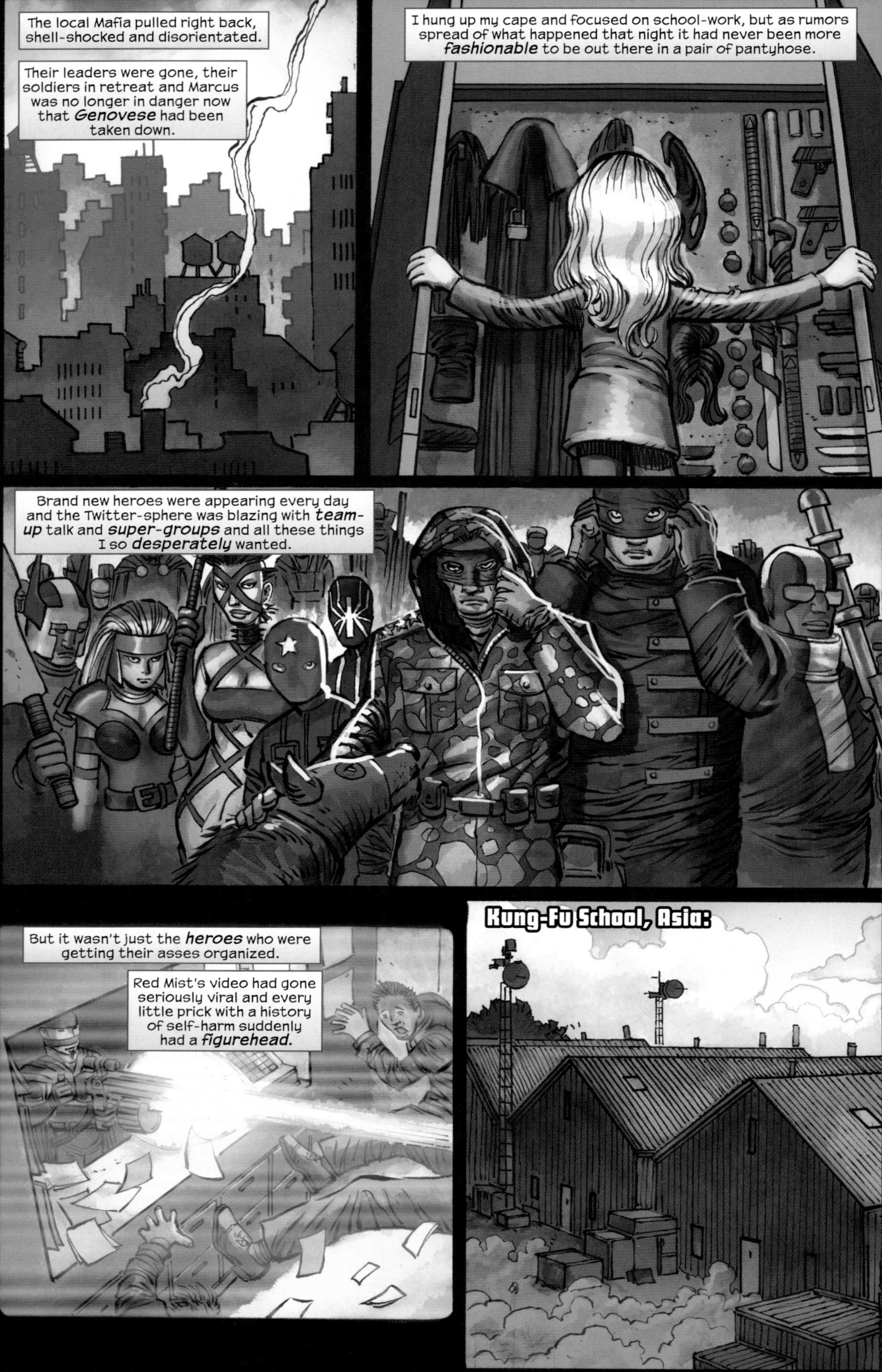

The local Mafia pulled right back, shell-shocked and disorientated.
Their leaders were gone, their soldiers in retreat and Marcus was no longer in danger now that *Genovese* had been taken down.
I hung up my cape and focused on school-work, but as rumors spread of what happened that night it had never been more *fashionable* to be out there in a pair of pantyhose.
Brand new heroes were appearing every day and the Twitter-sphere was blazing with *team-up* talk and *super-groups* and all these things I so *desperately* wanted.
But it wasn't just the *heroes* who were getting their asses organized.
Red Mist's video had gone seriously viral and every little prick with a history of self-harm suddenly had a *figurehead.*
Kung-Fu School, Asia:

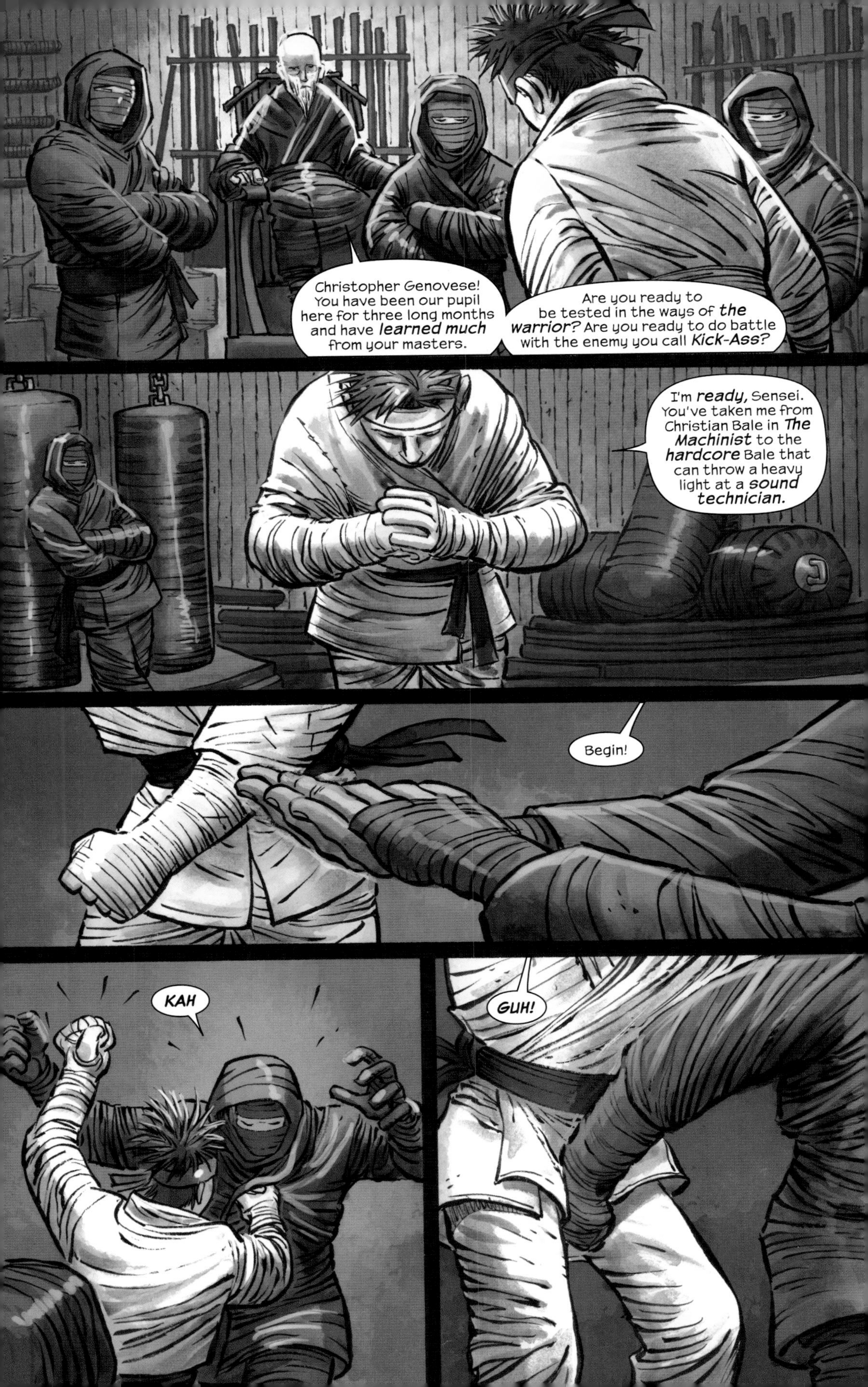
Christopher Genovese! You have been our pupil here for three long months and have *learned much* from your masters.
Are you ready to be tested in the ways of *the warrior*? Are you ready to do battle with the enemy you call *Kick-Ass?*
I'm *ready,* Sensei. You've taken me from Christian Bale in *The Machinist* to the *hardcore* Bale that can throw a heavy light at a *sound technician.*
Begin!
KAH
GUH!

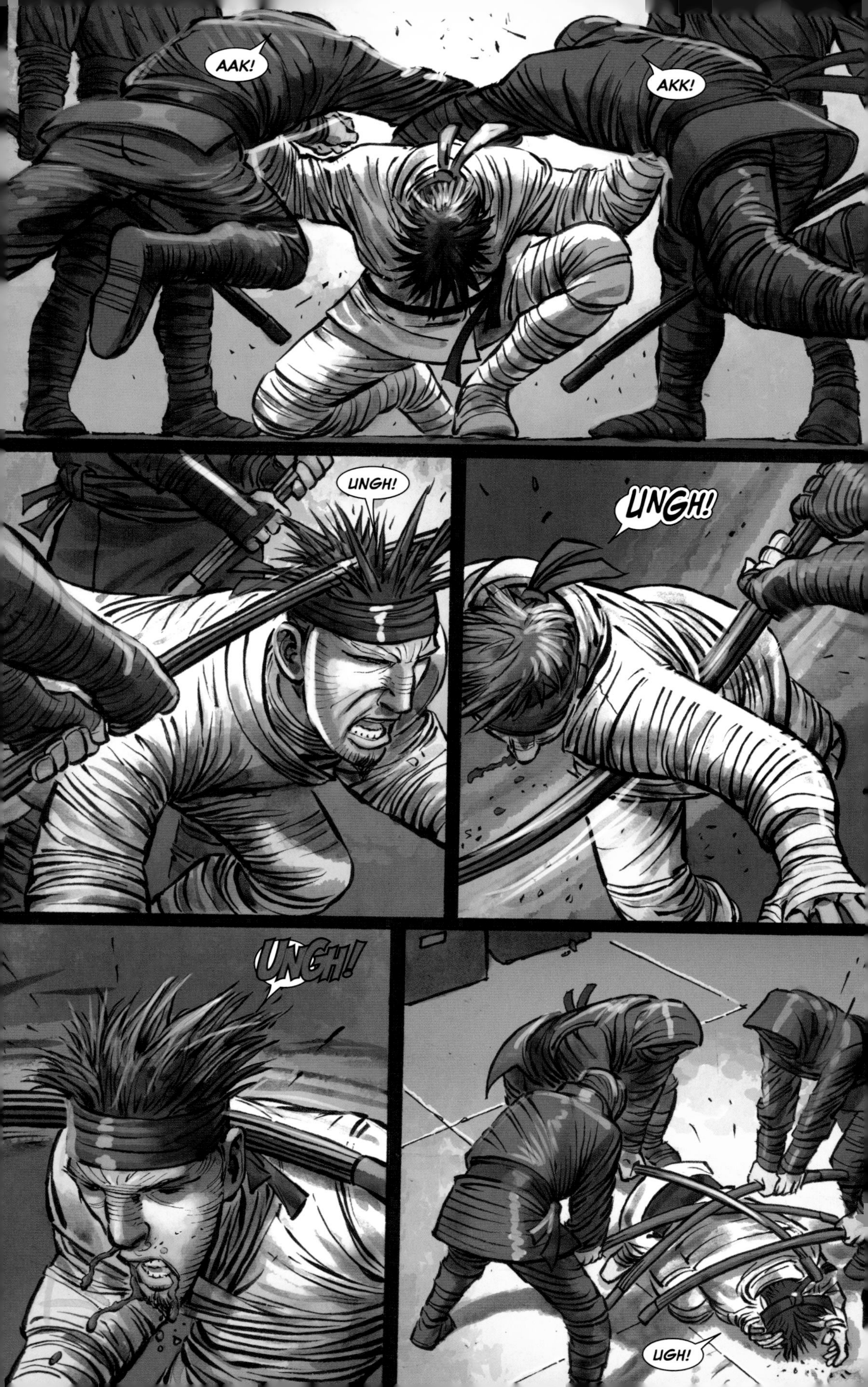
AAK!
AKK!
UNGH!
UNGH!
UNGH!
UGH!

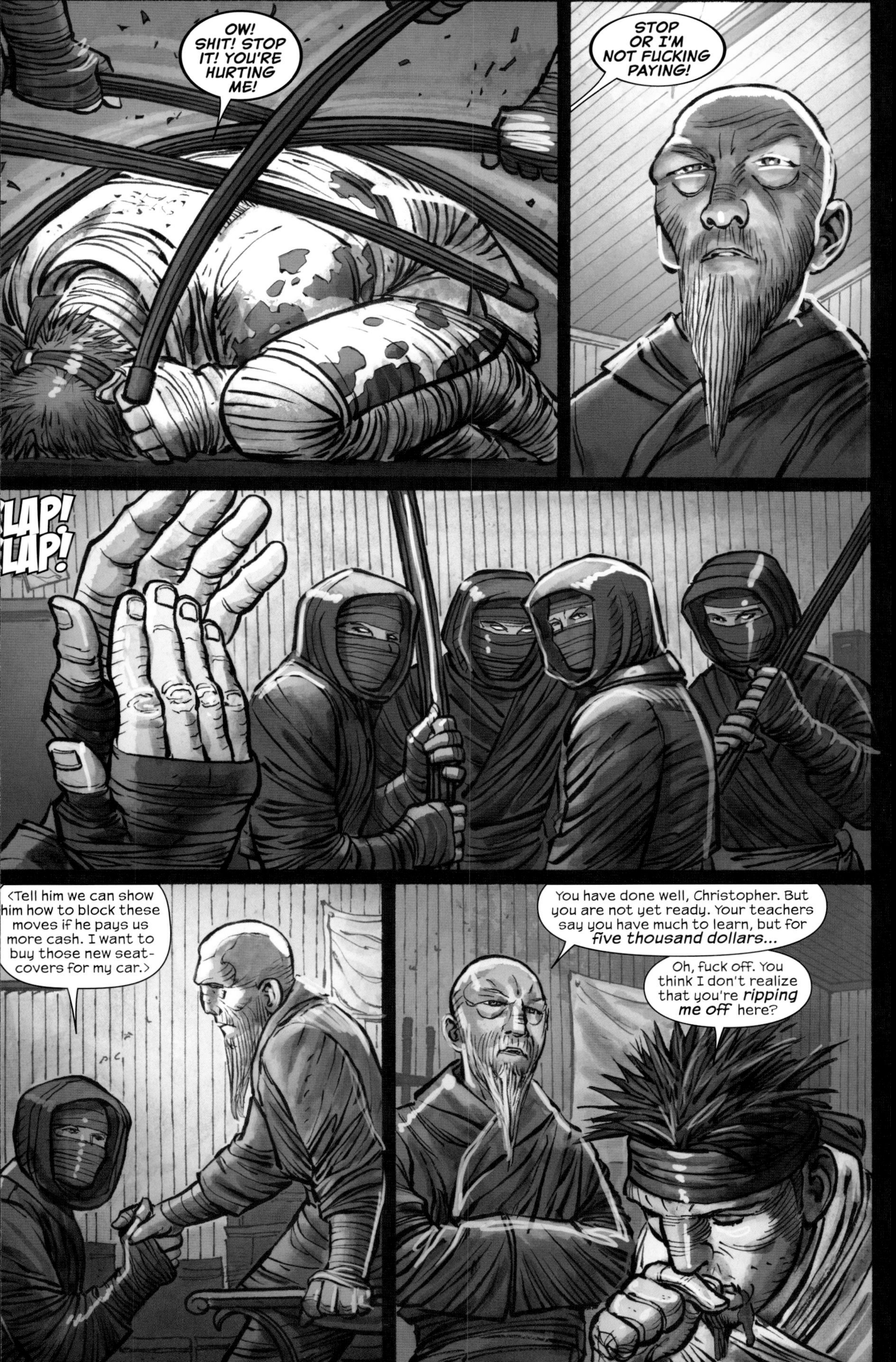
OW! SHIT! STOP IT! YOU'RE HURTING ME!
STOP OR I'M NOT FUCKING PAYING!
LAP! LAP!
<Tell him we can show him how to block these moves if he pays us more cash. I want to buy those new seat-covers for my car.>
You have done well, Christopher. But you are not yet ready. Your teachers say you have much to learn, but for *five thousand dollars...*
Oh, fuck off. You think I don't realize that you're *ripping me off* here?

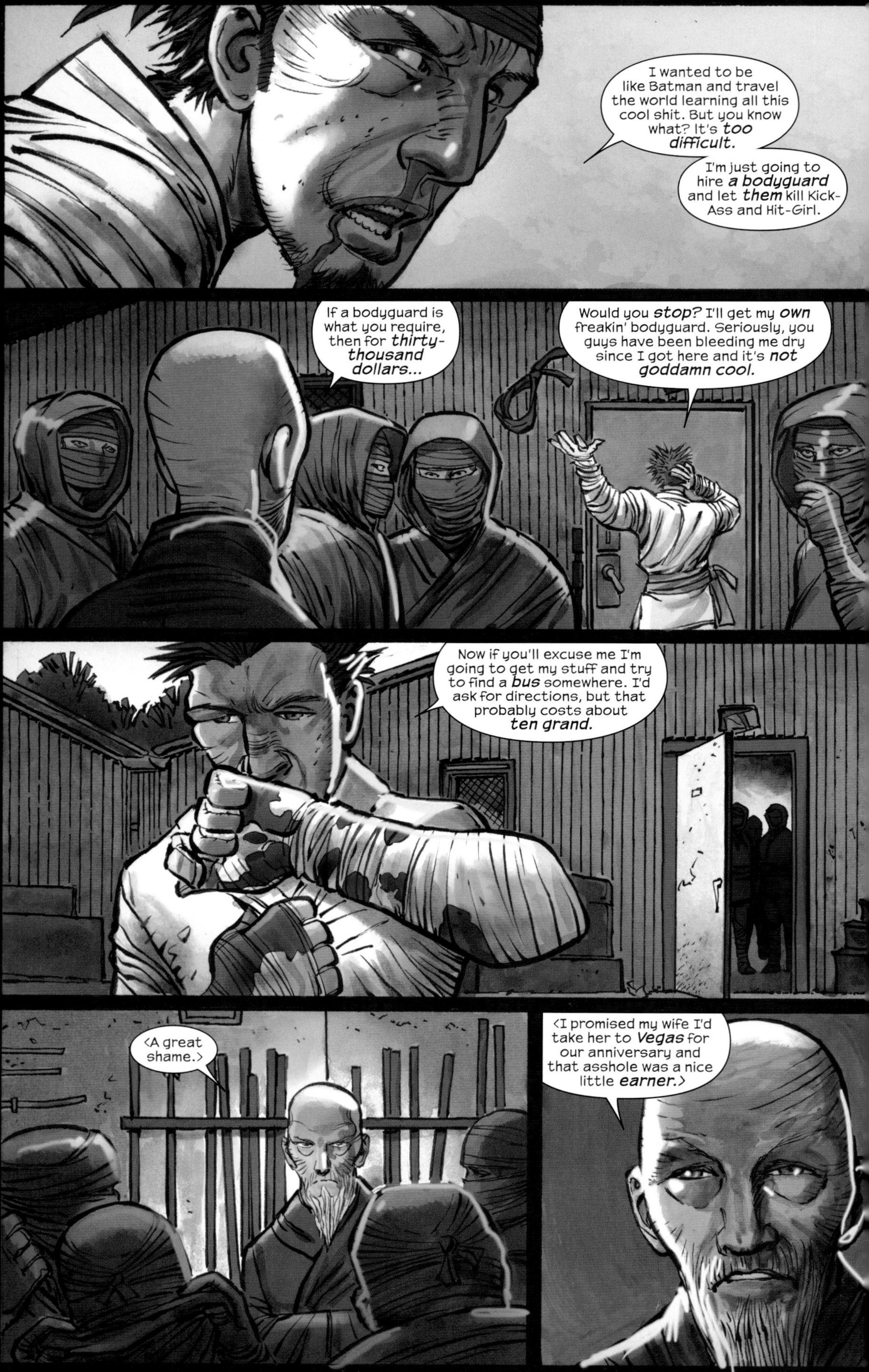
I wanted to be like Batman and travel the world learning all this cool shit. But you know what? It's *too difficult.*
I'm just going to hire ***a bodyguard*** and let ***them*** kill Kick-Ass and Hit-Girl.
If a bodyguard is what you require, then for *thirty-thousand dollars...*
Would you *stop?* I'll get my *own* freakin' bodyguard. Seriously, you guys have been bleeding me dry since I got here and it's *not goddamn cool.*
Now if you'll excuse me I'm going to get my stuff and try to find a *bus* somewhere. I'd ask for directions, but that probably costs about *ten grand.*
<A great shame.>
<I promised my wife I'd take her to *Vegas* for our anniversary and that asshole was a nice little *earner.*>

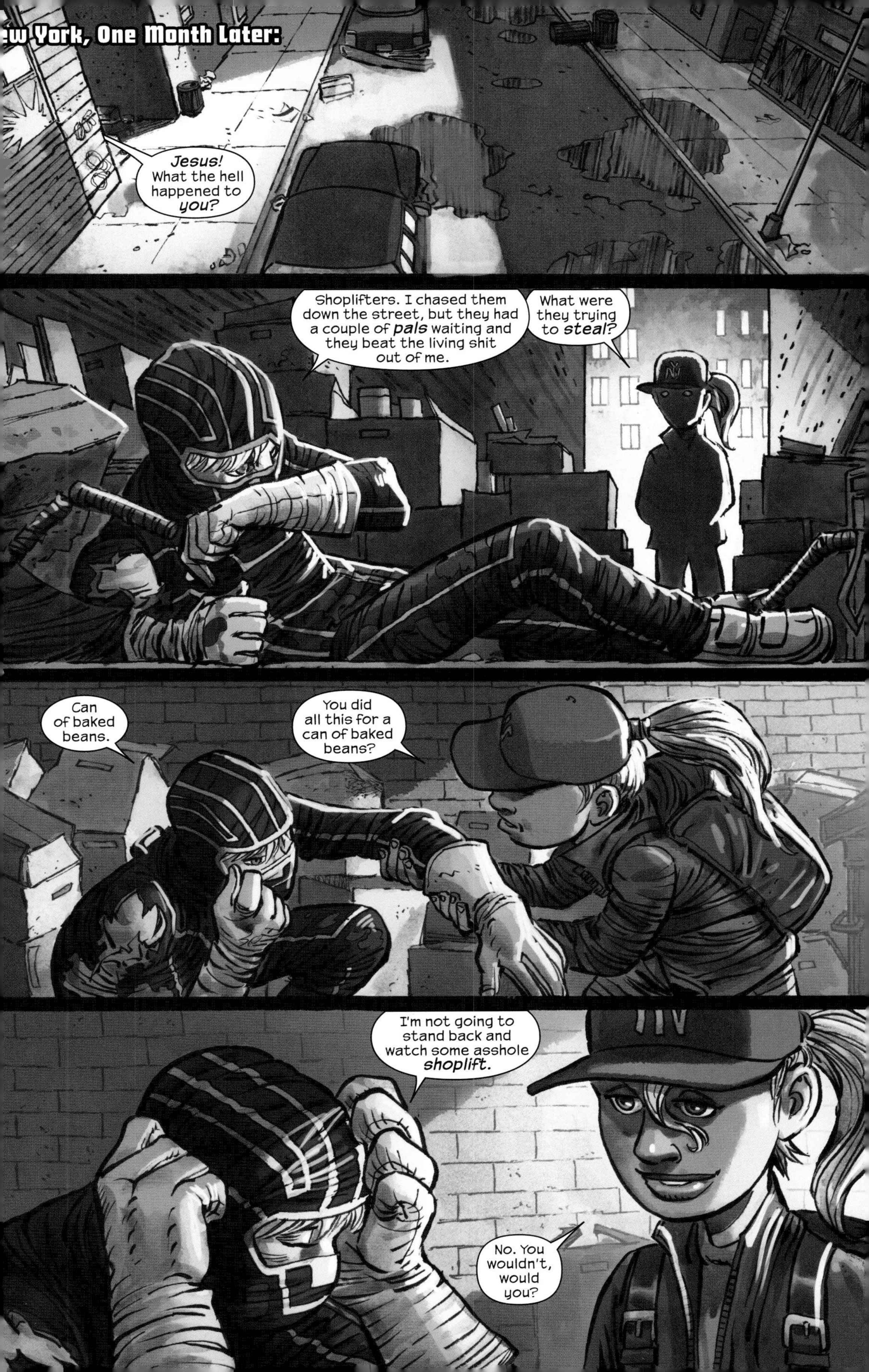
ew York, One Month Later:
Jesus! What the hell happened to you?
Shoplifters. I chased them down the street, but they had a couple of pals waiting and they beat the living shit out of me.
What were they trying to steal?
Can of baked beans.
You did all this for a can of baked beans?
I'm not going to stand back and watch some asshole shoplift.
No. You wouldn't, would you?

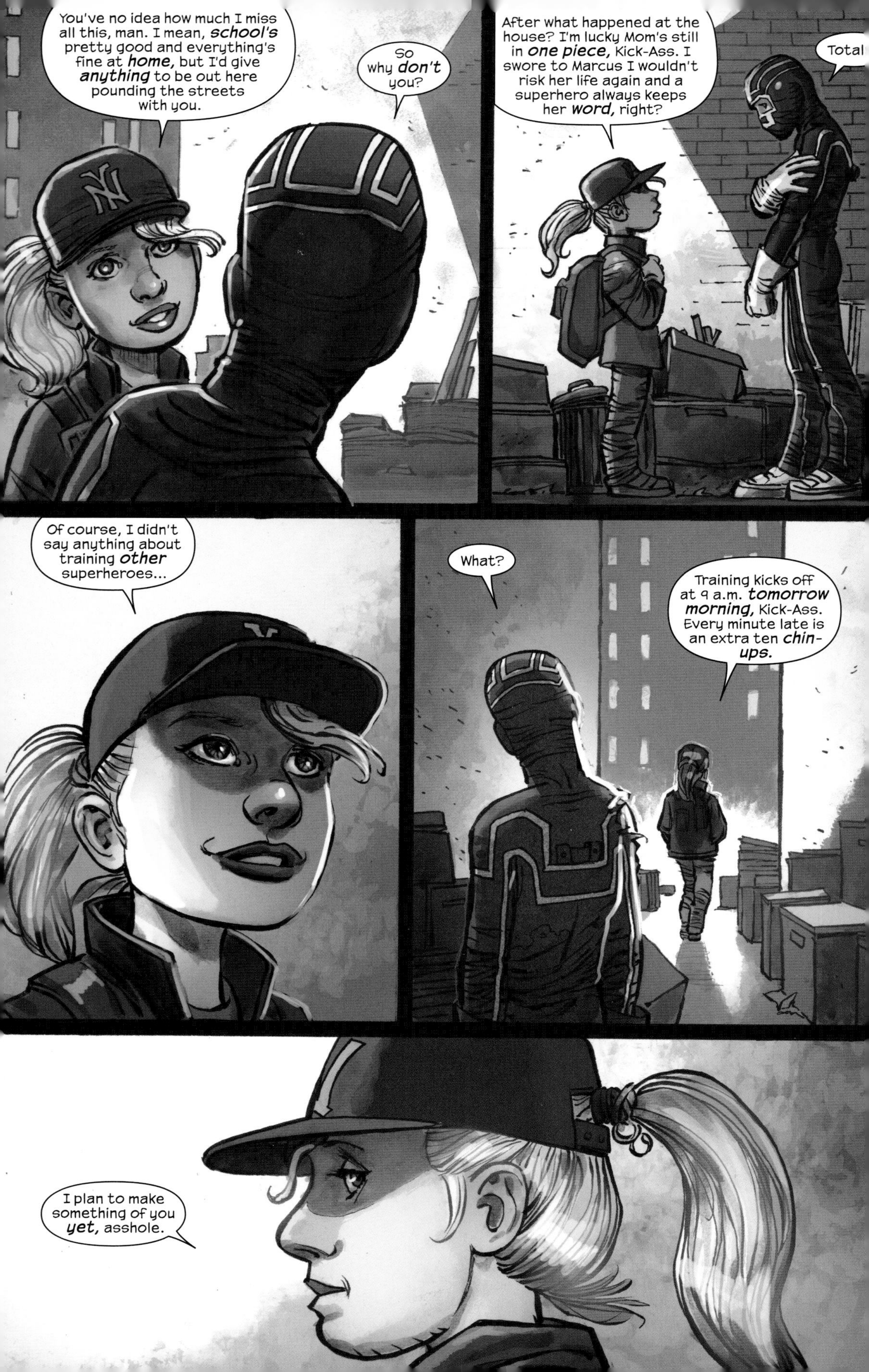

You've no idea how much I miss all this, man. I mean, school's pretty good and everything's fine at home, but I'd give anything to be out here pounding the streets with you.
So why don't you?
After what happened at the house? I'm lucky Mom's still in one piece, Kick-Ass. I swore to Marcus I wouldn't risk her life again and a superhero always keeps her word, right?
Total
Of course, I didn't say anything about training other superheroes...
What?
Training kicks off at 9 a.m. tomorrow morning, Kick-Ass. Every minute late is an extra ten chin-ups.
I plan to make something of you yet, asshole.

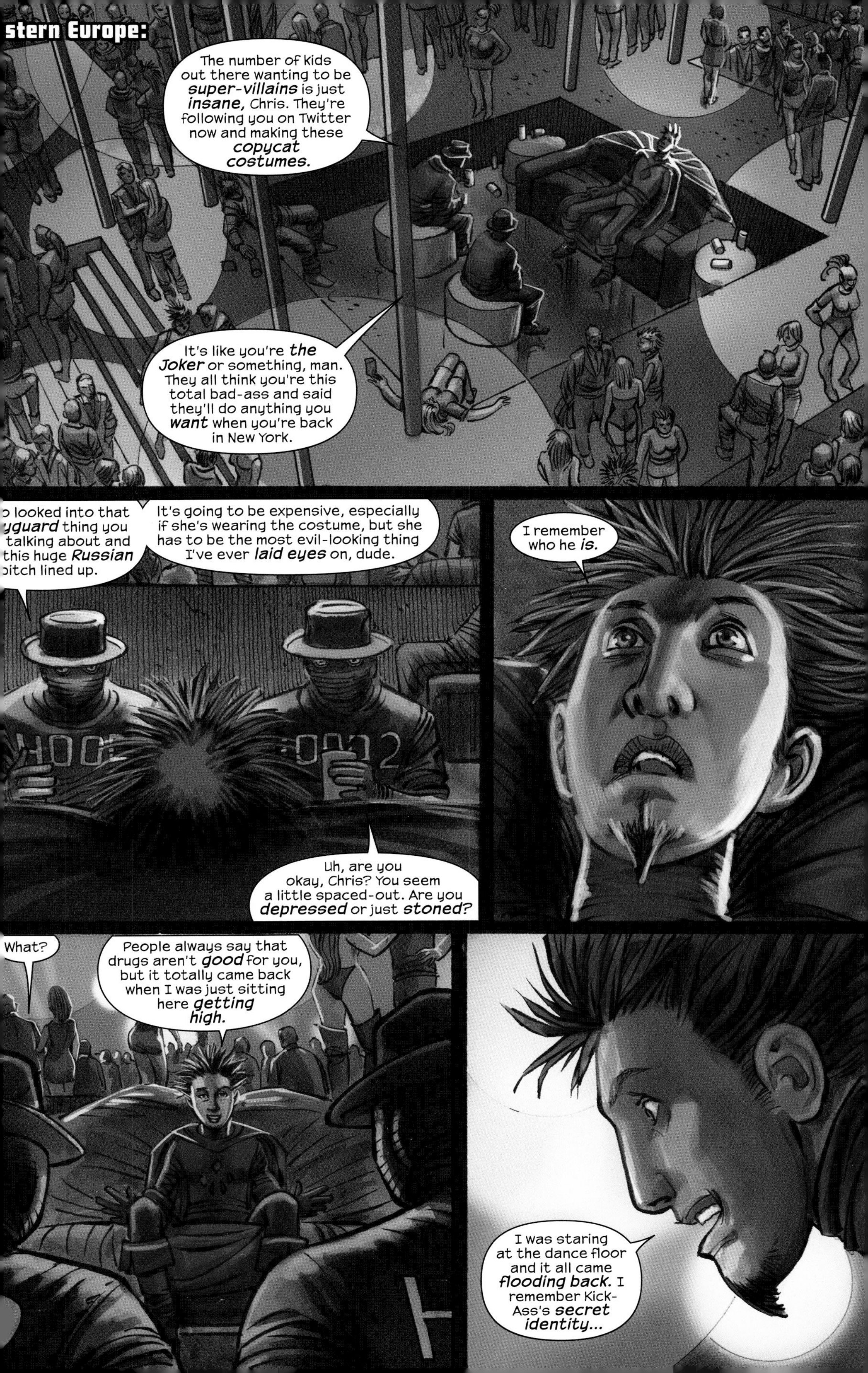
stern Europe:
The number of kids out there wanting to be super-villains is just insane, Chris. They're following you on Twitter now and making these copycat costumes.
It's like you're the Joker or something, man. They all think you're this total bad-ass and said they'll do anything you want when you're back in New York.
o looked into that yguard thing you talking about and this huge Russian bitch lined up.
It's going to be expensive, especially if she's wearing the costume, but she has to be the most evil-looking thing I've ever laid eyes on, dude.
Uh, are you okay, Chris? You seem a little spaced-out. Are you depressed or just stoned?
I remember who he is.
What?
People always say that drugs aren't good for you, but it totally came back when I was just sitting here getting high.
I was staring at the dance floor and it all came flooding back. I remember Kick-Ass's secret identity...

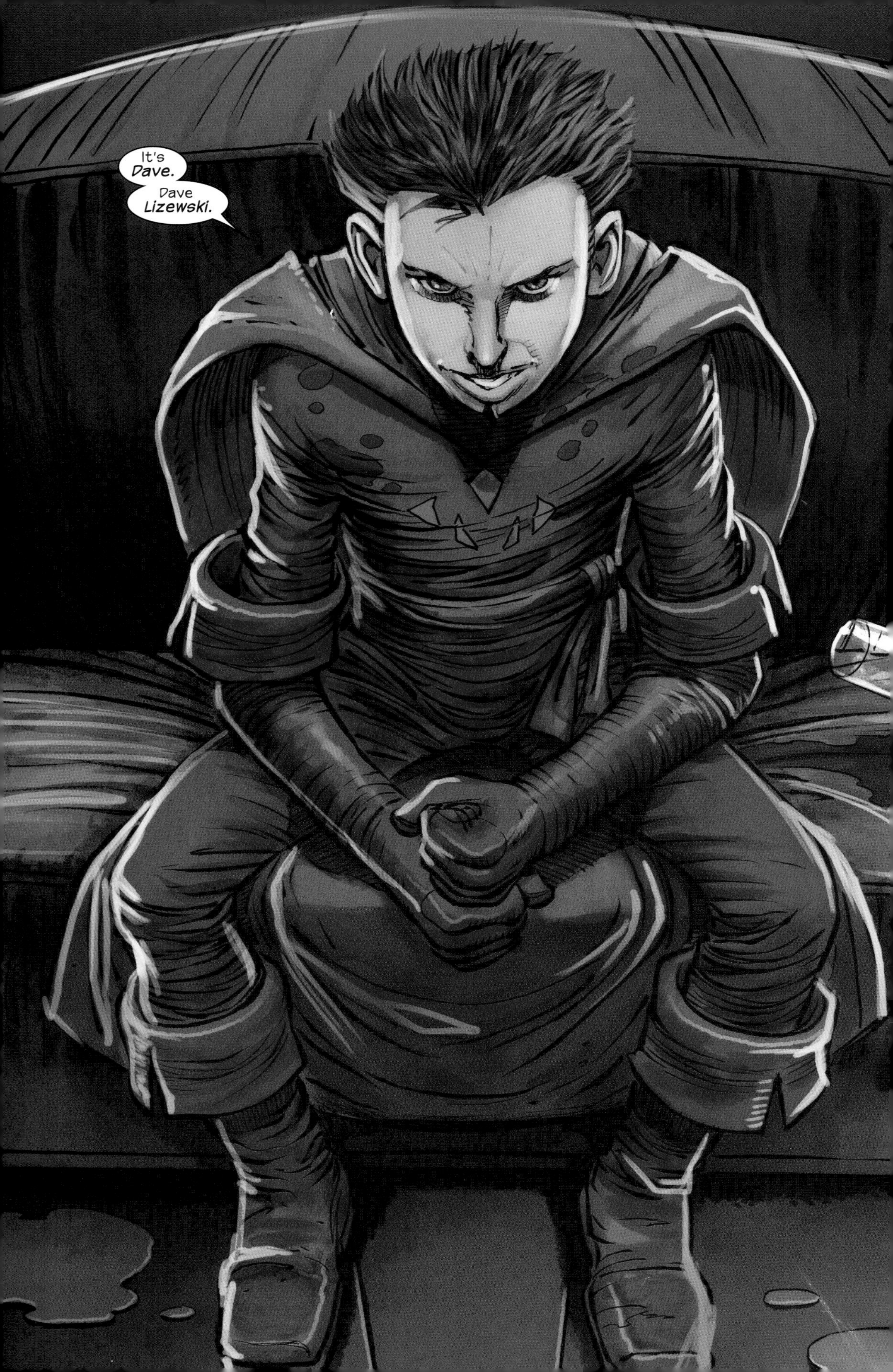
It's Dave.
Dave Lizewski.

END OF BOOK TWO

MARK MILLAR has been one of Marvel's key writers in the 21st century. His first major contributions were *Ultimate X-Men* with Adam Kubert and *The Ultimates* with Bryan Hitch, which *Time* magazine named 2010's Best Comic Book of the Decade. His *Wolverine* and *Marvel Knights Spider-Man* runs were also best sellers, but it was his epic *Civil War* series that reshaped the Marvel Universe and remains the publisher's best-selling title of the last decade. His Millarworld company boasts a roster of creator-owned books such as *Wanted*, turned into a blockbuster movie starring Angelina Jolie; *Kick-Ass*, which starred Nicolas Cage; and *Nemesis*, with Steve McNiven. Millar's other creator-owned works include *Supercrooks* with Leinil Yu, *The Secret Service* with *Watchmen*'s Dave Gibbons, and a new superhero series with fellow Scot Frank Quitely. In his native U.K., he's the editor of *CLiNT* magazine, an advisor on film to the Scottish government, and managing director of TV company Millarworld Productions. He was recently named the creative consultant for the Marvel franchise movies developed at FOX

JOHN ROMITA JR is a modern-day comic-art master, following in his legendary father's footsteps. Timeless runs on *Iron Man*, *Uncanny X-Men*, *Amazing Spider-Man,* and *Daredevil* helped establish him as his own man artistically, and his work on *Wolverine* and *World War Hulk* is arguably the most explosive comic art of the last decade. In addition to *Eternals* with writer Neil Gaiman, JRJR teamed with Mark Millar on the creator-owned *Kick-Ass*, later developed into a blockbuster feature film starring Nicolas Cage. Avid Spider-Man fans rejoiced at the artist's return to *Amazing Spider-Man* with the Brand New Day storylines "New Ways To Die" and "Character Assassination." He later joined writer Brian Michael Bendis on the relaunched *Avengers*. Recent titles include the blockbuster crossover *Avengers vs X-Men*, and the relaunch of *Captain America*.

TOM PALMER has worked as an illustrator in the advertising and editorial fields, but has spent the majority of his career in comic books. His first assignment, fresh out of art school, was on *Doctor Strange*. He has since gone on to lend his inking talents to many of Marvel's top titles, including *X-Men*, *The Avengers*, *Tomb of Dracula*, and more recently *Punisher, Hulk,* and *Ghost Rider*. He live and works in New Jersey.

WHITE is
he comic
's best and
ught-after
ists. Well-
or his work
such as *The
g Spider-
nisher*, *Dark
rs*, *Captain
, *Black
, *Wolverine*,
ntless more,
envelope-
rendering
r palette
sense of
and power
page he
.

CHRIS ELIOPOULOS
is a multiple award-
winner for his lettering,
having worked on
dozens of books during
the twenty years he's
been in the industry –
including Erik Larsen's
Savage Dragon, for
which he hand–
lettered the first 100
issues. Adding to his
success as a letterer,
he also publishes his
own strip *Misery Loves
Sherman*, wrote and
illustrated the popular
*Franklin Richards: Son
of a Genius* one-shots,
and wrote Marvel's
*Lockjaw and the Pet
Avengers* series.

JENNIFER LEE is a stor
editor and producer
working across film,
comics, and prose. She
edited for both Marvel
and DC Comics, and he
books include *Daredev
Black Widow*, *100 Bulle
Transmetropolitan*, and
the award-winning
illustrated prose novel
*The Sandman: The
Dream Hunters*. *Hit-Gir*
marks Jenny's reunion
with Mark Millar and
John Romita Jr, whom
she edited during their
seminal run on *Wolveri*
Film credits include *Tru
Adolescents* starring M
Duplass and Melissa Le
*Small, Beautifully Movi
Parts*; *Union Square*
starring Mira Sorvino
and Tammy Blanchard;
Arcadia starring John
Hawkes; and *The Skele
Twins* starring Kristen
Wiig and Bill Hader. She
lives in New York with
her husband, comics
illustrator Cliff Chiang.

VARIANT COVERS

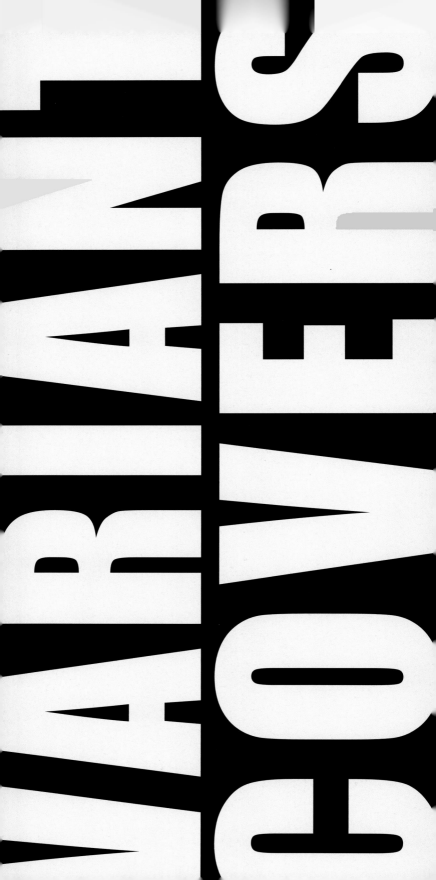

ONE

(VARIANT BY PHIL NOTO)

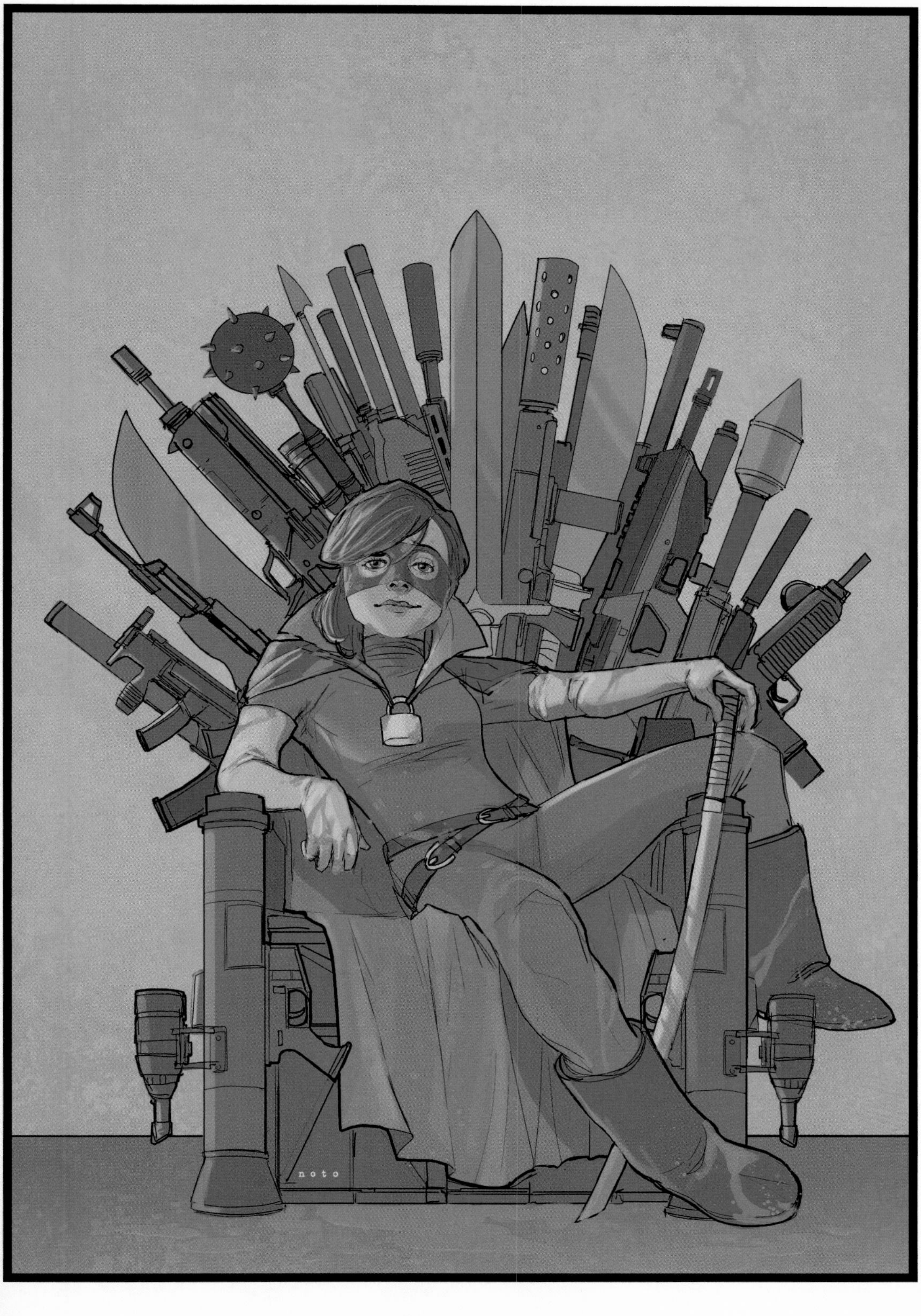
noto

ONE

(SKETCH VARIANT BY JOHN ROMITA JR. & TOM PALMER)

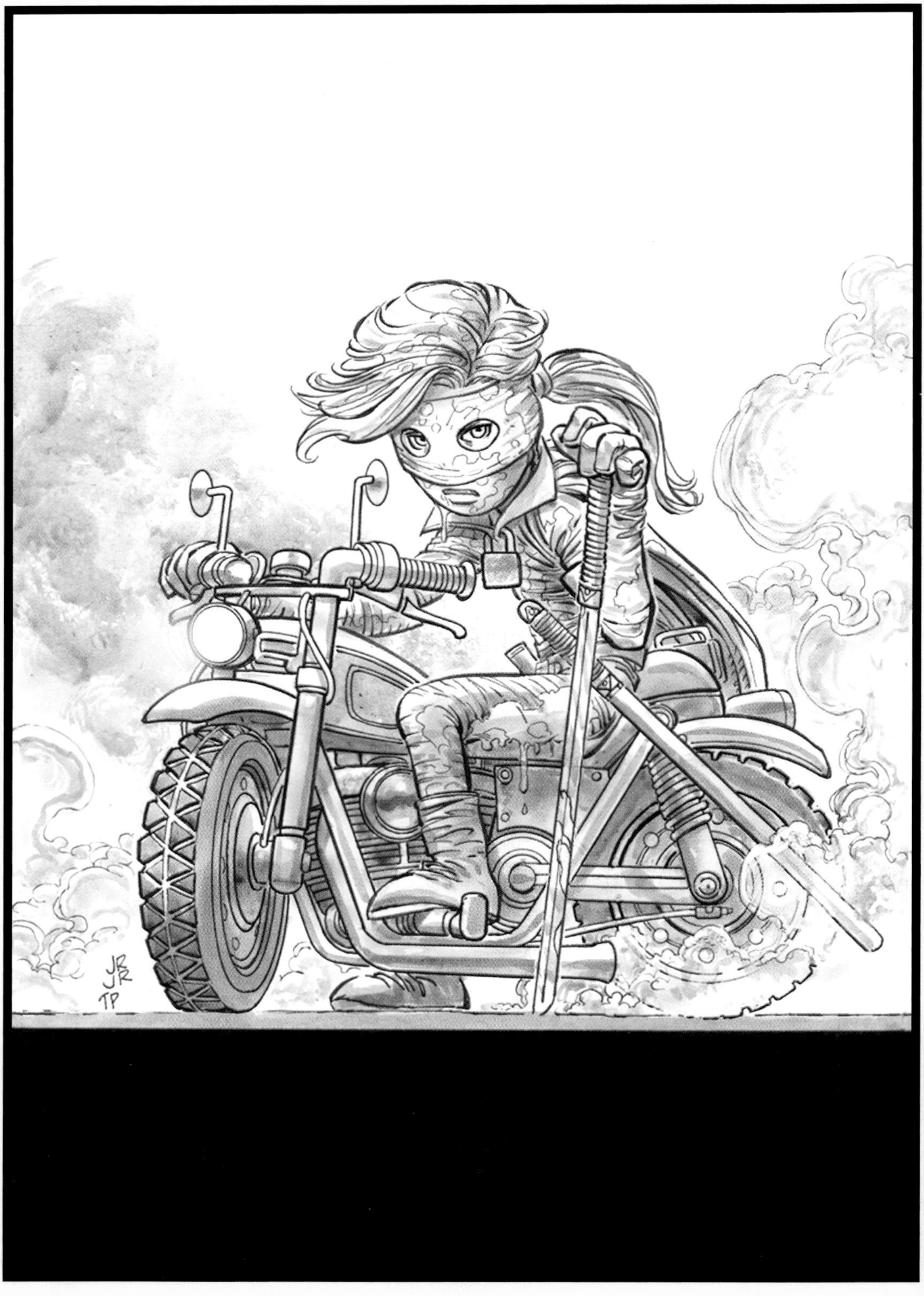
JR JR
TP

ONE

(VARIANT BY LEANDRO FERNANDEZ & ILEANA MONTECHIARINI)

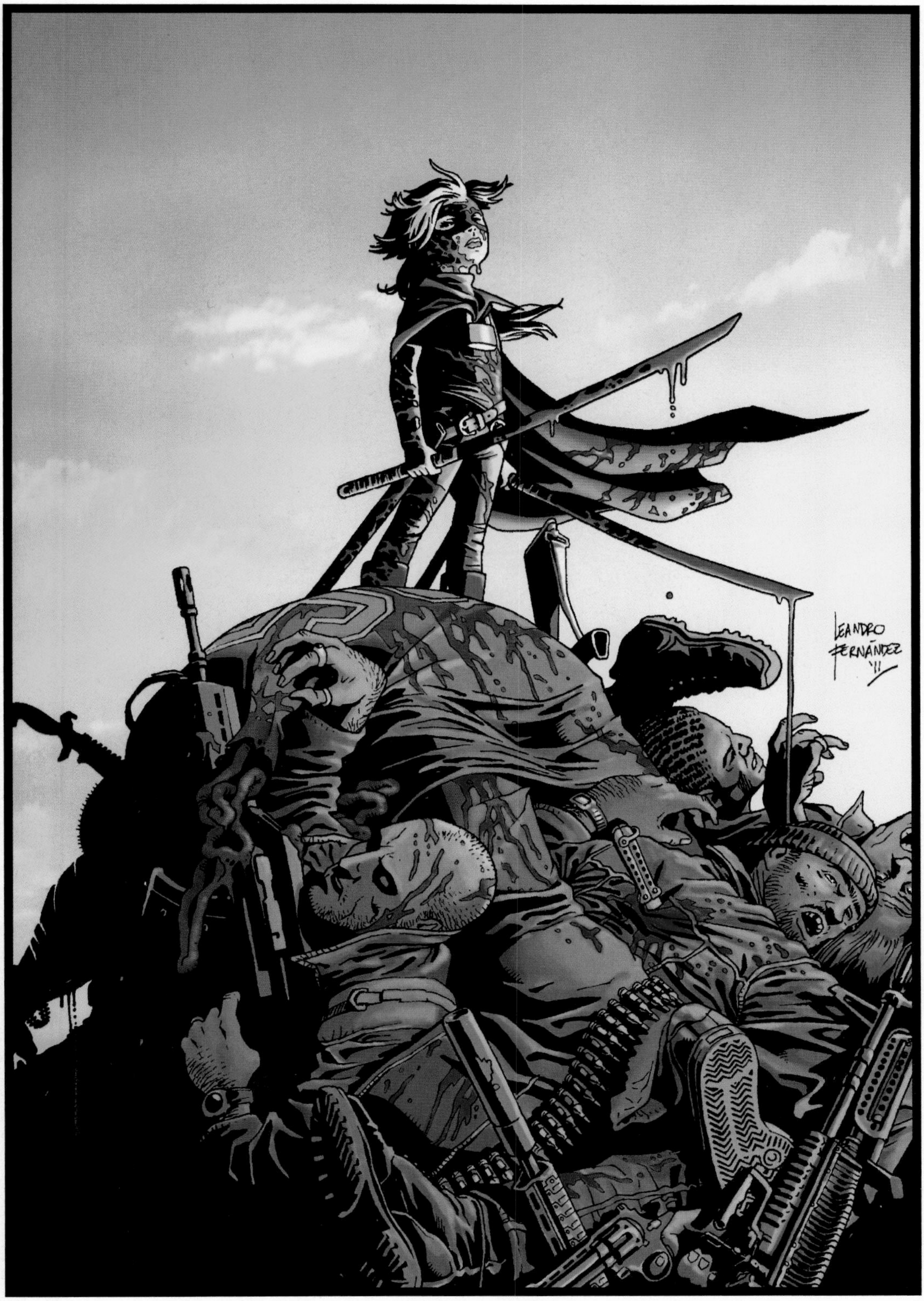
LEANDRO FERNÁNDEZ '11

TWO

(SKETCH VARIANT BY JOHN ROMITA JR. & TOM PALMER)

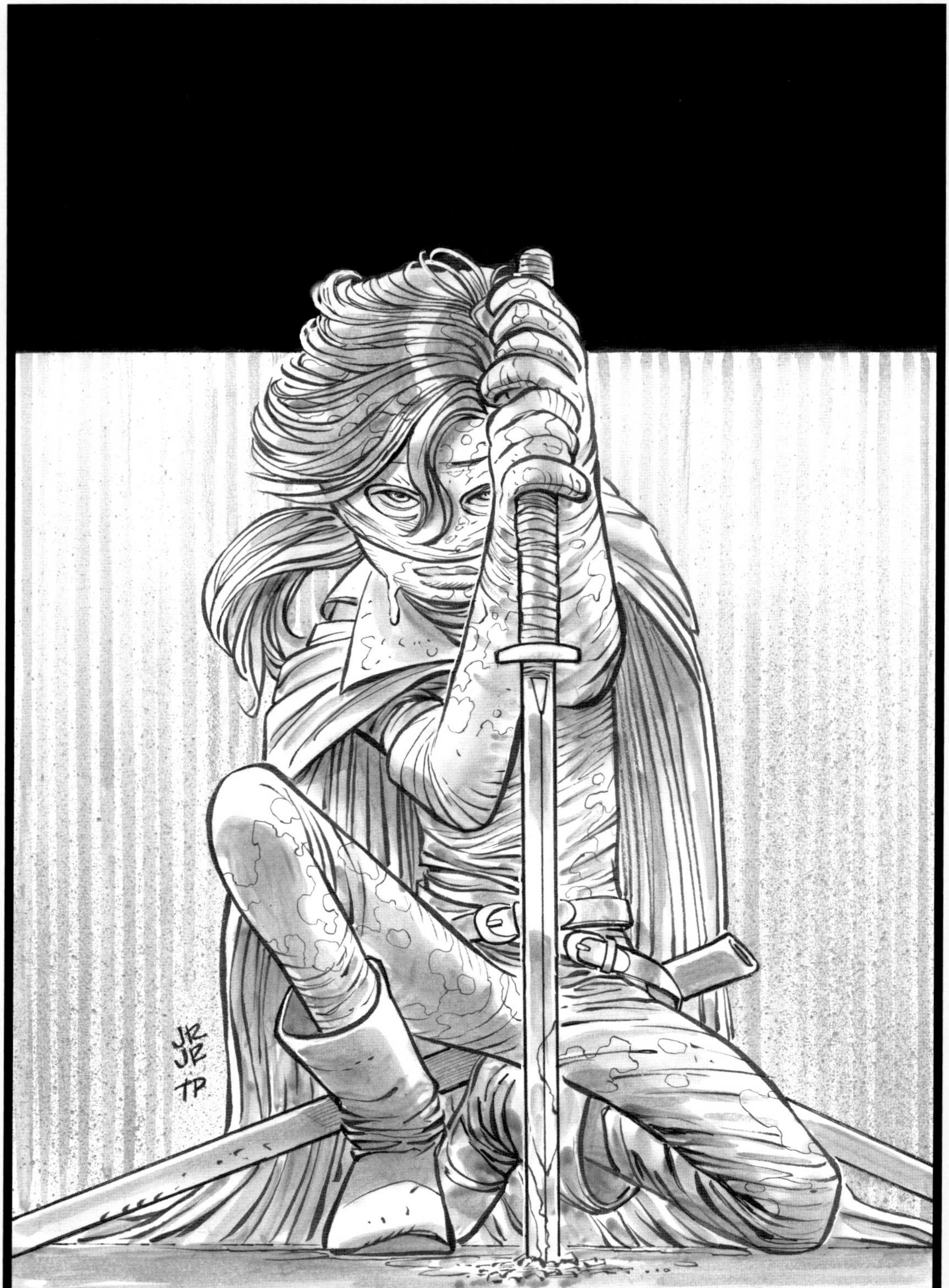
JR JR TP

TWO

(VARIANT BY DAVE JOHNSON)

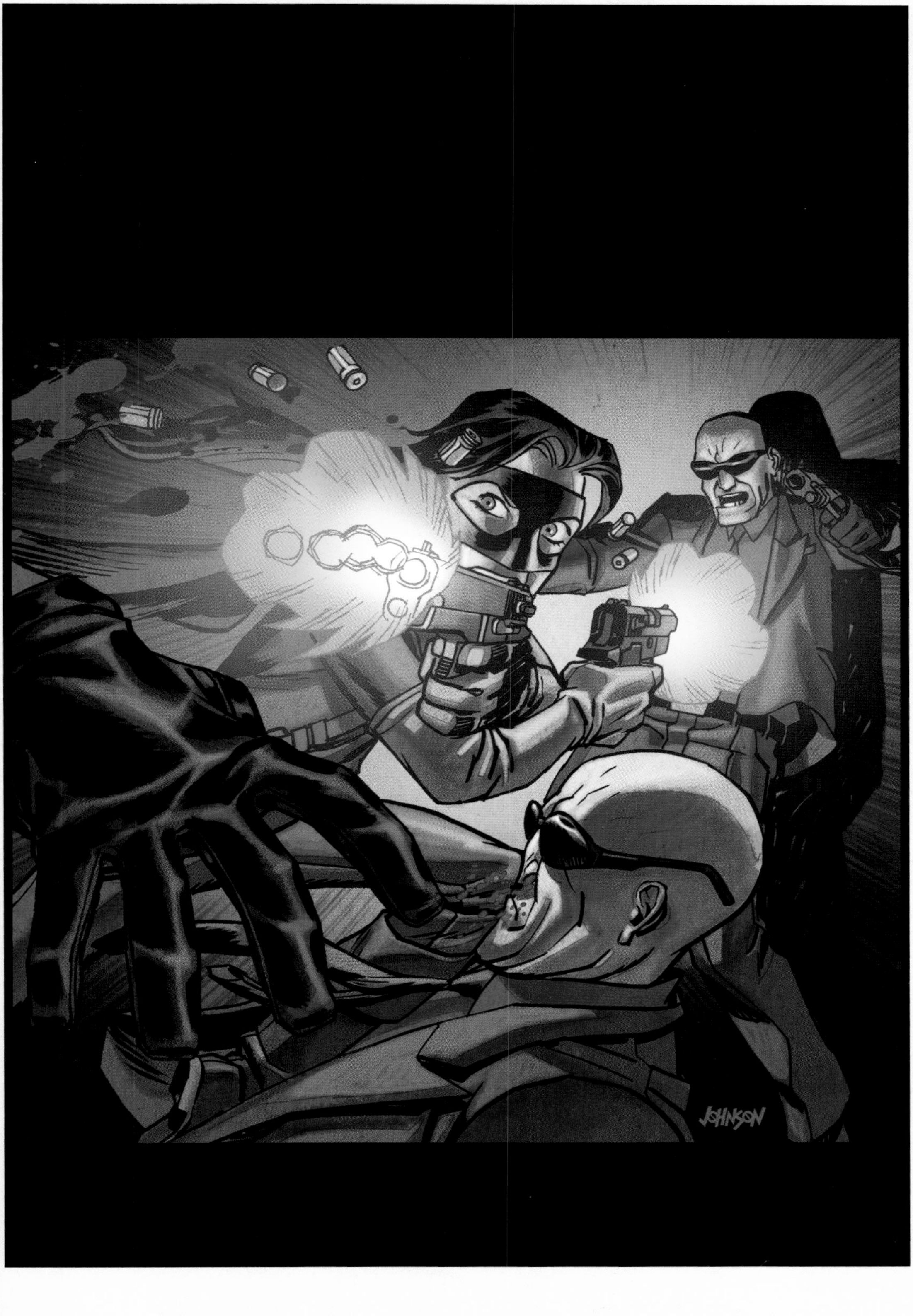
JOHNSON

THREE

(SKETCH VARIANT BY JOHN ROMITA JR. & TOM PALMER)

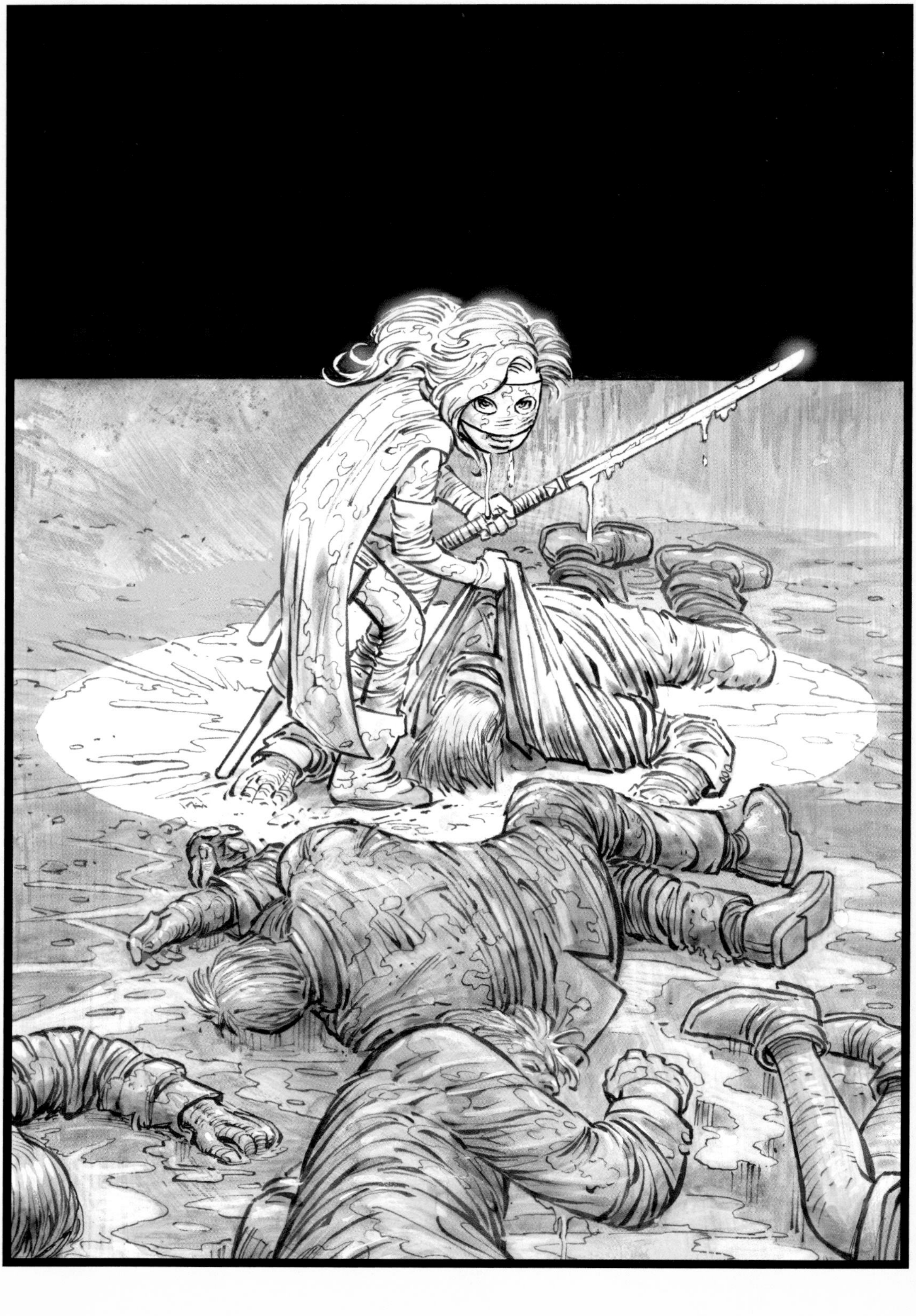

THREE
(VARIANT BY JOCK)

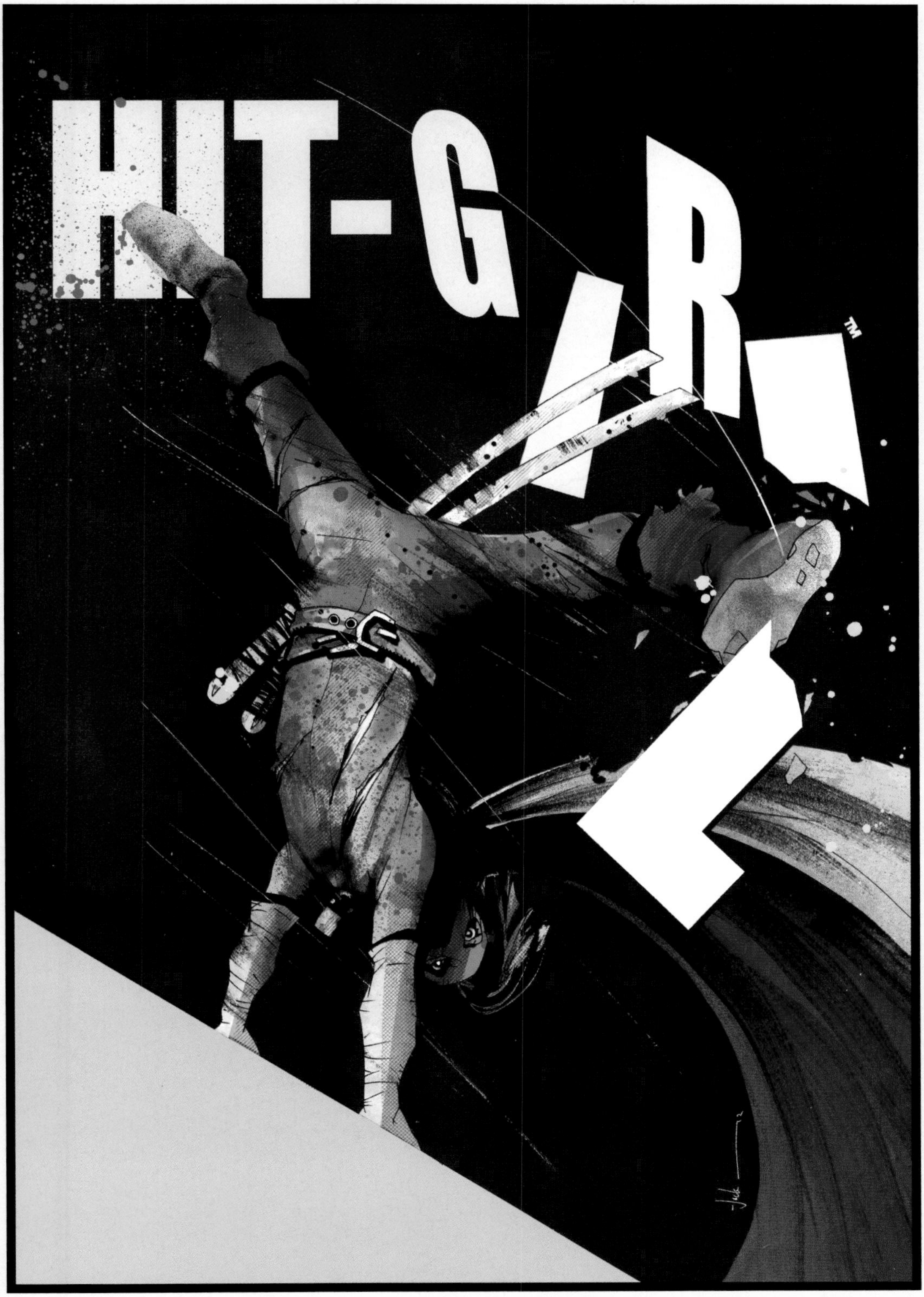
HIT-GIRL™

FOUR

(SKETCH VARIANT BY JOHN ROMITA JR. & TOM PALMER)

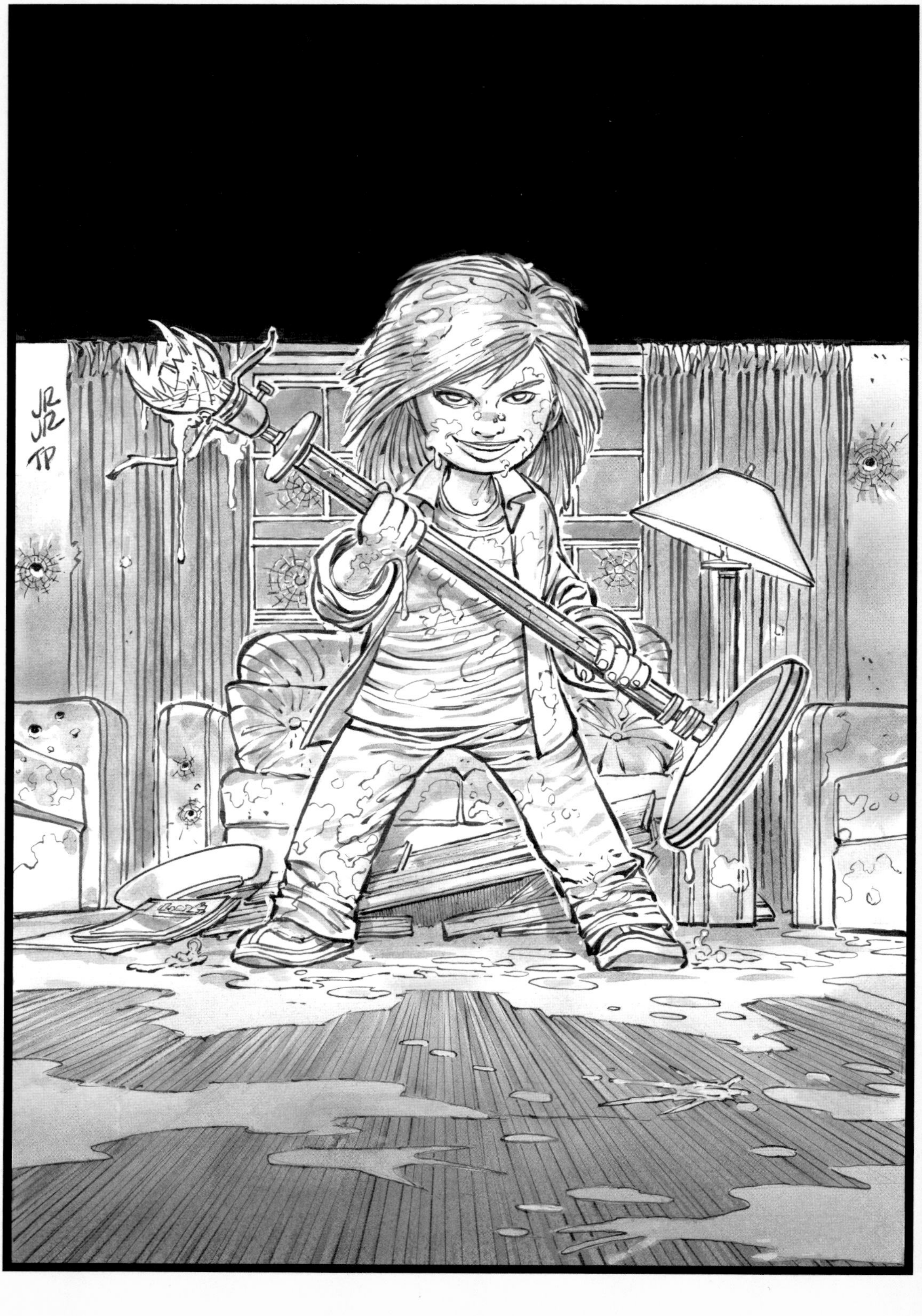
JR
JR
TP

FOUR

(VARIANT BY GEOF DARROW & PETER DOHERTY)

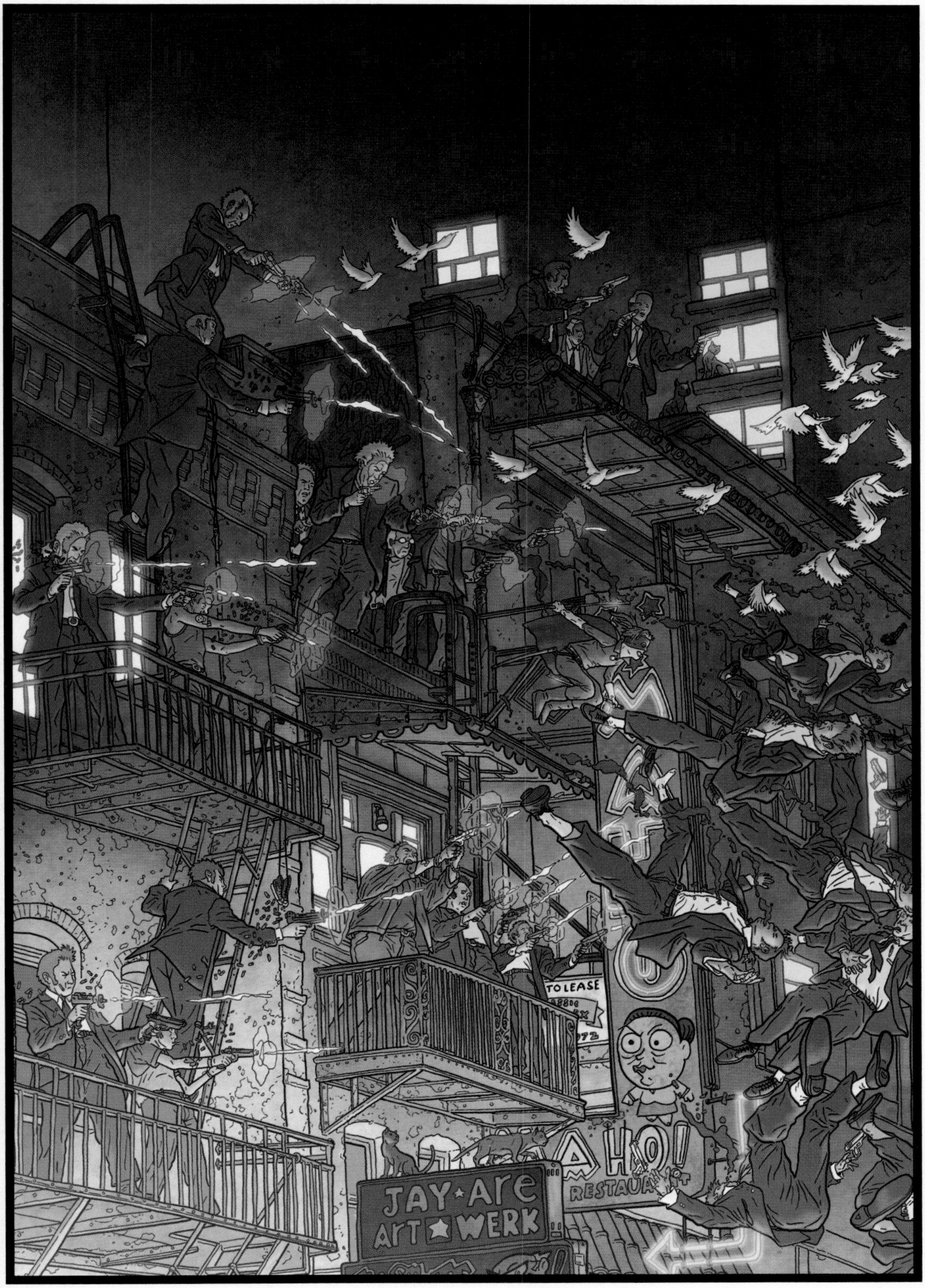
TO LEASE
JAY ★ ARE
ART ★ WERK

FIVE

(SKETCH VARIANT BY JOHN ROMITA JR. & TOM PALMER)

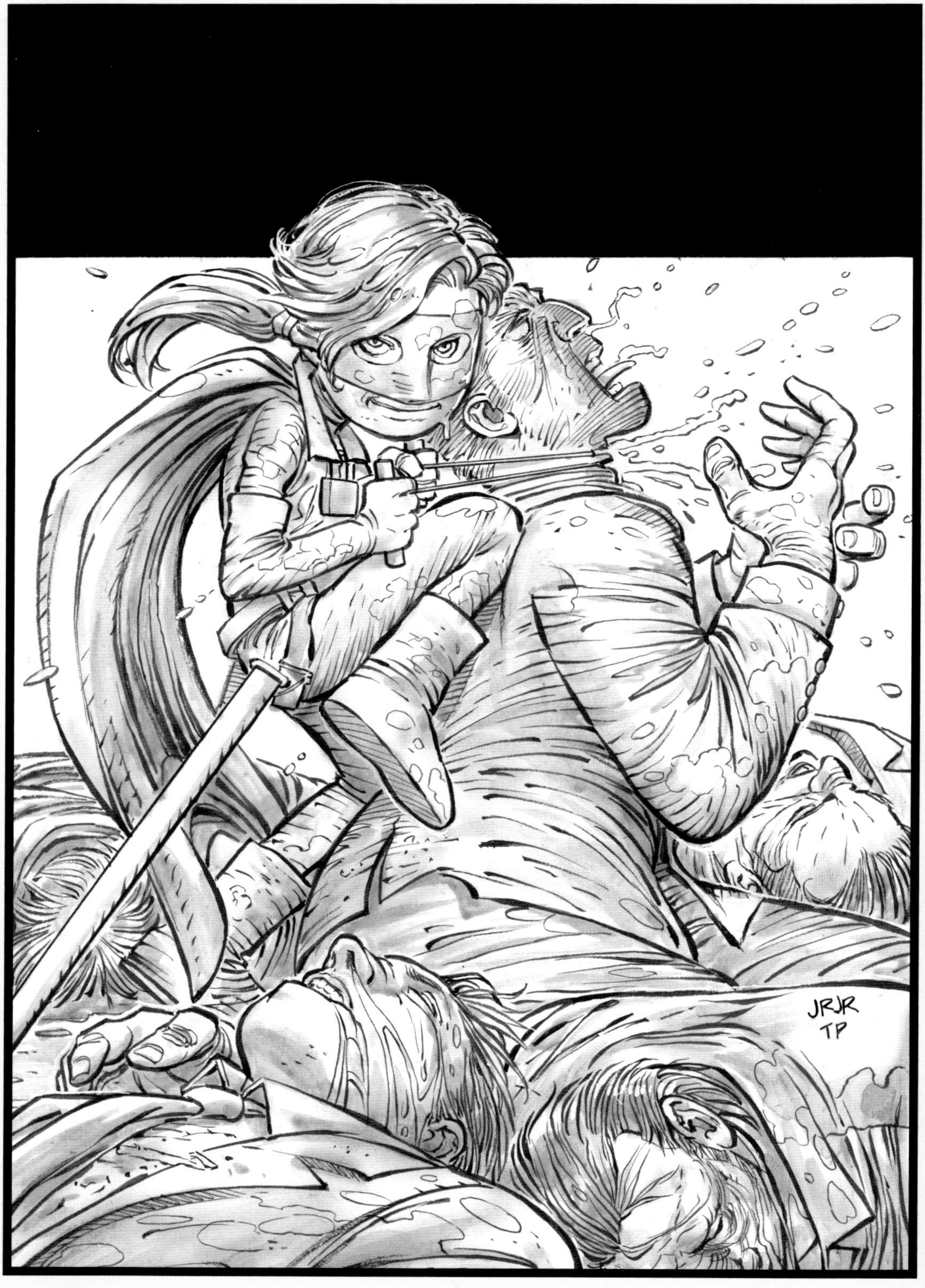
JRJR
TP

FIVE

(VARIANT BY BILL SIENKIEWICZ)

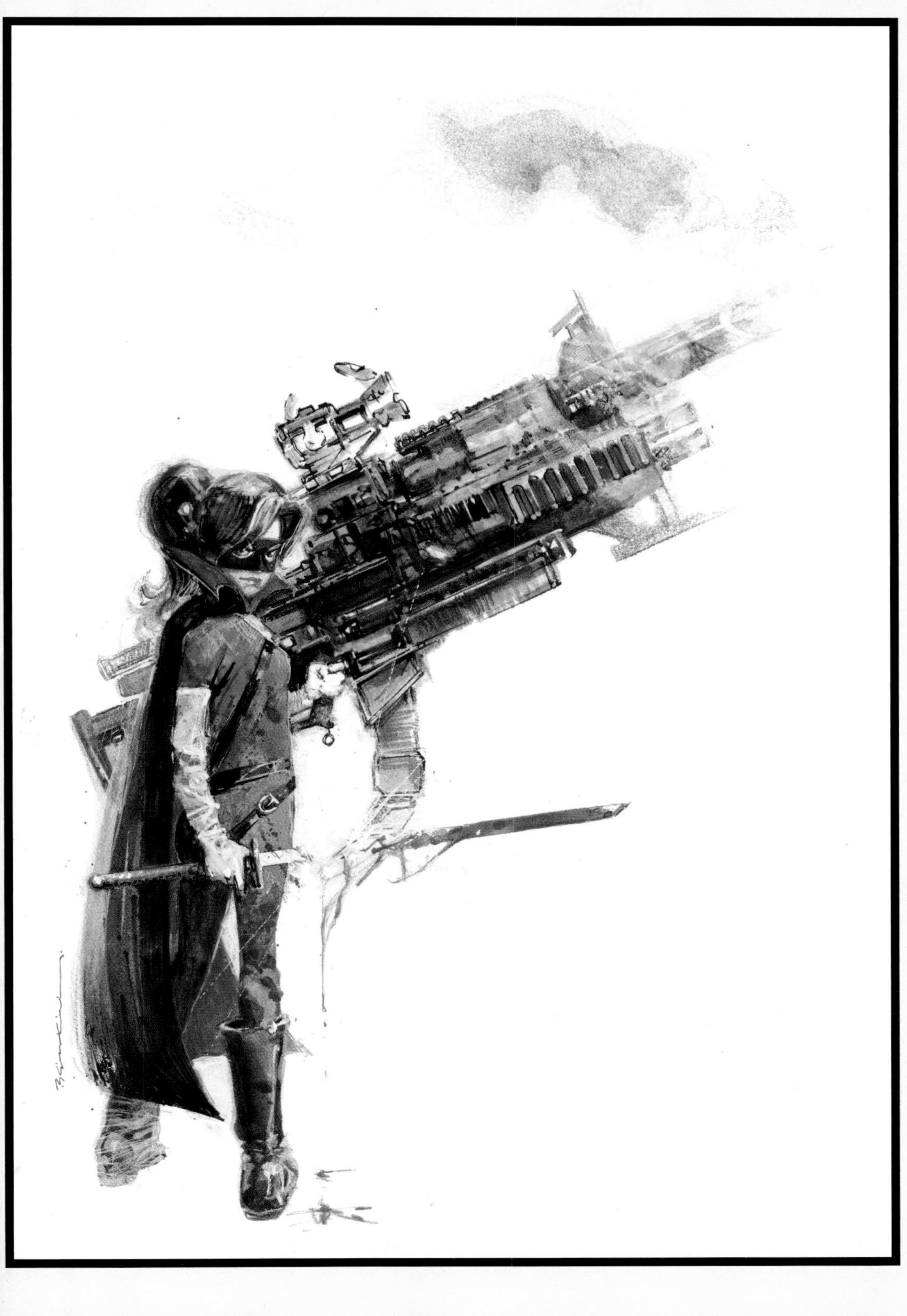

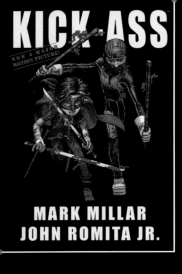

KICK-ASS

NOW A MAJOR
MOTION PICTURE!

MARK MILLAR
JOHN ROMITA JR.

MARK MILLAR · JOHN ROMITA JR.

HIT-GIRL

THE MILLAI

KICK-ASS 2

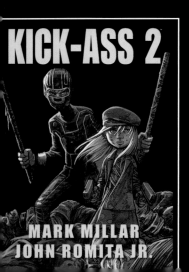

MARK MILLAR
JOHN ROMITA JR.

WANTED

MARK MILLAR · JG JONES · PAUL MOUNTS
NOW A MAJOR MOTION PICTURE FROM
UNIVERSAL PICTURES
WWW.MILLARWORLD.TV

MARK MILLAR & LEINIL YU
SUPERIOR

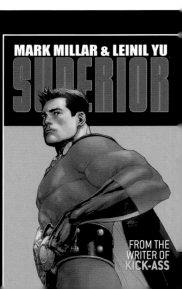

FROM THE
WRITER OF
KICK-ASS

WORLD COLLECTION

MILLAR & McNIVEN'S
NEMESIS

MARK MILLAR   DAVE GIBBONS
the **SECRET SERVICE**

6
$2.99

MARK MILLAR · FRANK QUITELY
JUPITER'S LEGACY

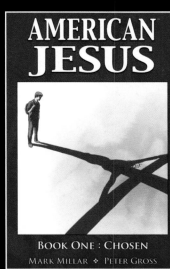

AMERICAN JESUS

BOOK ONE : CHOSEN
MARK MILLAR ✦ PETER GROSS

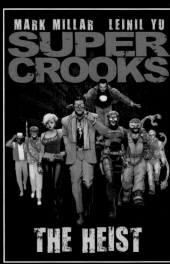

MARK MILLAR   LEINIL YU
SUPER CROOKS

THE HEIST

KICK-ASS READING ORDER

PART ONE

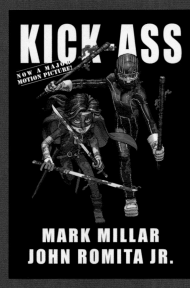

KICK-ASS
NOW A MAJOR MOTION PICTURE!
MARK MILLAR
JOHN ROMITA JR.

PART TWO

KICK-ASS 2 PRELUDE:
HIT-GIRL
MARK MILLAR
JOHN ROMITA JR.
TOM PALMER and DEAN WHITE

PART THREE

KICK-ASS 2
MARK MILLAR
JOHN ROMITA JR.

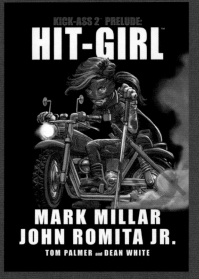

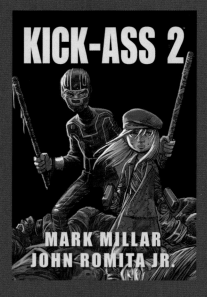

PART FOUR

KICK-ASS 3

THE GRAND FINALE

MAY 2013